CLIMBERS

Pain, panache and polka dots in cycling's greatest arenas

PETER COSSINS

For Clive Smythe
No mountain is too high

First published in Great Britain in 2022 by Cassell, an imprint of
Octopus Publishing Group Ltd
Carmelite House, 50 Victoria Embankment, London EC4Y 0DZ
www.octopusbooks.co.uk
www.octopusbooksusa.com

An Hachette UK Company
www.hachette.co.uk

First published in paperback in 2023

Distributed in the US by Hachette Book Group
1290 Avenue of the Americas
4th and 5th Floors, New York, NY 10104

Distributed in Canada by Canadian Manda Group
664 Annette St., Toronto, Ontario, Canada M6S 2C8

ISBN 978-1-78840-313-9

A CIP catalogue record for this book is available from the British Library.

Printed and bound in Great Britain

1 3 5 7 9 10 8 6 4 2

Typeset in 10.26/15.4pt FreightText Pro by Jouve (UK), Milton Keynes

Publisher: Trevor Davies
Editor: Sarah Allen
Copy Editor: Nick Fawcett
Art Director: Jaz Bahra
Picture Research Manager: Giulia Hetherington
Senior Production Manager: Peter Hunt

This FSC® label means that materials used for the
product have been responsibly sourced.

Contents

Introduction

It's the afternoon before the start of the 2021 Critérium du Dauphiné and I'm sitting in a rural hotel garden with Pierre Rolland, one of the great climbers of the twenty-first century, a bike racer whose career has been completely defined by the mountains and is best known for his Tour de France victory at Alpe d'Huez, cycling's most iconic ascent. Now in his fourteenth season as a professional rider, Rolland is, as the best climbers almost always are, an individualist, his 80-day racing season built around just a handful of clear-cut opportunities for success.

As actors on the most magnificent and exacting sporting stage of all, climbers have always been a breed apart, providing us with a spectacle that matches the dramatic setting they're racing in, drawing us into awe-inspiring mountain terrain, offering a sense of its intimidating and sometimes frightening scale, and, vitally, bringing it to life for us with their exploits and suffering. Always vulnerable to falls, crashes in form, to the sudden and unexpected, theirs is a precarious high-wire act – one that everyone who watches a bike race is captivated by.

Meeting Rolland is a first step towards understanding what sets climbers apart and why we're so enthralled by these sporting mavericks and the terrain they race in – the setting, according to cycling historian Serge Laget, for as much as 95 per cent of the Tour's legends while comprising barely 15 per cent of the route.

As we start to talk, Rolland reveals that his first – and still his favourite – experience of the mountains took place on the Puy Mary, just 80 kilometres to the west of where we're sitting in the village of La Chomette, in the Allier valley that lies between the volcanic peaks of the Auvergne to the west and the steep inclines of the Forez massif to the east . . .

'I can still remember my first experience of the mountains. It was in the Cantal with my best friend when I was 16 or 17. They aren't high mountains, but are nevertheless very impressive, especially when you come from a very flat region like the one where I grew up not far south of Paris. Right away, I felt very comfortable in that environment, because of the calmness that it instilled in me, the kind of effort that it drew out of me. Coming from a region where climbing could only be enjoyed very briefly, being in the mountains increased the amount and degree of pleasure that I felt. I knew right away that this was the kind of terrain I needed to focus on.

'Not long after that, I competed in my first Classique des Alpes as a junior. I'd barely climbed a mountain pass in my life and I couldn't believe the speed that everyone raced at on these long ascents. That increased my desire to climb for longer, to ride higher and higher.

'There's a mystical aspect to the mountains, something very particular about riding there. The atmosphere's imposing. It makes you feel small when you're in the midst of a huge chain of peaks, looking up and seeing them all around you as you're climbing towards them. It's a bit like being out on the ocean: there's an immensity to it that makes you realize how tiny you are.

'There's also a degree of romanticism to it. It's a bit like you're going back in time. When you're climbing, you know that thousands of people have gone up there before, by bike or on foot, and there are all kinds of stories that could be told. Then, when you're climbing all alone, it's a very particular sensation. It's beautiful, but hard at the same time, and there's a sense of reward as well. That's when you sense the romanticism. When you're climbing all alone like that, it's just you against the mountain, an obstacle that has to be conquered.

'When you're approaching the mountains, you know that you're going to suffer. There are two different aspects to it, depending on whether you're climbing a pass for training or in a race. Anyone can climb for a long time, but not everyone can do so quickly. When you're racing and your intention is to climb fast, it's very different. You're absolutely focused: on your physical resources and reserves, on staying well hydrated, on trying to go as fast as possible using as little energy as possible – the eternal contradiction of bike racing.

'There's also a sense of excitement, of course. You know that you're going to reach a vital point, no matter whether it comes at the beginning, the middle or towards the end of a climb. It's always there when you start up a long pass, where you know you will be climbing for 40 or even 50 minutes.

'I think of racing in the mountains as a three-sided contest. There's the battle going on within ourselves, where we're making the choice to keep going all out for as long as we can. You've also got to deal with your rivals, and with the mountain itself, every one of which is different in its characteristics – some you're more suited to, others less so. That's why I describe it as a three-sided contest, because on the one hand we set our own limits on the degree of pain and suffering we can tolerate, but at the same time, our rivals also impose limits, as does the climb we're on, both of those equally making us suffer. Ultimately, that's the contest we love so much.

'What I live for as a climber is those moments when I'm out on my own with fans on all sides. You have the feeling of "opening the road", of having the fans to yourself. It's a moment of absolute egotism. When you're on a great climb – perhaps the Tourmalet, Alpe d'Huez or the Ventoux – that pioneering sense of opening the road is heightened still further because you're leading the way on a celebrated ascent. In moments like that, you draw energy from the fans, who are so overwhelmingly present that you can't hear yourself breathing or sense your heart beating. It's absolute madness, but somehow you're not aware of the climb unfolding, you don't sense the gradient. You're so full of adrenaline. It's like being in a stadium, or on a theatre stage: an absolutely extraordinary feeling.

'On days like that when you're at your very best in the mountains, you get the impression that you're no longer within your own body, that somehow you're watching yourself perform. That's when you know that everything is going well. As you're pedalling, you get a feeling that's close to ecstasy, because you've thought about and dreamed of such moments for so long; you've visualized the images that are buzzing through your head, and now you're actually experiencing them. You feel a sense of well-being permeating your body, as if you're going beyond yourself, almost like you're having some kind of out-of-body experience.

'While the sense of pleasure in the mountains is fleeting, pain is almost ever-present, but it manifests itself in different ways. When you're at the front and your form is good, the pain isn't all-consuming, you can regulate it. When you're right in the thick of the action in a big race, you set the cursor on the degree of suffering you impose on yourself. You can manage it, set your own limit.

'You can feel the pain almost anywhere. When you're at altitude, it can be in the lungs, due to the violent efforts you're making. Your legs will be burning. You may feel as though your back's breaking.

Sometimes it's like your head's going to explode. But the thing is, as long as we're in pain, we're alive and we're fighting with all the resources we have left. When you can't hurt yourself any more, you're dead. It means that your body's got nothing left. When we suffer, we sometimes say to ourselves, "I'm hurting, that means my body is working well."

'When you're in the third week of a Grand Tour, your tolerance grows. You can't hurt your legs more than you did before. At that point, you're hurting everywhere, but it's not as intense as it was. If I were to climb a mountain pass at full speed today, the pain I'd feel would be far more intense than it would be after three weeks of racing because, with repetition, you develop a tolerance to it. The sensation of pain diminishes as you become accustomed to racing at speed. You have to learn to live with that pain, to deal with it, no matter what part of your body you feel it in.

'Over the course of my career, I've felt closer and closer to the mountains. I increasingly relish being in this terrain. I feel good there, it refreshes me. Sadly, there aren't so many of the great solo rides or breakaways now, the ones that tend to feature riders like me who lose time on purpose early on in a race in order to be able to make a great escape. My romantic side pushes me towards racing like this. I want to cycle in the same way I saw riders doing when I was a teenager. That goes against the current flow, where teams and tactics are more organized in the mountains. But I'll keep racing like it, in that all-or-nothing style.

'I'll never lose that sense of being a climber, even when I'm 15 kilos heavier than I was at the peak of my career. I'm sure I'll continue to set myself challenges to go up this or that big pass. I don't know where exactly – perhaps in Nepal or some similarly mountainous country – climbing passes that reach 3,500 metres in height or crossing an entire mountain range. That's the kind of challenge I would like to take on. It's just you and the mountain, no need to focus any more on time, speed or watts. It's a thrill, a personal challenge, exactly the same kind of test that any cyclist looks for in the mountains: a journey into themselves . . .'

Chapter 1

From Pottier to Pogačar

I'm woken up by a sudden blaze of yellow headlights little more than a metre from where I'm lying. *What the hell is going on?* Cocooned in my sleeping bag, I try to shift as far out of the vehicle's direction of travel as my tiny one-person tent allows. The driver grinds the gears, attempting to locate reverse, while I frantically fumble with the zip securing the door flap, trying to escape confinement, the engine growling loudly as the gear is missed, the car edging a few centimetres closer in the fraction before the driver stamps on the brake.

At that instant, the flap falls, and I caterpillar myself out, knees coming up to my chest, then propelling me forwards, the action repeated until I'm out of the lights' beam range. As I hop clumsily to my feet, I glance back and realize that my ten-speed Peugeot is almost completely under the front of what I can now see is a Spanish-registered car. The driver attacks the gears again, finds one, revs hard, and back the vehicle goes, the final glare of its headlights revealing that my bike has also survived unscathed.

I glance around. The sun's not yet up, but I can see that the Pyrenean meadow that I camped in with my best friend Andy and a few dozen other cycling fans the night before is now almost filled with tents, cars and camper vans. Poleaxed by five days in the saddle and the anaesthetizing effect of cheap French red the evening before,

I'd not been aware of this mini-Glastonbury forming until the cars were almost right on top of me. On my left, to the west, I can see the road heading into semi-darkness, the woods hiding the final kilometres to the Col de Marie-Blanque cloaked in the gloom. To the east, the mountains of the far side of the Ossau valley are backlit by the rising sun. I'm too awake to try to sleep again and it's too early to rouse Andy, so I pull my foam bed roll out of the tent and sit down, watching an increasing flow of vehicles come up the pass from Bielle, some stopping to fill a small space by the roadside, most continuing upwards towards the summit.

The journey to this, my first day at the Tour de France, began years earlier, sitting on the foot of the stairs scanning the report and results from the previous day's stage in my dad's *Daily Telegraph* right after it had been popped through the letter box of our home in the west of England. Even then, when my exposure to the race was limited to the printed page, I was enthralled above all by the mountains and the riders who thrived in them. We'd driven through the Alps on a family holiday and I'd marvelled at the terrain, at the roads twisting up and up for mile after mile, wondering how anyone could possibly race up them.

Later, I'd been on a mountain sports holiday with the school to Tignes in the French Alps. I still remember going into my room in our hotel close to the dam at one end of Lac du Chevril, opening the doors onto the balcony and taking in the breathtaking view across the water to the mountains towering over the resorts of Tignes and Val d'Isère, the sensation of wonder and, at the same time, insignificance so overwhelming that my roommate wondered why I had tears in my eyes.

My passion for the mountains was stoked further by Channel 4's coverage of the Tour de France; by the internecine battle between Bernard Hinault and Greg LeMond in 1986 and their hand-in-hand finish at Alpe d'Huez; by Stephen Roche's emergence from the mist at La Plagne and his collapse at the finish line in 1987; and by the ding-dong duel between LeMond and Laurent Fignon in 1989. Now, I was at last set to witness the race for myself.

My anticipation of seeing the riders race over the last climb on the final mountain stage of the 1990 Tour had been heightened considerably by our journey from south-east London. A few evenings before, we'd ridden to Paddington Station, caught the train to Plymouth and ridden to the docks to take the ferry to Santander. Having arrived in the wonderfully picturesque Spanish port first thing on a mid-July morning, we'd headed south into the Cantabrian mountains, where the heat was ferocious. Climbing the final pass of a long day, I'd succumbed to the conditions. Affected by heat stroke, I first sat, then slumbered, then slept at the side of the road. Andy coaxed me back to my feet, before pushing both bikes up the mountain while I staggered along in his wake, looking every inch the drunken Englishman in Spain. When, three days later, we reached the Spanish side of the Pyrenees, just to the east of Pamplona, that experience had convinced me that I had no hope of making it over the Port de Larrau into France.

As we started up, I looked high above towards the Pic d'Orhy astride the border and could see huge birds circling on thermals – eagles perhaps or a group of bearded vultures – and wondered how I would ever reach that altitude. After an hour or so of steady plodding, I was looking down on them, exhilarated by the landscape and, more than anything, by the knowledge that I was sure to make it to the top. I arrived soon after, feeling drained but virtuous as I watched a group of German motorcyclists high-fiving each other and taking pictures next to the summit sign having ridden in high-powered style up the pass. While we stood there contemplating the peaks as cloud began to swirl in around them, I was moved in the same way I had been a few years earlier looking out over Lac du Chevril. There was something else too – the realization of the incomparable majesty of the mountains as a setting for sport, an arena where the competitive challenge and the joy of spectating is thrillingly amplified.

Having plunged through the gloom into France, our pannier racks providing a rattling accompaniment on the frost-eroded surface, we hopped over the little but lovely Col d'Ichère, swept down the narrow valley carved by the Gave d'Aspe to Escot, then climbed the western flank of the Marie-Blanque, its 1,069-metre height belying the difficulty of the climbing test it presents over the final four kilometres to the pass, which average a touch more than 10 per cent and were horrible. But we'd made it.

Looking back, the stage the next day was rather mundane, although it seemed magnificent to us at the time. Claudio Chiappucci, the firecracker Italian climber who was the revelation of that race and was still in the yellow jersey, passed right next to us, closely marked by Greg LeMond, who had trimmed his lead to a mere five seconds and was waiting for the time trial a couple of days hence to make his final swoop. There were few dramatics. It was one of those rare mountain stages of transition between two critical phases of the race, best remembered now as the first in the Tour's history to be won by a Russian rider, Dmitri Konyshev proving victorious in Pau. My clearest memory is of the last man on the road, Banesto's Javier Lukin, a Basque climber who should have been in his element on the mountain roads on which his name had been daubed again and again by Spanish fans, but was struggling off the back. He looked haggard, tormented, and was quite unable to rouse himself as we all urged him on.

Why was he putting himself through this? And why were we enjoying watching him do it?

Understanding this requires some knowledge not only of the history and nature of bike racing, but also of humanity's relationship with the mountains, an examination of what writer and mountain climber Robert Macfarlane has described as 'the industry of ascent'.

In his book *Mountains of the Mind*, he says this began with the Italian poet Petrarch's climb to the summit of Mont Ventoux in April 1336, although few cyclists would recognize this infamous peak as the 'benign 1,910-metre lump in the Vaucluse' that Macfarlane depicts it as.

It turned out that Petrarch's expedition in the company of his brother Gherardo proved something of a false dawn for climbers, as another four hundred years would pass before the mountains were regarded as worthy of exploration and, ultimately, veneration. Until the eighteenth century, they were essentially viewed with trepidation to the extent where, says Macfarlane, 'travellers who had to cross the Alpine passes often chose to be blindfolded in order to prevent them being terrified by the appearance of the peaks'.

Interest and exploration of the natural landscape began to flourish from the late eighteenth century, prompted by the influence of the Sublime, an intellectual doctrine that suggested there was pleasure to be found in fear. Among its principal proponents was Anglo-Irish philosopher Edmund Burke, who was interested in the human psychic response to wild landscapes that captivated and terrified at the same time, producing an intoxicating combination of pleasure and terror. According to Burke, Sublime sights induced a sense of terror, which 'always produces delight when it does not press too close'.

The inclination to savour the sublime, to venture into and explore highlands, could be seen in the fashion among upper-class young men from Britain to spend time in the Alps during the Grand Tour, which was often undertaken after they had completed their education. It was also evident in the advent of Alpinism. After the first ascent of Mont Blanc was completed in 1786, most of the major peaks in the range were conquered over the next fifty years. Writers and artists were also drawn to these highlands, among them John Ruskin, who wrote in his 1856 book *Of Mountain Beauty*:

> Those desolate and threatening ranges of dark mountain, which, in nearly all ages of the world, men have looked upon with aversion or terror and shrunk back from as if they were haunted by perpetual images of death are, in reality, sources of life and happiness far fuller and more beneficent than all the bright fruitfulness of the plain . . .

Stirred by works such as Ruskin's, tourists began to travel in numbers to the mountains, some on the first package holidays as the travel industry began to flourish. Health resorts and spas opened up for those looking for the restorative qualities of the clean air and spring waters to treat lung, liver and other complaints. Towards the end of the nineteenth century, as the popularity of the bicycle as a means both of transport and of leisure spread through the industrialized world, cyclists began to explore the uplands as well.

When, in 1903, the Tour de France was first run and instantly became an enormous popular success, it was inevitable that the race would venture into the country's massifs. Just two years later, the organizers included a stage through the Vosges on France's eastern frontier. In 1910, the Pyrenees were introduced for the first time, followed by the high Alps in the next edition. These innovations changed not only the Tour, but also the perception of bike racing, setting it far from the urban velodromes where it had initially flourished and in a markedly different arena, the most spectacular and challenging in sport. 'The mountains were not simply a component of the Tour, but were its driving force', Serge Laget asserts in *Cols Mythiques du Tour de France*. 'The passion, the tension, the dramatic side of the Tour, its suspense, only emerged with the Aubisque, the Tourmalet and the Galibier.'

The fascination with these highlands was fed by the hyperbole of the press in that pre-radio era. When the racers first tackled the 'circle of death' comprising the Peyresourde, Aspin, Tourmalet and Aubisque passes during that 1910 Tour, the papers played up fears of possible attacks by bears and wolves. The roads were described as 'impassable' and even 'non-existent'. The race reports read almost like journeys of exploration, Tour boss Henri Desgrange depicting 'pedalling pygmies nibbling at . . . mountainous giants'. These portrayals might seem overblown now that we've become so familiar with these extraordinary landscapes, but they captured the epic nature of the setting and of the riders' exploits, while establishing the mountains as the stage for racing excellence.

At the same time, just as we've come to venerate high-altitude locations such as the Galibier, Stelvio and Angliru, we've also developed a fascination and reverence for the riders who thrive in these high-rise temples of sport. They have become, suggests Laget, 'the true and only aristocrats of the peloton'. Although the reality is more nuanced than that, the kings and queens of the mountains captivate us because in a sport where the riders are often so closely packed that it's difficult to work out who they are and what their tactics might be, there is beautiful simplicity to racing in the mountains. Slowed by gradient, gravity and, gradually, diminishing physical resources, a natural selection takes place, the anticipation building among spectators until the inevitable acceleration comes and the real drama starts to unfold.

From René Pottier riding away from his rivals on the Ballon d'Alsace in 1905, which was cycling's first great climbing exploit, all the way through to Tadej Pogačar's ruthless confirmation of his dominance at the summit of Luz Ardiden in the 2021 Tour de France, that basic racing scenario has remained essentially unchanged, even though the art of climbing and the nature of climbers has changed considerably. So too has our fascination with these enthralling athletes, each hoping to *fare il vuoto*, to get a gap – a moment described by iconic Italian climber Marco Pantani as 'the most beautiful thing there is . . .'

Chapter 2

The first King of the Mountains

Until the late 1860s, early incarnations of the bicycle were regarded as hobbyist machines rather than a means for racing. This began to change in May 1868 when a Paris-based manufacturer of velocipedes, which featured cranks and pedals mounted on the hub of the front wheel, organised the first recognized races in the French capital's Parc de Saint-Cloud. The success of this event led to the running of the first organized bike race, held over 123 undulating kilometres between Paris and Rouen on 7 November 1869. Over the next two decades, the racing scene flourished in France, Britain, Belgium, the USA and other industrialized countries. Competitions were track-based for the most part, the results published in a crop of specialist newspapers that were established, such as *Véloce Sport*, *Sport Vélocipédique* and, in the UK, *Cyclist*.

One of cycling's early competitive steps towards the mountains was taken on Westerham Hill in south-east London on the final Saturday of August 1887. That day, 24 riders signed up to take part in the inaugural Catford Hill Climb. On a course of around a mile and a half where the gradient touched one-in-six, or 18 per cent, on its steepest section, only a dozen of them managed to finish, S F Edge of Anerley Bicycle Club the quickest of them on a bike that weighed 15.8kg.

Perhaps even at that point, but certainly soon after, the most intrepid French riders were already exploring the Pyrenees on early editions of the 'safety' bicycle, the forerunner of the modern bike, so called because its design with two wheels that were the same or at least a similar size was an alternative to the far more hazardous penny-farthing. Among them was Louis Bonneville, a friend of Charles Terront, winner of the first edition of the Paris–Brest–Paris race in 1891.

Inspired by the rides he'd done with Terront, who was the first great champion of French cycling, and particularly by the duels they'd had 'when climbing certain hills', Bonneville organized France's first hill climb on the first Sunday of September 1892 at Villeneuve-sur-Lot. A Monsieur Malaure won the event, ascending a four-kilometre hill averaging 6 per cent in ten minutes and sixteen seconds, ten seconds quicker than runner-up M. Labénédie, with François Barlangue another sixteen seconds back in third place. The short report on the event in the weekly newspaper *Véloce Sport* noted that, 'The first three were riding machines with pneumatics weighing around 16kg, a gear of 1.47m.' It added, 'The most remarkable performance was that of the third-placed rider, young Barlauge [*sic*], a young cyclist just 14 and a half years old.'

Over the decade that followed Bonneville's event, bike racing flourished as a popular spectator sport, although it was mostly on tracks in the dozens of velodromes that opened across France, a phenomenon that was mirrored in Britain. Road racing, meanwhile, remained a niche interest, logistical issues making them difficult to organize. Yet, as the bike's popularity as a mode of transport boomed in the final decade of the nineteenth century, manufacturers sought out new ways to gain a commercial edge on their rivals.

In March 1902, *La Vie au Grand Air*, a weekly illustrated review, announced:

> The Touring Club of France is organizing, in the month of August next, a competition for touring bicycles that will comprise:
>
> 1. A preliminary examination of the machines taking part
> 2. A road route designed to test the function and resistance of all parts of the bicycle
>
> This test will take place on 18 August 1902 on a very hilly 225-kilometre course (Tarbes, Lourdes, Luz, col du Tourmalet, Bagnères-de-Bigorre, Loucrop, Lourdes, Luz, col du Tourmalet, Bagnères-de-Bigorre and return to Tarbes).

The route had been chosen because it was in such poor condition and would therefore provide an extremely rigorous test of the bikes and their componentry, although the two descents from the Tourmalet pass were neutralized, the organizers stressing that the event wasn't a race and that the riders' safety was paramount. It attracted a number of the leading manufacturers and racers of the era, including that year's Paris–Bordeaux winner and Paris–Roubaix runner-up Édouard Wattelier and three riders who would figure prominently in the inaugural Tour de France the following season: Hippolyte Aucouturier, Jean Fischer and Rodolfo Muller. The latter, a French-nationalized Italian, was the first to finish what actually became a 215-kilometre test with a reported 4,158 metres of climbing. Muller, riding a two-speed Clément shod with Dunlop pneumatics, completed the course in 11 hours and 39 minutes, 8 minutes ahead of Fischer, known as 'Le Grimpeur', The Climber. Riding a one-speed BSA, Fischer was the first rider to top the Tourmalet on both crossings, but Muller overhauled him on the return to Tarbes when he was waylaid, *Le Vélo* reported, due to 'multiple punctures that deprived him of first place'.

The papers were unanimous in their praise of the event's 'perfect' organization. It was, though, an extremely taxing challenge, as Muller revealed. He told the reporter from *La Vie au Grand Air*:

> I was delighted with my race; I consider this event as the most terrible of all those I've participated in, that's to say Marseille–Paris 1902 (second place), Paris–Brest and back 1901 (sixth), Bordeaux–Paris 1902 (third), and finally the record for Paris–Madrid which I still hold. The road's surface is very good, but terribly undulating and there were lots of riders who, having finished the first crossing, were already completely spent.

Marseille–Paris, it's worth noting, had taken place the previous May in weather so horrific that little more than half of the starters had made it to the finish and one ill-fated rider was found dead at the roadside.

What stands out from the photographs that appeared in *La Vie au Grand Air* is the dustiness of the unpaved roads, riders walking to the summit of the Tourmalet, the familiarity of that mountain landscape that has featured so often in the Tour de France, and the almost complete absence of spectators. Designed essentially as a test of bike and bits, as many events were during that period, it didn't attract much popular interest. Yet it was undoubtedly very significant, gathering a lot of attention – within the sporting press, at least, where it was front-page news – and demonstrating that the high mountains weren't beyond the bounds of either racers or their equipment.

This wasn't enough, however, to convince Henri Desgrange to consider sending the first edition of the Tour de France into the mountains in 1903, as he sought to boost the flagging sales of *L'Auto*, the daily sports newspaper he edited. With hindsight, this might be seen as an opportunity missed by Desgrange and his reporter Géo Lefèvre, who proposed 'a tour of France' as an unprecedented event that could capture the popular imagination and rescue the ailing title. But the six-stage race running between most of France's major cities that they proposed, the first multi-stage race the sport had ever seen, was so extraordinary in its scale that most expectations were that it would fail. Even Desgrange wasn't convinced of its prospects for success, especially when he saw the turn-out at the start in the Paris suburb of Montgeron. The new race drew a decent crowd, but not the kind of throng that suggested the race would prove a sporting sensation.

Yet as soon as the 60 riders in that inaugural Tour left Paris for the provinces, the popular response was staggering. Roadsides were lined in every village and town, checkpoints were packed, the riders were acclaimed as sporting heroes, and, at the same time, the rise in *L'Auto*'s fortunes was stratospheric, as daily sales rose tenfold and more.

There were some significant climbs on the route too, the highest of them being the 1,161-metre Col de la République, on the southern outskirts of Saint-Étienne, which the riders tackled in the early hours of the morning on the second stage between Lyon and Marseille. The stage-winner, Hippolyte Aucouturier, who was also the first to the summit of the République, described it as 'a terrible climb' and it must have felt that way to Jean Fischer, who attacked its lower slopes too quickly and paid the price further up the 17-kilometre ascent, 'The Climber' reduced to crawling pace.

Oddly, the Col de la République tends to be overlooked as the Tour's first pass in Tour histories for reasons that are not obviously apparent. It lies on the eastern side of the Massif Central, which is one of France's five major mountain massifs along with the Alps, Pyrenees, Vosges and Jura. What's more, it's a mere 17 metres lower than the pass that is usually credited as providing the Tour's first encounter in the mountains, the 1,178-metre Ballon d'Alsace.

This statistical anomaly is generally put down to the fact that Desgrange had overlooked the myth-making possibilities that climbs like the République offered. Indeed, these may not even have occurred to him until he assigned chief correspondent and key confidant Alphonse Steinès to carry out 'Operation Martini', a four-week vehicle-testing trip in the Alps that took place in the wake of a 1904 Tour that was beset by all kinds of cheating and chicanery and eventually saw the top four finishers disqualified and banned. Desgrange had toyed with the idea of not running the Tour again, but, once he had returned to Paris, Steinès encouraged the Tour boss to move on from this scandal by expanding the scope of the race route, specifically by seeking the mountains deliberately for the first time.

The Ballon d'Alsace, Col Bayard and Côte de Laffrey are comparative small fry for modern-day climbers, but for the riders in the 1905 race they offered a rare and extremely demanding challenge and were, according to cycling historian Serge Laget, presented as 'authentic giants'. When the Tour's third edition reached the first of those ascents on 11 July, L'Auto's hyping of the challenge these mountains presented and the heroic exploits they would likely produce was vindicated by the performance of a Tour debutant who was consecrated as cycling's first 'king of the mountains'.

The fifth of seven children born to carpenter Léon Pottier and his wife Anna Berthe Guillerot, René Pottier grew up in a well-to-do household at Moret-sur-Loing, 90 kilometres south of Paris. Like his four brothers and two sisters, he spent a good deal of his time swimming in the river next to the mill where they lived and riding bikes that their father's comparative wealth made available to them. René and his younger brother André, who would also become a professional cyclist, raced handicap events against their older brothers Léon and Charles. The four brothers then began racing in local events, where they proved almost unbeatable.

In 1903, towards the end of his three-year national service, Pottier joined the well-renowned Vélo Club de Levallois (VCL), winning a handful of races that season in their distinctive white jersey with a black band around the chest. That October, he set a new mark for the French amateur hour record of 40.080 kilometres at the Buffalo velodrome in Paris, *L'Auto* reporting that 'Pottier confirmed his undoubted qualities with this performance'. Watching the 24-year-old Pottier that day, Lucien Petit-Breton, who was also a member of the VCL and would very soon become one of his biggest rivals, described him as 'a slender, dark-haired boy who's rather taciturn. He has a mystic's piercing gaze, prominent cheekbones and a forehead that's ready to welcome the wrinkles of internal torment even before those that come with age.' His analysis would prove to be prescient.

Pottier turned pro in 1904 and soon afterwards set new world records for the paced kilometre and paced 20-kilometre marks. The following season, he joined the powerful Peugeot team and began to make a significant impact on the road, finishing runner-up at Paris–Roubaix and then losing out narrowly to Aucouturier at Bordeaux–Paris. Regarded as a strong sprinter with almost unparalleled powers of endurance, he made his Tour debut that summer, when he quickly revealed he had a special talent on the climbs too.

The second stage between Nancy and Besançon had the Ballon d'Alsace pass as its high point and it produced the first significant mountains duel in racing history between Aucouturier, Léon Georget, Louis Trousselier, defending Tour champion Henri Cornet and Pottier. The contest beautifully described by Victor Breyer in *L'Auto*. He recounted how first Trousselier, 'to our unutterable surprise', and then Georget, 'betrayed by his resources', fell off the pace. Aucouturier was the next to yield, leaving Cornet and Pottier locked in a duel. 'Gasping, dripping with sweat, both of them gave everything they had. Cornet fell two lengths back, then got bridged back up, then fell back again, and that was it,' wrote Breyer. Pottier pressed on alone to the summit, not easing up until he reached the top.

Pottier's startling performance in completing the nine-kilometre ascent in forty minutes, averaging eighteen kilometres per hour, led to the press dubbing him 'the king of the mountains'. His rivals were hugely impressed, too. Comparing his fluid climbing to Cornet's more pugnacious and punchy style, Lucien Petit-Breton said that Pottier 'looked much more beautiful on his machine, lighter, more harmonious in his pedalling technique. His speed didn't drop for a second in the final kilometre, the hardest. It was very beautiful to see and moving even. It made you forget fears that all of the riders would be forced to complete the climb on foot.' The description suggests that Pottier was a *rouleur-grimpeur*, a racer who in the style of Fausto Coppi, Eddy Merckx and Bernard Hinault, would climb at a consistent and high pace, as opposed to a pure climber, who tend to advance with short bursts of speed, repeated again and again, often breaking the rhythm of their rivals.

Breyer's boss, Desgrange, was equally effusive in his praise of Pottier's exploit. He wrote, contrasting the Frenchman with Welshman Arthur Linton, joint winner of Bordeaux–Paris in 1896, who died two months after that success as a result of typhoid fever:

> The ascent of the Ballon d'Alsace by the lead group, comprising Pottier, Aucouturier, Cornet, Georget and Trousselier, was one of the most exciting things I've ever seen and confirmed the opinion of many others that man's courage is limitless and that a well-trained athlete can strive for incredible results . . . Pottier's courage compared to that of Arthur Linton, and I don't think I could give higher praise than that to this new arrival on the professional scene who will, if he continues, leave us with the memory of unparalleled endurance . . .

Although he didn't know it, Desgrange's assessment of the two men would prove to be even more apposite, for wholly tragic reasons.

Dropping the whole field on the Ballon d'Alsace proved to be Pottier's final mark on that Tour. Caught by Aucouturier on the descent, who later rode clear to win in Besançon, he finished second on that stage, but was forced to drop out of the following one, some said due to the exertion of his effort scaling the Ballon, but actually as a result of injuries sustained in a crash.

He returned the next year to a race that looked wholly different, its distance extended, at the instigation of Steinès, by 50 per cent to 4,500 kilometres, a genuine Tour de France that also ventured beyond the borders of *l'Hexagone* for the first time thanks to brief incursions into Germany, Italy and Spain. Winner of the second stage into Nancy, having spent a good part of an hour making a repair and then needing to chase for 200 kilometres to reel in his rivals, Pottier, described by one writer as having 'dry and robust muscles' and 'without an ounce of excess fat on him', began the third stage to Dijon via the Ballon d'Alsace as race leader.

Approaching the foot of the climb, Victor Breyer's car slotted in behind the 19 riders in the lead group. In his report in the next morning's edition of *L'Auto*, he described Pottier going straight to the front as the road began to rise, moving so quickly that it was 'as if the bell had just rung out to signal the start of the final lap in a track race'. His injection of pace had an instant effect, scattering his rivals as he sped away 'like a wild boar escaping from the dogs.' Never looking back to assess the damage that he was doing, Pottier had just two riders on his wheel as he passed the three-kilometre marker stone on the Ballon d'Alsace: Augustin Ringeval and Georges Passerieu. The latter was the first to lose ground, at which point, said Breyer, 'There was a short, but terrible duel between Pottier and Ringeval'. Pottier opened a gap of five metres, Ringeval closed it, but in doing so he'd reached his limit. 'This time it was over!'

Pottier, wearing a distinctive, shapeless cloth cap with a wide and floppy brim that hung down over his face, rode the final four kilometres to the summit alone, building up a lead of four and a half minutes. It was an astonishing and, at that time, a completely unprecedented feat. Asked to give his perspective at the finish, Petit-Breton commented, 'As if it weren't enough for him to leave us standing, I saw him, with my own eyes, overtake an official race vehicle that was driving in front of us. He was, after all, the only one who wore a hat like that . . .'

Unlike the previous year when he'd been reeled in and dropped by Aucouturier, no one saw Pottier again until they reached Dijon, where his winning margin was 48 minutes. This gap was doubly astonishing, not only because it was so large, but because the general classification (GC) was decided on points and not accumulated time. In other words, he gained no competitive advantage from continuing to ride at such a ferocious pace, apart from demoralizing his opponents. What's more, he continued to race in this unbridled style. Legend has it that he got so far ahead of the rest on stage five that he stopped in a restaurant for lunch and a bottle of wine, drank most of it, then remounted, caught the riders who had passed him and went on to clinch his fourth consecutive stage win. A fifth stage win on the final day into Paris wrapped up the overall title.

'If Pottier managed to drop his rival on a climb, it was finished, he would never be seen again, he would press on alone and the others would have to achieve the impossible in order to bridge back up to him, it was game over', Robert Dieudonné said of him in *La Vie au Grand Air*. This confirms that he was, in effect, Coppi's forerunner, beautifully smooth in his pedalling action, devastating when he produced an acceleration. The harder it was, the better he was. The press and his rivals describe him as looking as fresh at the end of one of these all-annihilating performances as he had at the start. 'For him, racing was a natural function, an instinctive need; he needed to exhaust himself physically,' said Dieudonné.

This hints at another characteristic that has been ascribed to many great climbers: internal torment that fuels a need to find physical oblivion through racing. Pottier was known by his racing peers as 'the man who never laughs' due to his lack of joviality. What stands out in almost every picture of him is his sternness when viewing the camera. There's seldom the hint of a smile below his bushy, Asterix-like moustache. He purveys a sense of suspicion and ill-humour, even when brandishing a victory bouquet.

Such was the extent of Pottier's guardedness that Petit-Breton described it as making him impossible to warm to and immensely intimidating. He stated candidly:

> That boy leaves me utterly cold, gives me stage fright, annihilates me. With Pottier, nine times out of ten, I start already beaten. When it comes to him, I have to write a word that I detest and that I thought I'd never have to use: I have a complex about him. Yes, he's very strong René Pottier, he's got real class, but there's something more that I can't avoid. He's far from being unfriendly, and he shows exemplary loyalty . . . He's always correct, but reserved, with a severe look, unfathomable. It's impossible to gauge his feelings . . . The one thing René Pottier and I have in common is that we don't get on with each other . . . He was really the best, and by far, he completely outclassed us all.

Pottier highlighted that superiority again that September, setting a new record of 925.2 kilometres in winning the prestigious Bol d'Or 24-hour event at the Buffalo velodrome, which proved to be the last race of his career. At half past one in the afternoon of 27 January 1907, Arthur Berthélémy, the director of Peugeot's *service course* on rue Chaptal in the Paris suburb of Levallois-Perret, called Pottier's manager, the journalist Robert Coquelle, to inform him that he had found the Tour winner hanging in the team's workshop. Although Berthélémy quickly cut Pottier down, he had arrived too late to save cycling's outstanding racer.

Having had lunch with Coquelle, during which they'd discussed racing contracts for the upcoming season over a pale ale, Pottier had borrowed Berthélémy's keys to the Peugeot bike store on the premise that he wanted to tidy some things up. After entering the workshop, he first locked himself in, then took his bike down from a hook set in a beam and replaced it with a rope from which he hanged himself. The 27-year-old Pottier left nothing to explain the reason for his suicide.

In his statement to the police, Berthélémy – painting a rather different picture of Pottier to that of his fellow racers – said:

> Pottier was very happy in every respect. He'd got married about two years ago and loved his wife; what's more, everything seemed to make him smile. As it was me who initiated him in his sporting career, he was very close to me and I was in some way his confidant; in other words, if he had any kind of serious concern or was worried in any way, I would have known. Pottier was happy and in good health.

His younger brother, André, suggested that some kind of impropriety had been committed by Pottier's wife, Marie Zélie Herbert, who was four months pregnant at the time. The Pottier family subsequently shunned her, although no evidence was ever produced to substantiate the claim André Pottier had made. Madame Pottier gave birth to a daughter on 25 June and named her Renée in tribute to the father she would never meet.

As would be the case more than a century later following the death of iconic Italian climber Marco Pantani, another rider who won the Tour thanks to his exploits in the mountains, questions surrounding Pottier's unexpected demise triggered considerable conjecture, including suggestions that he might have been murdered. Bearing in mind his Tour win and other successes that had made him a wealthy man, together with the fact that he was at the peak of his competitive form and that his first child would soon arrive, why, the papers asked, would he have hanged himself? One of Pottier's friends noted that the Peugeot ace had carefully cut out the soap-opera strip in that morning's paper so that he could add it to his collection. 'That's not the kind of thing that a man who wants to end his life does,' this friend was reported as saying.

Berthélémy revealed that Pottier's pocket watch was broken, which added to the sense of mystery. This was further heightened on the day of his interment when Pottier's home was burgled and all of his trophies were stolen. Decades later, his grandson, Bernard Marty, said that his grandmother had wanted an autopsy to be carried out on his body. 'She didn't believe he had committed suicide,' he said. The riders' family apparently refused her request to exhume the champion so that this procedure could be carried out. The fact was, there was no clear evidence of any wrongdoing. As one paper summarized, 'the unfortunate Pottier's suicide can only be attributed to a sudden act of madness'.

What did become very clear following the death of the Tour de France champion was the esteem in which he was held by his peers and the press. Robert Dieudonné wrote in an obituary in *La Vie au Grand Air*:

> The harder a race was, the more it seemed to his taste; the greater the effort he had to make, the more his quality shone through . . . During the toughest stages of that long race, he was always at the front, unbeatable, winning from a long way out, winning from so far out that his performances were almost unbelievable; those following him were amazed by this incomparable endurance, of this tenacity that no other rider of repute could equal.

Dieudonné also made the point, 'Always consistent, always serious, he won without showing any joy, remaining silent, severe and stubborn.'

Robert Coquelle described Pottier as 'king René . . . so evident was his huge superiority'. His tactic was simple, Coquelle explained: 'go to the front and ride as hard as he could until there was no one left on his wheel, then keep going'. This strategy, relying on relentless pace-setting from the front, would be employed in the same devastatingly impressive fashion by most of the Grand Tour victors who followed him.

In the wake of Pottier's death, a monument was erected in his memory at the summit of the Ballon d'Alsace following a public subscription. The plaque reads: 'In the Tour de France, an annual race of 5,000km organized by *L'Auto*, René Pottier 1879–1907, was the first to arrive at this point in 1905–1906 after having maintained an average speed of 20 kilometres per hour on the climb of the Ballon d'Alsace and dropped all of his rivals.' Although it's not clear who finally did beat Pottier's record time for the Tour's 'first' ascent, no one in the next half-dozen editions improved on it, and it is believed to have survived until at least the 1933 Tour, when Vicente Trueba was first to the top on his way to victory in the inaugural King of the Mountains competition.

According to Serge Laget, Pottier's performances 'opened up a new world, the mountains, and what was essentially a new discipline, climbing'. More mountain tests were added in the following years, but these didn't prevent strapping *rouleur* François Faber, a Luxembourger like Steinès, from dominating the 1909 Tour, winning six stages including a consecutive run of the five most difficult ones. Faber squeezed all suspense out of the race, leaving Desgrange perplexed about how to reinvigorate it as a contest. Steinès, inevitably, had the answer.

'And what if we made the riders go through the Pyrenees?'

Chapter 3

The mythologization of the high mountains

While the significance of the 1903 Tour de France and the half-dozen editions that followed it can't be understated, as they transformed road racing totally, the 1910 Tour changed the sport in a wholly different way, for the introduction of the high mountains elevated it to epic status, for the sporting public and press at least. The riders had a very different perspective on this initiative, as we shall see.

Although frequently portrayed as occurring on a whim, a depiction that fits with the myth-making consensus within French cycling writing about the introduction of the Pyrenees, this pivotal moment was a natural step for Tour boss Henri Desgrange and his organizing team to take in order to boost circulation figures for *L'Auto*. It occurred as a consequence of exhaustive planning and reconnaissance, prompted by the growing realization that the high peaks would likely raise the Tour into the realm of the extraordinary. In short, rather than being accidental, it was inevitable.

Following the successful introduction of the Ballon d'Alsace in 1905 and the gradual addition of other mid-range passes in subsequent years, a Prix de Côtes was introduced for the 1908 Tour. Also known as the Prix Labor-Hutchinson, after the bike manufacturer and tyre company, respectively, who were its sponsors, it was won in both that year and in 1909 by Lucien Petit-Breton. This competition's title is significant because it highlights the extent of the climbs that featured in the Tour and other races in the final decade of the nineteenth century and the first of the twentieth. They were *côtes*, or hills, and the riders that thrived on them were known as *côtiers* rather than *grimpeurs*, hill climbers rather than mountain climbers.

This changed with what Victor Breyer, the Tour's race director, described as 'a leap into the unknown'. Interviewed in *But et Club* in 1950, he confirmed that the initiative was very much the idea of *L'Auto* correspondent Alphonse Steinès. 'He was convinced that the new formula was going to transform the chrysalis that had already become a butterfly into an eagle,' explained Breyer. He suggested that, as had been the case when Géo Lefèvre had suggested the possibility of a 'tour of France' to Desgrange in late 1902, Steinès's initial hurdle was in convincing *L'Auto*'s editor-in-chief that the scheme was viable. This fits with the well-established narrative that has developed around the Tour's first flirtation with the high mountains, but there isn't convincing evidence to fully support the claims that Desgrange was as reluctant as he's generally portrayed to be. In actual fact, the tale that has been spun around these events doesn't stand up well when set against articles that appeared in *L'Auto* between the end of the 1909 Tour and the race's arrival in the Pyrenees a year later. These stories also highlight the extent of the myth-making involved, a common trait among certain French cycling writers who would interweave embellishment with fact.

Let's begin with the well-known tale that depicts Desgrange as hesitant when it came to venturing into the Pyrenees. This is recounted by Pierre Chany, *L'Équipe*'s chief cycling writer for the best part of fifty years, in his histories of the race including *La Fabuleuse*

Histoire du Tour de France, and in Marcel Diamant-Berger's *Histoire du Tour de France*, which was published in 1959 and, therefore, fifty years on from these events taking place. Both depict Desgrange as conflicted. On the one hand, the Pyrenees would make the race a quite different test and a true tour of France, as the race would venture right to the edges of *L'Héxagone*. On the other hand, he was concerned that the initiative risked pushing the riders beyond their physical limits and, subsequently, rebounding on the popularity of his newspaper. This was, it should be remembered, a time when Frenchman Arthur Latham's world altitude record for an aeroplane stood at 1,100 metres, lower than some of the passes lined up for the Tour route, including the Port, Aspin, Peyresourde and Aubisque, and only half the height of the Tourmalet.

The starting point for both accounts is a meeting that is said to have taken place early on in 1910 between Desgrange and Alphonse Steinès, one of his chief correspondents whose role also included helping to draw up the Tour route each year. Diamant-Berger describes Steinès telling his vacillating boss that the Pyrenean initiative 'would be a huge success'. Desgrange responds to this by exclaiming: 'I'm telling you again that I don't agree that the race should pass through the Pyrenees. You just don't realize! The Pyrenean passes . . . You're going to make me kill them!' Steinès retorts by insisting: 'Not at all . . . I'm even convinced that this will be the key to the Tour.'

Desgrange's biography is silent on this encounter, and it appears that first Diamant-Berger and then Chany have drawn on an account provided by Steinès in 1952 in what is described as 'a delightful pamphlet' by renowned cycling historian Serge Laget in *L'Équipe*'s 2005 book *Cols Mythiques du Tour de France*. Prior to this point, though, Desgrange had already indicated within the columns of *L'Auto* that the Pyrenees would be on the programme for the 1910 Tour. He had hinted at this during the 1909 edition, which was a cakewalk for powerful Luxembourg rouleur François Faber. The high mountains, the Tour director opined, would provide a very different athletic test than the flat stages into Toulouse from Nîmes and then on to Bayonne.

On 30 September, Desgrange penned an article on his paper's front page confirming this route change: 'Faithful to the line of conduct that we've been following and that, for eight years, has been pushing us on to continually widen our Tour de France, here are the modifications that we've made to certain routes: the Tour de France will enter the Pyrenees . . . the Tour de France will head from Perpignan to Bayonne. The first stage will go from Perpignan to Bagnères de Luchon (289km), and the second from Bagnères to Bayonne (325km).' The only regret he voiced was that the race wouldn't be passing through Toulouse, as it always had previously, and he expressed the hope that the Toulousains would understand the reason for the decision.

During the spring of 1910, *L'Auto*'s Georges Abran and Charles Ravaud surveyed the Tour route, providing reports, published in the newspaper, that covered the state of the roads, the landscape and any other relevant factors. They were unable, though, to cross a few of the Pyrenean passes that were still blocked by persistent falls of snow, including the Tourmalet, Aubisque and Aspin. These snowfalls continued into June. In the middle of that month, Alcyon team manager Alphonse Baugé led his riders on a reconnaissance of the Tour stages in the south, including the pair in the Pyrenees. In a letter to Ravaud that was published in *L'Auto*, he asks: 'My friend, where the devil is Monsieur Desgrange taking us? In truth, it's frightening . . . What climbs and, above all, what descents . . . this passage will certainly go down in legend in the annals of cycle sport.'

Lucien Petit-Breton, the first rider to win two editions of the Tour and a teammate of defending champion François Faber on that Alcyon squad, voiced his concerns in *La Vie au Grand Air*, writing: 'When I was doing a reconnaissance, a month before the race, of the two new stages added by *L'Auto* to the Tour itinerary, I felt a real sense of fear at the idea that I would have to tackle them again in the race, that is to say for real, climbing that terrible giants' staircase that those two stages comprise, especially the second one, from Luchon to Bayonne.'

On 24 June, less than ten days before the Tour was set to start in Paris, another missive from Baugé appeared in *L'Auto*'s pages, this one written following a failed attempt to cross the Tourmalet by six Alcyon riders, five from Legnano and two independents. He detailed how Louis Trousselier had fallen into a torrent and Georges Cadolle had been badly injured in a crash. Ominously, he also declared: 'The road over the Tourmalet doesn't exist. It's disappeared beneath 6 to 8 metres of snow, and the poor devils, after an extremely difficult descent, were obliged to descend the formidable slope sitting on the snow, holding their machines behind them as a brake.'

In the adjacent column, Ravaud, who had met the riders when they'd returned by train to Paris, wrote that the race organisers were hoping that the roads would be passable four weeks hence. He added, though: 'If it happens that, contrary to preceding years, the Tourmalet and the Col d'Aubisque are still impracticable, we would consider modifying the route.' Ravaud went on to explain that Alphonse Steinès would travel in the coming days to inspect the route for himself, specifically that of the tenth stage over the Tourmalet and Aubisque and on to Bayonne.

It's hard to believe that Desgrange would have been alone in the *L'Auto* office in having second thoughts about the wisdom of sending the riders over these two passes. However, everyone's fears must have been eased a little when Steinès reported back that he had crossed the Peyresourde and Aspin without any problem on his first day of reconnaissance. On 29 June, the final story on *L'Auto*'s front page announced that Steinès had crossed the Tourmalet, the news revealed to them in 'a brief dispatch that has been sent from Barèges by our devoted correspondent, Monsieur Lanne Camy'. Beneath this they printed the message sent: 'BAREGES, 28 JUNE. – Alphonse Steinès crossed the Tourmalet on foot, yesterday evening, at 10 o'clock. – Lanne CAMY'.

On 30 June, the paper reported that Steinès had crossed the Aubisque and would deliver a fuller description of his experiences on the Tourmalet the next day. However, before examining that, let's hark back to Diamant-Berger's account of Steinès's travails on that latter pass, which describes how, together with *L'Auto*'s local correspondent, Paul Dupont, Steinès sets out from the auberge where the pair stayed in Sainte Marie de Campan, travelling in a roadmender's vehicle. After climbing for 15 kilometres, they reach the snowline and before too long the only way to pick out the road is by the poles planted alongside it.

At seven in the evening, the car is forced to a stop by drifts and Steinès is reported to have told Dupont: 'Listen, the car can't get over, you go back down and go all the way around the Pic de Midi massif. As for me, I'll cross the pass on foot. There's no snow on the other side, and I'll walk down to Barèges where you can meet me again.

There's still about four kilometres from here to the col, and from the col to Barèges there's another twelve or so, or sixteen in total. It's seven o'clock, I will be in Barèges at ten. I must get over the pass; the Tour must too.'

Anyone with even a little experience of walking in the high mountains would instantly realise that Steinès's timetable was laughably optimistic. Covering 16 kilometres in three hours on terrain like that would test even the hardiest of walkers, let alone one preparing to find their way through deep snow wearing leather brogues and carrying a cane. As he sets off, Dupont warns him that bears come over from Spain when there's snow in order to feast on the French flocks. 'But we're not sheep,' Steinès replies.

He soon finds himself in snow so deep that the four-metre-high roadside poles aren't apparent. By fortune, he stumbles upon a young shepherd and gives him a 20-franc gold piece in exchange for guiding him to the summit of the Tourmalet. When they reach it, at somewhere between half past nine and ten in the evening and with darkness closing in, they discover that the snow is just as deep on the far side. The shepherd turns back, while Steinès, using his cane for support, slips his way downwards.

He soon loses his footing in a mini-avalanche and ends up in a muddy stream. He follows the cascading watercourse down the valley, finally finding a track dug out of the snow and soon after comes across a stone kilometre marker and sits astride it, sobbing with relief. While sitting on the marker stone, he spots lights and figures walking up the road towards him, and it turns out to be a group of gendarmes who have come up from Barèges searching for Steinès after he hasn't appeared as expected. They escort him to the Hôtel de France et de l'Angleterre, where he is welcomed by the proprietor and newly anointed *L'Auto* correspondent Lanne Camy, who informs him that's it's three in the morning. He has a warm bath, eats dinner and goes to bed. The next morning, he sends a telegraph to Desgrange: 'Henri Desgrange. L'Auto. Paris. Passé Tourmalet, stop. Très bonne route, stop. Parfaitement faisable.' The crossing of the Tourmalet is practicable.

Comparing Diamant-Berger's version with the detailed report that Steinès described in the 1 July edition of *L'Auto*, it quickly becomes apparent that the latter doesn't need any embellishment at all. It's full of gripping detail, and begins with him saying:

> I did indeed cross it, but God knows how. If I lived to a hundred, I would always remember the details of this struggle against the mountain, the snow, the ice, the clouds, the ravines, the darkness, the cold, against the isolation, against hunger, thirst, against everything in a word . . . Nothing has been exaggerated. Given the state it's in now, it's madness to want to try to cross the pass. The mountain folk had told me that I couldn't cross it. But when I left Paris I'd promised our Director that I would see for myself and I tried to cross it no matter the cost. I almost paid for this mad recklessness with my life. Yes, almost.

Having stressed that it was likely the snow would melt away under July's powerful sun before the riders reached the pass little more than three weeks hence, Steinès reflected on the challenge facing them, saying: 'What's more, it is useful that everyone knows that crossing these passes, even when they're practicable again, won't be child's play. It will be the greatest performance that any rider will ever have produced.'

Focusing on the specific details of his adventure, Steinès said that his driver's Dietrich car was forced to stop two kilometres from the top of the Tourmalet at seven in the evening. Thick cloud cloaked the slopes, making it difficult for *L'Auto*'s correspondent to pick his path. But he was helped by a cowherd, who guided him to the pass, Steinès falling through the hard-packed snow into deep holes, some head-high, on a number of occasions. It took the pair an hour to reach the top, where the cowherd said he was turning back. 'I initially begged my shepherd not to leave me like that, to not abandon me in these Siberian steppes, in this desert of snow where I wouldn't dare to take a step because I would risk breaking my bones in this landscape I didn't know, where there wasn't a path or trail, on this path that is frequented by bears that come from Spain. After begging, I made threats, and I believe that if I had been carrying a gun I wouldn't have hesitated to make use of it,' he confessed.

He slipped, stumbled, rolled and tumbled down the mountainside. After four kilometres, he saw a slash of darkness in the snow and heard running water, then staggered on downhill, following the course of the stream that he had come upon, not sure of the time because his watch had stopped at 8.20 during one of his innumerable falls. This stream led to another, guiding him down the valley. Soon after, his spirits began to lift when he noticed the tread of a bike tyre on the track he was on and began to run in the direction it led, fatigue finally forcing him to sit at the roadside, 'where I cried abundantly'. As he hunkered down there, he noticed a light and shouted out. Two figures approached through the gloom, a pair of gendarmes who led him down to the Hôtel Richelieu at Barèges, where the proprietor, Monsieur Lanne Camy, gave him some dry clothes and then served him dinner. 'It was half past ten in the evening. The other travellers looked at me like I was some kind of phenomenon. I was the gentleman who had crossed the Tourmalet at night.'

His walk had been epic, but it hadn't taken eight hours and finished at three in the morning, as Diamant-Berger's account suggests. What's more, there's no mention of Steinès sending a telegraph to *L'Auto*'s Paris office with his renowned message that the Tourmalet was passable. However, Lanne Camy did contact them, with his assurance that their correspondent had arrived safely at ten o'clock in the evening. The discrepancies are minor, but quite significant, the result no doubt of back copies of *L'Auto* being difficult to access in the immediate post-war years, which certainly encouraged embellishment. As for the very precise details of conversations that Steinès had with Desgrange before his expedition and with various people during it, these may have been drawn from the 1952 pamphlet mentioned by Serge Laget in *Cols Mythiques du Tour de France*, or perhaps from an interview that Daimant-Berger carried out with Steinès before his death in January 1960.

To reach Luchon on the 289-kilometre route from Perpignan, the riders tackled four passes – the Col du Portel at Quillan, the Col de Port between Tarascon and Saint-Girons, then the Col de Portet d'Aspet, and, finally, the Col des Ares, followed by 25 flat kilometres into the finish. Watching the action unfold from the *L'Auto* car, Desgrange noted in his newspaper how the first two climbs weren't hard enough to split the best riders. The Portet d'Aspet was a different proposition, though. Nowadays, this eastern flank of the pass is a comparatively easy ascent for professional riders, but in the early twentieth century the road followed a different trajectory, one considerably steeper, averaging 10 per cent for four kilometres, the crest arriving at 'the end of a terrible and poor ascent', according to one of *L'Auto*'s correspondents. Here, Octave Lapize, known as 'Le Frisé' or 'Curly' for his distinctive hair, got a gap. 'Then, on the descent, which is extremely dangerous, I plunged down. Tough luck if I had some kind of mechanical failure, I was telling myself,' Lapize explained to Alphonse Steinès in Luchon, where he finished eighteen minutes ahead of Émile Georget, race leader François Faber being another four back in third.

Three things should be noted. First, at that time, the race was decided on points rather than accumulated time, so Lapize only cut two points from Faber's lead, reducing it to twelve. In addition, he was a member of the Union des Cyclistes de Paris club whose president was Steinès, who had of course plotted out the two Pyrenean stages. Unlike most of the other Tour favourites, Lapize hadn't carried out any kind of reconnaissance of them, choosing instead to rely on analysing the route on a map with Steinès, his 'friend and mentor'. Eventually, just three riders abandoned during the stage, underlining that it wasn't excessively difficult. Indeed, Lucien Petit-Breton, who had already been forced out of the race following a crash but was still following the Tour as a special correspondent for *La Vie au Grand Air*, described it as 'hard, but not any more so in terms of difficulty than the two stages in the Alps', which had, as always, avoided the high passes in the heart of the range.

Yet, as Petit-Breton highlighted, a far larger challenge now lay ahead for the 59 riders left in the race, 'that terrible giants' staircase'. *L'Auto* billed it in a similar fashion, headlining their preview 'Pygmies against giants'. The yellow-paged paper warned that:

> The test that they're going to take on is the most challenging that has ever been set since the creation of our

sport . . . tomorrow we're going to attempt the impossible; tomorrow we're going to try to make them achieve an exploit that's unprecedented in the annals of our sport . . . I've got an idea that the pygmies will surprise the world!

It's not clear who wrote these words, but almost certainly it was Steinès, who was the only member of *L'Auto*'s editorial staff who was completely aware of what lay ahead on the 326-kilometre route between Luchon and Bayonne. It got under way with a very notable departure, the organizing paper announcing that Victor Breyer was taking over as the Tour referee from Henri Desgrange, who, 'suffering a little bit at the moment, has decided to spend a few days at Luchon, then to return to Paris'. It may have been the case that Luchon's healing waters were precisely the remedy that the Tour boss required for his ills, although it's also been suggested that he wanted to put some distance between himself and his race as it negotiated 'the circle of death', teetering all the while on the edge of calamity. Whatever the reason, Desgrange missed what would prove to be a defining moment for road racing, one described by Petit-Breton as 'a Homeric struggle of men against mountain'.

The riders gathered in the early hours of the morning for the start in Luchon and were waved away at half past three, Octave Lapize and Gustave Garrigou being among the first to reach the initial ramps of the Col de Peyresourde on the western edge of the spa town. At Arreau, on the far side of the Peyresourde, Lapize and Garrigou had already opened up a two-minute lead. They rode on to the Col d'Aspin together, Lapize gaining three minutes on his rival on the ascent, then losing that advantage on the way down to Sainte-Marie-de-Campan, at the foot of the Tourmalet. It was five past six, the day dawning gloriously, as they began to follow the route where Steinès had almost lost his life just a few weeks earlier.

They were set to climb almost 800 vertical metres higher than any Tour stage had previously ventured and adopted very different strategies for this unprecedented test of skill, endurance and mental fortitude. Lapize, who had employed a gear of 5.10m on the previous stage – that is to say, his bike travelled 5.1 metres with each complete revolution of the pedals – had fitted a much smaller gear of 4.45m to cope with the steepness and length of these climbs. He also switched between riding his one-speed bike and pushing it briskly on the rough, gravelly road on which it was often difficult to maintain traction, particularly on steeper sections. This tactic enabled him to open up a 500-metre lead on his rival by the summit.

Garrigou, meanwhile, had opted for a gear of 4.30m and remained in the saddle all the way to the top of the Tourmalet, raising an arm in triumph at the summit as he claimed a special prize of 100 francs for being the first rider to achieve this feat; another two riders later emulated him. 'Ten times, twenty times, we felt that he wouldn't have enough strength to push the pedals through their "dead" point; but we were mistaken', wrote Victor Breyer, who timed Garrigou's ascent at 1 hour and 31 minutes. He added, though, that it was a pyrrhic victory because Lapize, alternating between riding and pushing his bike, reached the top of the pass 'in a clear first place.'

Breyer recounted that the descent, cut through banks of snow, was no more than three metres wide, and that their driver, Chrétien, 'literally had us sliding down to Barèges', riders speeding past *L'Auto*'s car with 'crazed audacity'. Once in the valley, the race director's vehicle once again had a significant speed advantage and worked its way past several riders until it was on the heels of Lapize and

Garrigou, who were back together again approaching the last significant hurdle, the Aubisque, then scaled via the Col du Soulor and a now disused road over the Col de Tortes rather than the modern route around the truly spectacular Cirque du Litor, where the road, perched on a narrow ledge hacked out of a towering cliff-face, is all but guaranteed to stir up awe and fear in equal measure no matter how many times you ride along it.

Breyer's account of the ascent is remarkably honest, the stand-in race referee confessing:

> I'll never forget that savage climb of the Aubisque. It was there, in fact, where I had a very clear vision of total defeat, that I considered the total annihilation of the enormous contest that I'd been made responsible for that same morning by the man who had conceived it . . . Yes, you can smile, as I'm doing now, but I feel no shame in confessing that I perceived disaster for an instant. Listen to my account and you'll understand.

He described how three riders started up the Soulor together, Lapize and Garrigou having been joined by Pierino Albini. The Italian slipped back with a gesture of resignation after just 500 metres. He dismounted and started to push his bike. A kilometre later, Garrigou yielded too, almost falling from his bike next to a stream, which he lay in to cool down. Soon afterwards, Lapize halted too, glancing back as he did, apparently set to abandon. Breyer's car stopped close to him and the stand-in race referee jumped out and ran across to the French rider.

'What's wrong Lapize?'

The man looked at me with revulsion in his eyes.

'You're criminals. Do you understand? Tell Desgrange from me; you shouldn't ask men to make an effort like this. I've had enough.'

Breyer was starting to despair, sensing that the race was over. He managed to persuade Lapize to continue, but was fearful that no one would be following behind the lone leader in what was now debilitating heat. Yet, at that moment, Basque rider François Lafourcade appeared, climbing without evident difficulty on a gear of 4.10m, and passed Lapize in the same steady style that he'd overtaken the other favourites earlier on the climb. An *isolé*, or independent rider, who had no team support at all, the rider from the finish town of Bayonne, continued alone to the summit, completing the whole climb on his bike. Lapize, again alternating between riding and pushing, was the second rider to reach the pass, 16 minutes later.

Most accounts of the leaders' passage through 'the circle of death' describe Lapize spitting out the phrase, 'Assassins! You're all assassins!' in the race referee's direction as he reached the pass. Yet there's no contemporary source for this. In Breyer's account, the pair did have that conversation in the early kilometres of the climb, while Steinès reported Lapize telling him: 'Desgrange is an assassin!' when he spoke at the end of the race in Bayonne to the rider he mentored. Although this discrepancy isn't really of any consequence, it does underline how exploits in the mountains were mythologized, in this case over the years subsequent to them taking place, including – as we shall see – on other occasions by Desgrange and fellow journalists too. In every instance, you're left wondering why they were embellished, because the athletic feats involved were so extraordinary that they didn't need to be inflated.

At Eaux-Bonnes, close to the foot of the Aubisque, Lafourcade had pushed his lead out to 18 minutes over Lapize and Albini, but it soon became apparent that the local rider had pressed too hard. He was reeled in just before Mauléon, with 92 kilometres remaining. At the finish, Lapize outsprinted the Italian by three lengths to claim victory, Lafourcade arriving ten minutes later on the heels of François Faber and Louis Trousselier.

Although it was initially feared that fewer than half of the 59 starters would reach Bayonne within the time limit, to general surprise no fewer than 46 riders managed this feat, while all of the other 13 completed the stage but were eliminated for being outside the time limit. They requested that they be allowed to continue the race as 'amateurs' and were given permission to do so, starting the next stage half an hour after the Tour peloton.

Breyer began his summary of this groundbreaking spectacle with a fulsome appreciation of the riders' efforts. The stage had, he admitted, 'had so much ink devoted to it and provoked such passionate discussion that L'Auto, stricken by fear, did at one moment consider suppressing it before the test that had been declared as impossible by so many experts had even been attempted'. He added that his hopes for it had also been doused by the previous stage into Luchon, which he'd found 'a bit of a disappointment'. Yet the stage to Bayonne had far exceeded his expectations. 'It was incredible! It was crazy! It was extraordinary. It was everything that you'd want it to be!' he declared.

Speaking to Steinès just after he'd finished, stage-winner Lapize uttered those immortal words, 'Desgrange is an assassin.' He didn't stop there, though.

> Ouf, finally it's over! What a stage! The one the day before yesterday was child's play compared to this one! What a struggle! What a battle! I'm certain that I'll never see anything like it again in my life. It was mad and defies all description.

Later on, he told Steinès, 'Don't compliment your boss!'

L'Auto's Charles Ravaud dubbed Lapize,

> the man of the Pyrenees. It's a title that will ensure his fame forever. He is arguably the most complete of our champions, but he's certainly the most extraordinary climber we've ever seen . . . he's clearly shown to the masses that nothing is impossible for our current champions, for our professors of energy among whom he figures within the first rank.

This seems rather harsh on François Lafourcade, however. Yes, Lapize had led for most of the stage and had eventually prevailed, but the Basque rider's performance had been pivotal to its success. By Breyer's account, he was the hare that the *cracks* were all forced to chase as a result of his unbroken ascent of the Aubisque. While Lapize, who continued to chip away at Faber's lead and ultimately won the Tour, is well remembered, most notably with that impressive sculpture atop the Tourmalet that's transported to the top of the pass each June with great fanfare and is returned to the valley below before snow closes the road in winter, Lafourcade is almost forgotten.

Ravaud described the Aubisque's conqueror as showing 'marvellous endurance and energy', as 'leading the dance with incomparable brio', and stated that 'his exploit will remain legendary'. But he also criticized his tactics. 'He could perhaps have been first on the stage if he hadn't so foolishly expended himself on the Pyrenean climbs,' he suggested. It appears, though, that rather than misjudging his strategy, Lafourcade's moment had arrived four decades too early. The Tour's first summit finish didn't take place until 1952 and, like Pottier before him on the 1905 stage over the Ballon d'Alsace and dozens more specialist climbers who would follow in his wheeltracks, Lafourcade's brilliance going uphill ended up being nullified competitively by his comparatively modest ability on the flat.

It's rather sad that the Basque rider's achievement hasn't remained as legendary as Charles Ravaud predicted and, what's more, that Lapize's 'assassins' outburst has become the most renowned moment of that first ascent of the 'terrible' Aubisque, because that inaugural ascent of what's a magnificently dramatic summit would be better remembered for a remarkable achievement on the part of the members of the Société Les Pyrénéistes de Lourdes, who were responsible for the checkpoint located on the pass. To honour the riders on their unprecedented achievement, they had erected an *arc de triomphe* that bore the words, *'Bon voyage et au revoir'*. What must the 59 Tour riders have felt as they passed beneath this temporary span? Huge relief certainly, exhilaration perhaps. What a moment it must have been for them.

The sceptics were quickly won round, Petit-Breton among them. 'Never has it been so well demonstrated how limitless human strength is. What a marvellous mechanism this human machine is, leaving all of man's creations far behind it in terms of suppleness and quality', he wrote in *La Vie au Grand Air*. As for the architect of the stage, Alphonse Steinès, he felt vindicated in advocating the passage through the Pyrenees, asserting:

> The pen alone can't translate our feelings. We were stupefied by the results that the human machine can achieve when it is well directed, well trained, well prepared . . . Of course, the tenth stage was hard: it was thought to be impossible; it wasn't, and now we have to keep it for the Tours de France to come.

It did, of course, reappear on the Tour route 12 months later, although it was overshadowed by an even sterner test as Desgrange and Steinès took the decision to send the race through the high Alps for the first time. The 366-kilometre fifth stage between Chamonix and Grenoble crossed the Aravis, Télégraphe and Galibier passes, this first incursion into the heart of the range resulting in this 1911 edition being dubbed 'the first modern Tour'.

The stage proved to be pivotal in the battle for the overall title, as Gustave Garrigou increased his advantage over his closest rival François Faber from a single point to ten. Both were, however, well beaten by Émile Georget and Paul Duboc, with Garrigou taking third place in Grenoble. Georget completed the 34-kilometre ascent of the 2,556-metre Galibier from Saint-Michel-de-Maurienne via the 1,500-metre Col du Télégraphe in two hours and thirty-eight minutes, averaging thirteen kilometres an hour, with just one very brief stop at a secret control point, a hugely impressive feat as the surface on the upper part of the Galibier was glutinous thanks to the meltwater running off the snow banks on either side of the road.

According to contemporary accounts, Georget's exploit was witnessed by just a few dozen spectators. But it was brought to life for hundreds of thousands more in Henri Desgrange's report, which is one of the most overblown and, consequently, memorable in the history of cycle sport. It began with *L'Auto*'s editor-in-chief delivering an exhortation of the bicycle's magical properties, which, it should be noted, also highlights the writer's unconcealed male chauvinism.

> Today, my brothers, we shall come together, if you so desire, in a common and pious thought for the divine bicycle. We will tell her with total piety and gratitude of the ineffable and precious joys she is willing to give us; of the memories with which she has filled our sporting memories, and for what she has made possible today.

He went on to describe the riders entering 'paradise on the shores of Lac Annecy as hell was already looming in front of them'.

Having watched them climb the Télégraphe, he described them readying their forces for the assault on the Galibier, drawing an unforgettable comparison between this 'monster' and what had hitherto been the Tour's most substantial hurdles:

> Oh Sappey! Oh Laffrey! Oh Col Bayard! Oh Tourmalet! It would be negligent of me if I didn't proclaim that compared to the Galibier you are but pale and vulgar babies; faced with this giant we can do no more than tip our hats and bow!

Looking ahead at one point, he described the riders looking like

> ants on the move; it was in fact our men nibbling away at the monster employing their pedals as teeth . . . It was freezing cold up at the summit, and when Georget passed, having

placed his victor's foot on the head of the monster, he passed close to us, dirty, his moustache full of snot and food that he'd eaten at the last control point and his jersey smeared with the grime from the last stream that he'd had to ford his way through, he directed at us the barbed but august comment, 'I bet that's surprised you!'

Another journalist, Paul de Vivie, who wrote under the nom de plume of Vélocio, questioned Desgrange's account, explaining in a rival publication that a friend of his who had ridden with Georget up the last two hairpins of the Galibier had never heard him say the words attributed by Desgrange, who was actually following François Faber further down the climb at the time. Vélocio asserted that Georget's only utterances were a query about the route ahead and, as he tried to clean the mud from his bike while negotiating the gloop in the tunnel cut beneath the top of the Galibier, his subsequent exclamation of, *'le mot de Cambronne'*. 'Shit!' in other words.

While a little irritating when viewed from the Anglo-Saxon journalistic perspective, where an emphasis has always been placed on accuracy, these discrepancies for the sake of colour and drama were and still are an accepted element of the lead story on the previous day's racing in what was *L'Auto* and is now *L'Équipe*. Desgrange's florid, lavish and hugely evocative style was taken up by his successor as race director and editor-in-chief Jacques Goddet and, in the post-war years by the likes of Pierre Chany, Philippe Bouvet and, in recent seasons, Alexandre Roos. Each of them has captured the otherness of road racing, its ever-changing locations, the uniqueness of its dramas, the often concurrent beauty and cruelty of the challenges and fates it serves up. Rather than reporting the who, what, when and why, their goal has been to transport their readers into the race, to praise, to chastise and to mythologize, and nowhere has this been more evident than in the mountains and the feats of Émile Georget, Gustave Garrigou and the 'fleshless men', as they've been described by writer and former *L'Équipe* correspondent Philippe Bordas, who have followed them.

Generally, the racers have been happy to play along with this myth-making. Interviewed by Alphonse Steinès in the wake of his triumph, Georget said of the stage, 'If I hadn't won it, I would have said that you were mad for making us do something like this, the most colossal thing that I've ever done since I started racing.' With that he got back on his bike and began to ride away, then turned back to Steinès to add,

> The guys that built the tunnel high up on the Galibier could have done it lower down and saved us the trouble of climbing in the snow, at 2,650 metres above sea level. It would have just needed to have been a bit longer! But I wouldn't have minded a little bit of racing on the Métro!

Chapter 4

Minimus versus Maximus

The stories that stemmed from the Tour de France's first incursions into the high mountains were a boon to both *L'Auto* and to those once frightening regions into which the race had ventured. In 1913, when Philippe Thys became the second Belgian to win the Tour, the organizing newspaper's sales averaged a record 320,000 per day, ten times the figure during the inaugural race a decade earlier. At the same time, the race's power as a marketing tool, with France itself as the main product in the shop window, helped to boost the profile of ski stations, spa towns and passes that featured on the route, which were becoming more accessible thanks to the expansion and improvements to the railway network. Already popular with the more affluent members of French society, resort towns such as Annecy, Chamonix and Pau saw visitor numbers rise rapidly.

Early editions of the Giro d'Italia, which was first run in 1909, also produced epic tales of perseverance and endurance in the country's highlands. Yet the script for these races stuck to type in the years that followed the First World War. The stages were immensely long, on occasions extending to almost 500 kilometres, lasted anything between 12 and 20 hours and frequently took place on appalling roads. What's more, bikes were heavy and prone to punctures and other breakdowns. Although ability and, to a lesser extent, tactical nous were critical, the overarching requirement for success was perseverance. 'In that decade, the Tour was a sadistic enterprise,' John Foot wrote of the race's editions during the 1920s in *Pedalare! Pedalare!*, his history of Italian racing. 'It was inhuman, a test of endurance and of an individual's willingness to tolerate pain.'

While this almost inevitably meant that the strongest man won, the racing lacked the flair and panache that is now associated with the mountains. It was brutal, as exemplified in this description in *L'Auto* by Henri Desgrange of Léon Scieur's calvary during the 1921 Tour stage from Bayonne to Luchon.

> I saw him crouch down next to a stream that was singing with freshness as it descended the mountain; I saw him drink like an animal stricken by thirst; in that same place, I saw him take his sandwiches out of his musette and soak them in the stream, then guzzle them down, paper and all . . . I saw him get back on his bike, then get off again, exhausted, and drag his machine by hand like beasts drag the lump of wood that prevents them from running; I heard this taciturn man call out, 'What a job! What a job!', sobbing as he did so.

Reading this, you'd imagine that the Belgian was one of the backmarkers, perhaps a Tour novice who was discovering the harsh nature of the competitive challenge. Yet he had been in the yellow jersey since the second stage and finished third that day in Luchon to retain a lead that he ultimately held all of the way to Paris. Tellingly, he was nicknamed 'The Locomotive'. Fuelled by sandwiches, their wrappers and who knows what else, Scieur could keep going for hours, for no fewer than fifteen and a half on that 326-kilometre day to Luchon. Like his rivals, he raced unrelentingly from the first day to the last. There was little thought of pacing themselves for particular stages, of perhaps saving their resources for the mountains. Why do so when you might be affected by some vagary of the road, usually a mechanical setback? It was better to race flat out from the off and take advantage of your rivals' travails, building up a cushion for those moments when you'd need to rely on your gains, as Scieur did that day in the Pyrenees.

The riders were also hampered by the rudimentary nature of the bikes they were racing on. These had to be sturdy in order to cope with the often atrocious condition of the roads, and most weighed in at around 16kg, compared to the 6.8 kilos that is the lower limit allowed by the Union Cycliste Internationale (UCI) in the current era. What's more, rather than two dozen beautifully indexed gears, racers competing on either side of the Great War were generally limited to two, using a smaller one when climbing, then taking out and flipping the rear wheel to engage a bigger gear when on descents and the flat. Loosening the nuts to make this change could be a lengthy process in cold and wet conditions when a rider had spent two hours climbing a long pass and was at the point of exhaustion. It wasn't until 1930 that Tullio Campagnolo started producing the first quick-release mechanism that made this procedure so straightforward, the wheels held in place with a skewer slotted through a hollow axle and fixed with a cone nut at one end and a cam assembly at the other.

Desgrange put a brake on technological progress too. While he regarded himself as something of a paternal overseer of the riders, he was far more concerned with the purity of the sporting contest. It meant he was a martinet as an organizer. Determined to ensure that strength and endurance remained the fundamental prerequisites for Tour success, developments such as the freewheel, which allows forward momentum without needing to turn the pedals, and the crude early gearing systems that allowed riders to change gear when they were on the move were generally prohibited to trade or, from 1930, national team riders, although they were often permitted for use by the *isolés*, or independents, who raced without team support.

The Tour director's view was that these advances corrupted the competitive challenge by favouring weaker riders who weren't durable diesels capable of riding flat out for hours on end. It may have been pure from a competitive sense, but it further encouraged racing that was sterile, that lacked athletic flamboyance, particularly in the mountains. Rather than dropping their rivals with one or a series of swift accelerations, riders would turn the one gear their bikes were equipped with for climbing at a very consistent cadence, inching rather than flying away from each other.

What's more, when anyone did attempt to get out of the saddle and 'dance on the pedals', their efforts could be ridiculed. During the infamous 1913 stage from Bayonne to Luchon when Eugène Christophe was forced to carry his bike down the Tourmalet to the forge at Sainte-Marie-de-Campan and repair his broken front fork, the unfortunate Frenchman had previously been engaged in a head-to-head with Belgian Marcel Buysse on the Col d'Aubisque. In Jean-Paul Rey's biography of Christophe, *Le Damné de la Route*, the writer describes 'the "Great" Buysse trying to stand up on the pedals from time to time, lifting his backside from the saddle to sway from left to right and back again. This position,' Rey continues, 'was the major novelty of the 1913 Tour; the era's cycling connoisseurs said it was a bad idea and described those who adopted it rather dismissively as dancers. One journalist had even gone so far as to evoke "a peloton transformed into a corps de ballet".' Christophe, on the other hand, stayed in the saddle and 'climbed with all of the serenity of a god from

Olympus'. Other reports on the Frenchman's style were, though, far less glowing, depicting him as dogged rather than godlike, more befitting his nickname as 'the Old Gaul', as a dependable rather than a flamboyant campaigner.

Yet there were riders in the 1920s whose power on the climbs was striking and could be stirring. Among the most notable were Italy's Ottavio Bottecchia and Alfredo Binda. The former was the eighth child – hence Ottavio – born to Italian peasants Francesco and Elena Bottecchia in a hamlet sixty kilometres north of Venice. Apprenticed to a cobbler in the pre-Great War years, he discovered the bike as a member of the Italian army's *bersaglieri* (sharpshooters), carrying messages and orders on a folding bike during the conflict with Austria's forces on Italy's northern border.

Tall and slim, his 'thin, bony face, aquiline nose and wide mouth, set in a sad smile', according to one journalist, he took up racing in the post-war years, the president of his local cycling association spotting his talent and gifting him a bike, on which he quickly enjoyed success, his winnings boosting his earnings as a bricklayer. He turned professional in 1922, but put his competitive career on hold when Elena, his first child with his wife Caterina Zambon, died from diphtheria in March at the age of seven months. He returned to racing late that season, and impressed with eighth place in the Tour of Lombardy one-day Classic and, in March 1923, a long solo break in Milan–Sanremo. Competing as an *isolato*, he finished fifth overall and first in that 'independent' category at the Giro d'Italia, standing out particularly on the climbs. There, he caught the eye of France's leading racer, Henri Pélissier, who encouraged the Automoto team he'd recently joined to sign up the little-known and visibly impoverished Italian, *La Gazzetta dello Sport*'s Bruno Roghi writing that 'You couldn't but notice his tattered and threadbare clothes.'

Two weeks after finishing the Giro, he travelled to Automoto's Paris HQ for the Tour. His new employers didn't expect the unheralded Bottecchia to last more than a stage or two, but he was part of the stage-winning group on both the first and the second stages, victory in the latter making him the first Italian to wear the yellow jersey. Although his inexperience and Automoto's team orders eventually led to Pélissier taking the title, Bottecchia finished second in Paris. The following year, he was, according to his French leader, 'untouchable' and led the race from start to finish. Already well clear of his rivals at the start of the Bayonne to Luchon stage through the 'circle of death', he cruised in 26 minutes ahead of the second rider. 'It wasn't simply the time he gained', Desgrange wrote in *L'Auto*.

> You had to see the ease with which he rode, the unity of his style, the perfection of the slaughter he carried out. I didn't see him dance on the pedals on a single occasion. He set off like a beautiful thoroughbred, making the most of the splendour of his form, destined for victory from the off.

Bottecchia retained the Tour title in 1925, when Binda won the first of his five Giro crowns. The pair should have been great adversaries, but this rivalry failed to develop, first because Bottecchia rode for a French team and prioritized France's national tour over his own, and then due to the still-unexplained events that took place during a training ride in June 1927. The Italian was found lying at the roadside not far from his home in the Friuli region in the north-east of Italy, his undamaged bike not far away. He was taken to hospital, but died 12 days later without regaining consciousness.

His injuries were reported as being too severe to have been sustained in a crash, and it was believed he had been beaten. But by who? There have been numerous theories. It was claimed that he was the victim of an attack by fascists irked by his liberal leanings, or that he'd been assaulted by a jealous husband. A local farmer claimed on his deathbed that he'd thrown a rock at Bottecchia, who had stopped to pick grapes from the farmer's vines, although the grapes would have been far from ripe at that time of year. Another suggestion was that his own family had paid for him to be killed for the insurance pay-out. The mystery has never been resolved.

For his part, Binda wasn't interested in racing the Tour, despite the fact that his racing career began in and around Nice where, as a teenager, he and his brother Primo worked in their uncle's plastering business. Although he did turn pro for La Française, a French team, in 1923, and started the process to take on French nationality, he switched allegiance to the prestigious Legnano squad the following season. His victories at the Giro, the first coming in 1925, the Italian Classics and his three world championship titles made him a sporting superstar in his home country and extremely wealthy. He made just a single appearance at the Tour, in 1930, when the Giro organizers paid him to skip their race after he'd won it in four of the previous five seasons, netting an astonishing thirty-three stages in the process. He claimed back-to-back wins in the Pyrenees in that edition, then abandoned on the subsequent stage after a mechanical issue left him in a vain solo pursuit of his GC rivals, who collaborated to ensure that the dangerous Italian was put completely out of contention.

Ranked by many renowned commentators as the greatest Italian racer of all time, better even than Fausto Coppi, Binda was one of the sport's ultimate stylists, often described as pedalling 'on air'. For René

Vietto, one of France's greatest climbers whose early career coincided with the latter years of Binda's, the Italian was incomparable in terms of his technique and class. 'He was at one with his bike. Elegance, purity, an artist. He was the epitome of beauty in action,' said Vietto. According to John Foot, 'If he did have a fault . . . it was that he was *too* good, so much so that nobody else could get a look-in. He had no fragile side, no weak points, no Achilles' heel. Binda was great, but he inspired admiration, not adoration.'

His all-round ability meant that he would almost always win sprints from the small groups that tended to contest the spoils in big races, could time trial better than anyone, and was exceptionally gifted as a climber, to the extent that he was dubbed 'the Lord of the Mountains'. He was also recognized as one of the great cycling tacticians, as a racer who didn't put his nose in the wind unless it was absolutely guaranteed to provide him with a competitive advantage. Backed by a supremely strong Legnano team that was totally committed to his service in what was already the traditional Italian style for their supreme champions, Binda was almost unbeatable. Yet his clinical dominance was so complete that the racing in Italy followed the same predictable script as the Tour.

Spice was added with the arrival on the Italian scene of Learco Guerra, a builder from Mantua who came to cycling late. He started racing in the mid-1920s and was 27 when he rode his first Giro in 1929. He finished second in the Giro the following year, then achieved what was then the extraordinary feat of finishing runner-up at that year's Tour, the race that Binda abandoned. Prodigiously durable, he was known as 'The Human Locomotive', his nickname reflecting qualities that compared extremely well to gifted stayers in the recent past such as 1921 Tour winner Scieur. Although he shared many of the same racing attributes as Binda, notably in time trials and when racing for victory from small groups, he was the antithesis of Binda. He was exuberant, impulsive, aggressive.

During the early 1930s, the pair divided Italian fans in a similar way to Gino Bartali and Fausto Coppi a decade later. Yet, unlike this illustrious duo, Binda and Guerra came from the same racing mould, the difference between them being one of personality rather than style. The sense of unpredictability when they were racing only extended to which one of them would win having crushed the competitive life from the rest of the opposition.

Change was coming, however, both on the technological side, thanks to the widespread introduction of 'on the move' gearing such as the dual-rod design that was introduced by Tullio Campagnolo and his fast-flourishing componentry company, and on the racing side, as specialist climbers began to emerge and, most significantly, capture the hearts of fans. René Vietto would soon become the most cherished of these pure climbers, but others led the way, including two French flyweights, Victor Fontan and Benoît Faure. They epitomized this new breed, described by writer Philippe Bordas as the first 'cyclists who climbed like chamois'. They were, he added quite unforgettably, 'Hermits fed on grasshoppers. On twigs.'

I have a particular affection for Fontan, a rider whose exploits are little remembered outside his native Béarn region centred on Pau in the Pyrenees. When, in 2010, the Tour organizers announced they were going to commemorate the centenary of the race's first foray into this mountain chain with back-to-back stages focused on the Col du Tourmalet, I was equipped by collector and restorer Tim Gunn at the Old Bicycle Company with a Fontan bike dating from the late 1920s. Kitted out in woollen jersey and shorts and Léon

Jeantet aviator-style goggles also from that era, I climbed the famous pass on the Fontan, with its two gears on the flippable rear wheel and wooden-rimmed wheels, braking coming courtesy of rubber blocks rather than the originals, which would have been cork- or leather-faced.

Naturally, I picked the smaller of the two gears, which was a mighty – for me at least – 46×18, a ratio that I'd more likely use on a very shallow and short gradient than on a nineteen-kilometre pass. Fontan and strong climbers like him would have spun this gear seated in the saddle for the most part, only rising to 'dance' on the pedals on the steepest sections. I, on the other hand, was up on them right from the off in order to keep the gear turning. I bobbed upwards, progress steady, if not serene, until I reached a section of road under repair, the top surface eroded and gravel-covered. Standing on the pedals, it was close to impossible to maintain traction, but in the saddle I couldn't maintain any forward momentum. The degraded section was only 300 metres long, but that was all I needed to get a more complete idea of what racing up the Tourmalet and other passes would have been like on a rutted surface mixing stone and compacted earth. In a word, hellish, and even worse than that in the wet. Descending on bikes so rudimentary on roads like that must have been a lottery, although Tim wasn't willing to let me assess the accuracy of this judgement because he feared for the welfare of his beloved Fontan. I confess that I was happy to go along with his demand that the bike should complete the descent back to Luz-Saint-Sauveur in the back of his van.

Born in the village of Nay, just south of Pau, in 1892, Fontan was the youngest of six children born to clog-maker Isidore Fontan and his wife Maria Cazenave. As a teenager, he became an apprentice carpenter and also showed real talent as a bike racer, lining up in the Tour de France des Indépendants in 1910 in what proved to be a vain effort to make a breakthrough in the sport. After spending five years in the French army during the Great War, when he was wounded twice, he returned to the Béarn and, from 1921, to competition. He was a frequent winner in his home region and finally made his Tour debut in 1924, abandoning on the fifth stage. He subsequently told his wife that his competitive career was over and devoted himself to his work and young family for the next three years, but then felt the itch to race again.

He made his return to the Tour in 1928, this coming on the back of an impressive Giro debut where he was engaged by Legnano to work as a *gregario* for the all-conquering Binda, who won the title and no fewer than seven of the twelve stages. Despite his duties as a domestique, Fontan was fourth overall. Riding at the Tour for the team run by the Bordeaux-based manufacturer Elvish, which drew its riders from France's south-west, Fontan first won in that city and, two stages later, took a second success in Luchon after crossing the Aubisque and Tourmalet passes.

He was an unusual mix as a racer. Standing 1.62m tall and slightly built, he had the classic build of a pure climber, but he raced in the style of the *rouleurs-grimpeurs*. 'I never used to climb *en danseuse*, but always seated,' he said in an interview in 1981, a year before his death. 'All my strength was in my kidneys.' By this, he meant that his power came primarily from his lower back, enabling him to push a big gear consistently for long periods – 44×20 for the Aubisque, although he confessed he should have opted for a slightly smaller and easier 44×24. Yet he had the pure climber's ability to accelerate away from his rivals, Desgrange being among those who dubbed him a 'king of the mountains' because he was so adept at racing uphill. He also had the character of a mountain man, professing that he didn't understand the excitement of fans after he'd won in Luchon. 'What really annoys me is that embarrassing curiosity in the street,' he told renowned journalist Gaston Bénac in Luchon. 'As soon as I stopped, there were fifty hands slapping me on the back and I had deafening shouts resounding in my ear. But the mountain air doesn't make me deaf, I can assure you.' This trait of reluctant hero has been a common one among climbing specialists, partly because their art is all about creating the space to be alone, about shunning company. Taciturn, unsmiling in almost every picture, a Basque beret pulled down tightly on his head, Fontan looked more like a Pyrenean shepherd than one of the great endurance athletes of his time.

Seventh in that Tour, he returned in 1929, now aged 37, with a beefed-up team, Elvish-Fontan-Wolber, perhaps racing with the Fontan frame upon which I'd climbed the Tourmalet, and as one of the favourites for the yellow jersey. Following the stage into Bordeaux, he was one of three riders who found themselves in the unprecedented situation of wearing a leader's jersey, as they were tied on time. Two stages later, he took it for himself in Luchon, where he finished with just teammate Salvador Cardona for company, Fontan gifting his colleague the win as he himself opened up a ten-minute lead on the overall classification. 'The whole region is delirious with the celebrations of this victory by one of their own', said Henri Desgrange in *L'Auto*, adding that the elation was heightened by 'our now serious hopes of seeing one of our own win the great race'.

Those hopes evaporated just nine kilometres into the next stage through the Pyrenees to Perpignan. 'The headlights of our Hotchkiss revealed one of our riders walking on the right-hand side of the road.

He was wearing the yellow jersey. It was Fontan', reported Desgrange, who said the race leader's front fork had broken. 'The man was beside himself. He was walking like a drunk, incapable of pulling himself together.' A fan offered him a bike, then he found another that fitted him better and set off in pursuit, only to abandon at the halfway point when half an hour behind his rivals. While the race director admonished him for quitting the Tour, because he could still have gained much from continuing, Fontan revealed that his morale had been completely undermined as, he claimed, someone had used a saw to sabotage his bike. His great opportunity had been snatched from him. He might have been remembered as one of the great climbers of the early Tours, perhaps even as the race's oldest winner. Instead, those accolades went elsewhere.

Benoît Faure was one of Fontan's regular rivals during those years, a climber too, but of a different breed, the pure kind who had always been criticized for being one-trick ponies – good going up, but unable to stay the pace on the flat, essentially from the same mould as François Lafourcade, the first rider to conquer the Aubisque in 1910. Faure was nicknamed 'The Mouse' because of his diminutive stature – he was just 1.58m tall and weighed a mere 53kg – but also, according to Desgrange, due to the way in which he nibbled away at the mountains and often managed to sneak into the key break in races.

The third of five children, he was raised in the Forez region in central France, close to the bicycle-manufacturing centre of Saint-Étienne. As a child, he was picked on by his peers because of his size, and used to escape from this bullying on an old bike that was far too big for him, riding off through the steep, wooded hills typical of that eastern part of the Massif Central. Later, following his military service in the early 1920s, he worked on farms and in factories, always travelling to work on a hand-me-down bike, eventually earning enough money to buy a road machine to race on and quickly gaining a reputation for his ability on the climbs.

He made his Tour debut in 1926, finishing twenty-third, and had much more experience when he made his second appearance in 1929 for Le Chemineau, a Saint-Étienne-based bike manufacturer known principally for producing derailleurs – it had been established by a former racer turned componentry innovator, Joanny Panel, who in 1911 was the first rider to participate in the Tour using a bike equipped with a derailleur. Faure initially came to the fore with a darting attack on the Col de Puymorens in the Pyrenees, attacking at the foot of the pass and leading over it. Hamstrung by a puncture and a crash when victory in Perpignan looked likely, he received good reviews, *L'Auto* describing him as 'a little winged angel'.

Buoyed by his performance rather than dismayed by the setback, Faure went on the attack again on the short stage between Cannes and Nice that crossed the Braus, Castillon and Turbie passes, upping the pace on the first of those climbs, quickly dropping most of the GC leaders, who stopped quite soon on the Braus's steep ramps to flip their rear wheel onto its smaller gear. 'In intense heat, Faure climbed with the agility of a squirrel', reported *La Tribune Républicaine*, the Saint-Étienne newspaper. In *L'Auto*, meanwhile, Desgrange pitched the tiny Frenchman's duel with 77-kilogram Belgian Louis Delannoy as a contest between 'Minimus' and 'Maximus', detailing how 'Maximus's huge body fell to the road and there he was on the ground'.

The Tour director's report suggests that Faure's bike wasn't equipped with one of Panel's Le Chemineau derailleurs, as it relates how 'it was only when he felt that he had no serious rivals behind him that he decided to change his enormous gear, and did so with remarkable speed'. Desgrange's car followed Faure for the rest of the stage, *L'Auto*'s editor-in-chief describing his performance 'as an extremely attractive spectacle, because you can only imagine the ease with which this little gentleman not only turns the pedals, but pedalled for the whole day to win a stage against a coalition of stars'. He adds that his style was 'light and supple, quite interesting to see'. Although Desgrange doesn't at this point mention Faure standing on the pedals, the little Frenchman tended to accelerate by dancing away in this fashion, which must have offered a considerable contrast to the technique adopted by the bigger men in his wake, who were mostly *rouleurs-grimpeurs* who preferred to stay in the saddle and keep to a steady, more comfortable rhythm.

Desgrange having been so dismissive of this style in the past, was this the moment when he was won over by the beauty and exhilaration of a pure climber in full flight? To an extent perhaps, although there's no significant evidence for this apart from these comments. However, Faure's performance and the Tour director's fulsome response to it prompt a more fundamental question: what is a climber? Or, to put it a better way, what do we want to see from climbers? Should they be strong on the climbs and everywhere else, battling for the great titles with each other, often in dogged rather than flamboyant fashion? Or should they be virtuosos when racing uphill, capable of brilliance in this domain although they may be lacking in others? I'll offer no answer yet, but will say that these questions should be borne in mind from this point, when the contest between podiums and panache begins to become apparent.

Thanks to his enthralling performances in the mountains, Faure was one of the few riders to come out of that race with universally agreed distinction, as he finished fifteenth overall, winning the yellow-and-black jersey as leader of the *touristes-routiers* category in the process. On his return to Saint-Étienne, he was greeted like a conquering hero, with the roads blocked all around the city's velodrome into which he was driven in an open-top car. One local paper, swept up in the euphoria, recounted how 'Everyone wanted to see the happy Tour winner.'

Desgrange and his organizing team, meanwhile, set about a revamp of the Tour because the action was becoming increasingly sterile, controlled by the trade teams and their powerful *rouleurs*. In 1930, it returned to a national team format in order to break the control of these dominant squads, notably Alcyon, whose Belgian leader Maurice De Waele had won the previous edition despite falling ill. While the 1930 race was portrayed as a vast improvement on those that had preceded it, perhaps because it produced a French winner in André Leducq, it underlined how racing had changed. The number of stages increased, but they were shorter and – thanks to better roads, improvements in bikes and equipment, and improved tactical coherence within teams – the racing was more closely contested, more like what we'd expect of the modern-day Grand Tour.

Riding, as he had done in 1929, as a *touriste-routier* under the Sud-Est banner with four other riders, Faure once again stood out, first on the stage into Luchon. He led over the Aubisque and Tourmalet, but was reeled in and dropped by Binda, Leducq and Pierre Magne 20 kilometres short of victory, his reward being the yellow-and-black jersey as leader in his class. He also earned 300 French francs for being the first rider in this category to summit the Aubisque, and an equal sum for the same feat atop the Tourmalet. These two passes were among the seven that comprised the newly established Prix du Chocolat Menier. The prizes were significant, equivalent to a month's wages for most French workers, but were dwarfed by the 2,000 francs that went to the first 'As' (ace) or elite rider to reach these summits, both of whom were, of course, well beaten by Faure.

He re-emerged on the Cannes to Nice stage, leading over the Col de Braus once again. Desgrange, by now clearly captivated by Faure, wrote that he climbed with 'disconcerting ease . . . He's like a piano virtuoso whose hands fly across the keys with incredible speed. In his case, it's his legs that turn the gear in that same way and he honestly gives us the sense of seeing an art that nobody wants to acknowledge.'

While the Tour director was famed for his hyperbole, this is still an astonishing accolade. Faure, Desgrange suggests, had climbed into another dimension. Gripping though it was, racing in the mountains had always been about struggle, an agonizing endeavour even for the very best racers. The diminutive Frenchman, though, had found a new method and made it look beautiful. The likes of Fausto Coppi, Charly Gaul, Lucien Van Impe, Alberto Contador and Tadej Pogačar would follow Faure, gliding, darting, dashing along this same path, producing their own kind of magic in the most awe-inspiring and dramatic arenas in sport.

Unfortunately, on this occasion this little wizard was struck by bad luck, suffering several punctures caused by tacks that had been scattered on the road. Victory went instead to another rider from the lower rank, Louis Peglion, who just happened to be a Provençal, which perhaps explained the reason for the ambush. Yet Faure bounced right back, distinguishing himself on the long stage from Nice to Grenoble, leading over the huge Allos pass and then the Col Bayard, after which he was caught by Leducq and Guerra. Unlike in the Pyrenees, he managed to hang on, although inevitably 'The Mouse' had no chance in the sprint against the 'Human Locomotive'.

Faure was resurgent on the next stage, breaking clear on the climb from the Lautaret pass up to the Col du Galibier, although his previous efforts took their toll on the highest pass of them all at that time. Nearing the top, Pierre Magne, younger brother of the French team's co-leader Antonin, bridged up to him and the pair rode through the tunnel at the summit together. It meant that Faure had been the first *touriste-routier* to top six of the seven passes that featured in the Chocolat Menier competition. On five of those six occasions, he'd been the first rider from any class to reach the summit.

Faure finished eighth overall in Paris, retaining the yellow-and-black jersey he'd won in 1929. Desgrange had seen more than enough to declare, 'I'm going to award little Benoît Faure the title of King of the Climbers'. *Le Miroir des Sports* offered the same judgement. 'The extraordinary *touriste-routier*, according to the oldest Tour followers, is not only the most brilliant climber of the moment but is even one of the best seen since the war . . . he has become more aware of his astonishing gifts and, full on immense confidence, he deliberately goes on the attack on each possible opportunity,' it declared, adding that if he had a bit more speed and power on the flat, 'there isn't a rider around who would worry him in a hard race on a very hilly course'.

Desgrange offered a further tribute by insisting on Faure's promotion from the *touriste-routier* category to join the 'Aces', although the Frenchman wasn't entirely content with the honour as it meant falling in with the national team's goals and strategy rather than having the freedom to race how he wanted. Very much an individual who was happiest preparing and racing in his own way – a characteristic shared by many other climbing greats – Faure found it hard to adapt to racing in a supporting role during the 1931 Tour. After struggling in the Pyrenees, he came strong on the stage to Nice and was once again in the front group going over the Col de Braus. However, his team leader Antonin Magne, who was also in the yellow jersey, crashed during the stage and ended isolated from his teammates and losing half of his nine-and-a-half-minute lead. 'Benoît Faure rode his own race on the Col de Braus', declared *L'Auto* pointedly, while the atmosphere around the French team's dinner table that night was reported to be funereal, Faure sitting alone and saying nothing.

He redeemed himself in the Alps, helping the taciturn and sometimes tactically indecisive Magne to retain the yellow jersey, while he himself ended the race in a respectable thirteenth place. Even so, the accommodation with the national team was short-lived. Having ended the season without a single victory, he opted to return to the lower rank of Tour riders and to follow his own path. This quickly brought him his first victory since 1930, at the hilly Paris–Caen one-day race in April 1932. Jacques Goddet, by then Desgrange's deputy at *L'Auto* and the Tour de France, wrote of Faure: 'Dancing on the tips of his pedals as he climbed, swaying from thigh to thigh, in the style we saw on the Tourmalet in 1930, his body stock still, he dropped the four other men with whom he had ended up at the front of the race one after another.'

Released from the strategic shackles of the French national team, 33-year-old Faure went to the Tour looking to restore his reputation as cycling's best climber, only to find that a rider who had been inspired by him was about to take that mantle.

Chapter 5

First technique, then beauty and grace

Born in the village of Sierrapando in western Cantabria, just inland from Spain's Atlantic coast, in 1905, Vicente Trueba was the third of nine children whose parents ran a cattle farm. Like all of his siblings, he quickly developed a taste for cycling and showed an aptitude for it, finishing second in his first race, for which he won a Gillette razor. Particularly talented on climbs where his slight 1.59-metre frame gave him a natural advantage, he won his first race at 20, but had to fit his fledgling racing career around his work as a carpenter, then his military service, and later in the bike shop and repair business he set up in Torrelavega with his elder brother José, who was also a talented racer.

Mentored by Cantabrian pro Victorino Otero, who had finished the 1924 Tour, Trueba progressed steadily, his breakthrough moment occurring at the Tour of the Basque Country in 1929. There he lined up against several Tour stars, including that year's winner Maurice De Waele, former champion Nicolas Frantz and the new French climbing star, Benoît Faure, with whom the Spaniard went head-to-head on the Orduña pass on the race's opening day, Faure ultimately reaching the summit first. During the three stages that followed, Trueba learned a lot from watching Faure, who had a similarly diminutive build, but was more skilled at holding his own in the bunch and on the flat.

Twelfth place in the Basque Country, three places ahead of his brother José, followed by fifth in another strong field at the Volta a Catalunya, where his brave performance earned him plaudits from press and fans, in addition to selection for Spain's 1930 Tour de France team. That year, as part of Desgrange's attempt to undermine the sway of the bike manufacturers, the race organization supplied the bikes, built according to the riders' dimensions, or at least they should have been. Trueba, however, ended up with a 56-centimetre frame instead of the 54 he'd requested, and with 170-millimetre cranks instead of 165's. As a consequence, he struggled through the first half of the race, when he was affected badly by knee trouble until he reached the Pyrenees where both he and his brother were equipped with their own bikes by supporters from home.

He almost quit on the first day in the Pyrenees, but shone on the second, finishing tenth and in the front group in Perpignan, drawing a mention from race director Henri Desgrange, who dubbed him 'The Flea', a nickname that stuck with him for the rest of his life. The race director described him as being 'as tall as an apple, perhaps even not as high' and chasing across to the leaders at Bourg-Madame, at the stage's halfway point.

> Suddenly we saw a flea arrive, like a hurricane, finding his way up to the leaders. He was dropped, then jumped back up like a flea, rejoining the peloton again, which once again slapped him back with its pace. But he repeated his task, then did it a third time, a fourth, a fifth and a sixth time.

Desgrange clearly admired the way that the Spaniard rode, and his words made Trueba one of the race's most popular personalities, but the former was apparently unaware of the fact that the Spaniard's bizarre tactics were the consequence of his travails with the race organization bike. 'I picked up a bad knee injury that didn't allow me to pedal properly,' Trueba recalled in a post-career interview with *Semana* magazine.

> I always coped as best as I could until the mountains loomed. Then I had no other option: I had to keep standing up on the pedals again and again to deal with the slope, as a result dropping those who'd just been ahead of me. Climbing in that way reminded Desgrange of the way a flea jumps around and he gave me that nickname.

Although that interview took place more than thirty years later, he hadn't forgotten Faure either, revealing, 'In that race I had to battle like a demon against the best climber that I ever came across in my life: the Frenchman Faure. He was a monster on the climbs.'

Trueba finished twenty-fourth in Paris, the third-ranked Spaniard on a team that frequently rode for themselves rather than for a common cause. Lacking a manager, a masseur and a mechanic, and chased down by the French whenever he tried to go clear, Trueba was disillusioned and decided not to return to the Tour in 1931. His presence was missed, though. *Paris-Midi* stated dismissively, 'badly advised, he prefers to be first in Torrelavega than last in Paris', while other papers also expressed their disappointment that Faure wouldn't be tested by the best climber yet to emerge from Spain.

He returned to the Tour in 1932, the only Spanish rider in the 80-strong field, riding as a *touriste-routier*. The first opportunity for a duel between 'The Flea' and 'The Mouse' arrived as the race left Pau on stage five for Luchon. At Eaux-Bonnes on the lower slopes of the Aubisque, a group went clear and Trueba quickly scurried across to them, then went clear on his own. He led over the top, winning the 2,000 francs from Chocolat Menier – their competition no longer split into *As* and *touristes-routiers* categories – and led down the other side, but then got delayed when hit by a car going onto the Tourmalet, which enabled Faure to bridge up to him. The radio commentary described 'two titans climbing in a terrible battle to arrive, triumphant, at the Olympus of the Gods'. Faure was first to the top, helped, it's reported, by significant pushing by French fans.

In Perpignan, where he received a rapturous welcome from the local Spanish community, Trueba received a message from Desgrange, who informed him he was looking at the possibility of having a Hispano-Swiss team in the 1933 race. Riding on his own bike by that point, he continued to impress, finishing fifth in Nice, where he picked up a series of invitations for post-Tour events including the Tour of Lombardy, as well as another 1,900 francs in prizes. Second to summit the Allos on the next stage, behind Faure again, he gained another 1,000 francs.

Trueba's weakness, said the papers, was his ability on the descents, a criticism often laid against slightly built riders, whose lack of bulk meant they were always likely to be bucked about on the rutted roads as well as this making braking harder. Riding as an individual, the Spaniard also had to measure the risks he took, knowing that if he crashed and broke his bike his race would be over, unlike the riders on the big national teams who could always take one from a teammate. The Aces could also draw on the latest technology. That year's eventual Tour winner Georges Speicher, for instance, was peerless when descending, but the Frenchman benefited from a new braking system on the rear wheel that kept the bike steady on descents rather than causing it to wobble, a movement that's always sure to induce a cautious approach.

Fifth over the Galibier, Trueba won a special prize from the Hollywood sweets company as the race's best climber, while contracts continued to rain in. His fee for them was around 2,500 to 3,000 francs, which matched those of the peloton's major stars. This, it should be noted, was a rider who finished in a respectable twenty-seventh place in Paris, a long way out of the yellow jersey contest. In short, his notoriety derived completely from his ability on the climbs. As had been the case with Faure, the fans took him to their hearts and the press eulogized him, Spanish daily *ABC*, for instance, describing him as 'a pigmy physically, but with a gigantic Spanish spirit'.

The attention and acclaim that his climbing contest with Faure and Italy's Francesco 'The Chamois of Cumiana' Camusso received led to a very significant boost in the prizes on offer in the mountains for the 1933 race. On the one hand, Chocolat Menier raised its prize fund to 35,000 francs, which would be distributed over the race's eight major climbs: the Galibier, Vars, Allos, Braus, Puymorens, Portet d'Aspet, Tourmalet and Aubisque. At the same time, *L'Auto* introduced a prize for the best climber, who would receive 10,000 francs, with points awarded on 15 passes, the previously mentioned 8 plus the Ballon d'Alsace, Faucille, Aravis, Laffrey, Port, Peyresourde and Aspin.

Trueba prepared for this new challenge by participating in the inaugural edition of Paris–Nice, where he abandoned after the third stage after a car came onto the course and caused the six riders in the breakaway, including the Spaniard, to crash. In May, he travelled to Italy for his Giro debut along with compatriots Mariano Cañardo and Isidro Figueras. They formed the three-rider Bestetti-d'Alessandro team. But their bikes were abysmal, the racing was often slow and dull, the pace only rising when finishes neared. Trueba also complained that there weren't enough hills, and those that were on the route weren't hard enough to give the pure climbers a chance to lead their merry dance on the pedals. He finished forty-fourth.

Trueba knew the terrain at the Tour would be much more favourable to him, and quickly proved that. On stage four to Belfort, through the Vosges massif, he was the clear leader over the Ballon d'Alsace, Belgian stage-winner Jean Aerts hailing him as 'indisputably the king of the mountains', a status that Faure couldn't dispute after the Frenchman had finished outside the time limit on the second stage to Charleville run in horrendous conditions. In his race report, Desgrange recounted how the Spaniard was the last rider to flip his wheel halfway up the Ballon, having already opened up a lead, describing him not as a flea but as a *moucheron*, a gnat or a fly, with 'his legs cooked in the Extremadura sun', which paints a distinct picture, even if this region is about as far away as you can get in Spain from the rider's native Cantabria. Two riders passed him as he refitted his wheel, but both were quickly caught and passed, making Trueba the early leader of the new mountains competition.

The Spaniard, who was said to be the first racer to climb on 'the hoods', gripping the brake levers as he stood on the pedals rather than resting his hands on the top of his handlebar or on the drops, was even more impressive on stage seven over the Galibier into Grenoble. Having crossed the Col du Télégraphe and descended into Valloire in a small group, he cruised away from them on the mighty pass, opening up a gap of five minutes by the summit, beating Eugène Christophe's 1912 record for the climb by 23 minutes. One report notes that he was using a gear of 44×21 (4.8m), while most of his rivals were using 44×24 (4.2m), the difference highlighting his power-to-weight advantage.

Le Miroir des Sports hailed Trueba's ascent of the Galibier by putting him on their cover, the accompanying text reading: 'It's there, in a desert setting, devoid of vegetation and shade, that the Tour de France riders climb slowly, painfully, into the ranks of sporting heroes.' More significantly, given that another two decades would pass before there was a summit finish in the Tour, the paper also rued the fact that the stage had finished with a group sprint, noting,

> the responsibility for this paradoxical finish doesn't lie with the riders who have fought with energy and value that deserves every accolade, it's not even with the fearsome Galibier, which very conscientiously fulfilled its role as the Judge of Peace . . . The major culprit, if we can pick one out, was the route of the stage itself. Between the summit of the Galibier and Grenoble, there were exactly 95 kilometres of descent and flat. In these conditions, it was absolutely impossible that the gaps created climbing the pass would be the same at the finish . . . Nine times out of 10, when the finish is too far from the col, the stage is decided by a group sprint.

Further down the same page, another article also bemoaned, 'The winners on the major cols aren't given enough of an advantage.' It went on to blame Desgrange for being too cautious, asserting that he

> knows all too well that the cols are the big reason for the Tour's success, but he's haunted and understandably by the memory of former climbers, the Bottecchias and Buysses, etc., who gained on one mountain stage some 30 minutes and were able to sit on that lead until the end of the Tour, suppressing all interest in the race as a result.

It added that giving stage winners a two-minute time bonus was further skewing the race against the climbers.

Trueba was also well aware that the odds of doing anything other than competing for the mountains prize were heavily stacked against him. In a letter home that was printed in *El Diario Montañés*, he wrote: 'As you can see I can't win a stage, which is what I want to do.' He highlighted, as key factors, the long descents and flats into finishes, the fact that he was racing alone in headwinds, and that it was impossible for a single rider to hold off a peloton.

Desgrange would have been well aware of the criticisms made by rival publications, and on this issue persistently maintained that the yellow jersey should be contested by the most complete riders rather than those who were supremely talented in the mountains. Indeed, he said precisely this in the pages of *L'Auto* following the Galibier stage, offering qualified praise to Trueba and his lightweight rivals on that stage, Frenchmen Léon Level, Gaspard Rinaldi and Eugène Le Goff, who, he wrote, 'as they didn't all have a good position in the general classification had no other objective than to finish in the places of honour on the summit of the giant Galibier'.

Warming to his theme, he dismissed the climbers as serious contenders for the overall crown, affirming,

> We become ecstatic with their lightness at these altitudes . . . but once the Galibier had been crossed, our reason gradually returned and we're obliged to concede that ultimately they've not changed anything, that the race is almost going on without them, even when they're at the front of it.

He concluded that, 'we come back inevitably to those who have a more complete set of qualities . . . worthy of the yellow jersey'.

While Desgrange's desire to see the best all-round racer win the Tour is understandable, what opportunity did he give the climbers of doing so? Most of these specialist *grimpeurs* raced as independents and had little chance of winning a stage, even in the mountains, let alone the overall title. The route was rigged against the climbers too, leaving them no option but to compete for the rewards that were on offer in their preferred terrain. Thanks to Desgrange, they were effectively participating in their own two-wheeled freak show, always the warm-up act for the Aces. Like the derailleur, the Tour director didn't seem to think they deserved an overly prominent place in his race.

Further evidence of this posture came on the stage from Digne-les-Bains to Nice. Having led over the Vars and been third to crest the Allos on the previous stage, pushing his lead in the mountains competition to 19 points, Trueba was set on having an easier day as the Tour made for the Côte d'Azur. However, as the two breakaway riders built up a big lead, he sensed that he might finish outside the time limit, so chased across to the second group of three, which arrived in Nice twelve minutes down on winner Fernand Cornez, but inside the time limit, which the peloton, containing every rider above Trueba in the general classification, failed to do. Desgrange resolved this dilemma in what has become the standard fashion, by extending the time limit, in this instance from 8 per cent to 10 per cent of Cornez's finishing time. He made no excuses for doing so, for to continue with just half a dozen riders would have been a very poor spectacle. But it's easy to imagine Trueba feeling pretty peeved as he reflected on the day's events in his hotel room that night.

At Perpignan, where he was once again mobbed by Spanish fans, he spent the rest day working on his bike with a mechanic sent by his sponsor, Pierre Colin. Following a complete overhaul, which included the fitting of duralumin rims – an extremely strong but relatively lightweight metal that had been used in the aircraft industry since the 1920s – it was two kilos lighter, now weighing in at 9.12kg, and Trueba took full advantage.

'Tighten your toestraps tomorrow!' he warned his rivals before the short Tarbes stage. Although wise to his plans, they couldn't stop the little Spaniard from leading the way over the Peyresourde and then the Aspin. Held up beyond it by a puncture, he was caught by two others riders and finished third in the sprint, rising to sixth on GC. In Tarbes a vendor selling pictures bemoaned the fact that he hadn't printed more of Trueba, as his was the one fans wanted because they were so captivated by his flair.

On the next stage Trueba led over the Tourmalet, the next rider five minutes behind him. Caught by three other riders on the Aubisque after he sustained a puncture, and was then knocked off his bike by a passing car, he remounted and regained his place at the front to arrive a minute and a half clear at the summit, where hundreds of cars were parked – 987 according to French paper *Le Soir* – and a group of Spanish ladies, seeing how small he was, offered him rocks to put in his jersey to boost his weight for the descent. For once, though, as he raced downwards, Trueba increased his lead a little more, only to be thwarted by a railway worker on a level crossing. Listening in on the radio and apparently sensing a chance to assist the four French riders in the group of six chasing the Spaniard, the railwayman closed the barrier 'for a train that never came', as *Marca* put it in an historical account produced in 1964. Trueba was caught at Jurançon on the outskirts of Pau, where Learco Guerra was quickest in the sprint as the tearful Spaniard admitted he now had no chance of winning a stage.

Although he was both angry and disappointed, the Spanish press was euphoric. In *ABC*, José María Salaverría wrote: 'A little man sitting on a bicycle is the Spaniard who is making most of the noise in Europe at the moment.' He went on to compare him to the master painter Goya, the scientist Cajal, the conquistador Pizarro and to El Cid riding alone through the Moorish lines at Valencia.

In *Corriere della Sera*, the renowned journalist and novelist Orio Vergani painted a beautifully evocative picture of the little Spaniard, a depiction that still resonates watching Trueba's successors in the modern era. He's described as having a large chest and short, slim legs with 'disproportionately immense muscles.' His arms, meanwhile, 'were almost atrophied, used only to steer his path,' while the inward curve of his shrunken stomach made it look 'entirely possible to squeeze his navel and his spine between two fingers'.

With 'rivers of saliva' running down his chin and his pupils 'dilated by the hypnotic effort', Trueba sounds less like an athlete than a drunk, an impression bolstered by the way the Spaniard, with 'his devastated anatomy', staggered around when he stopped to flip his wheel and change gear. Yet his suffering, Vergani suggested, was nothing like the torment that he was inflicting on his rivals, for whom he was the most hated man in the race. 'Trueba will return home with his nickname and a little money and feed himself up a bit, and next spring, if he can, he will start jumping again,' the Italian writer concluded.

Trueba, after leading over nine of the fifteen climbs in the mountains competition, which he won by a distance, finished sixth in Paris, where he was acclaimed by thousands of fans as he stood on the balcony of the newspaper *L'Intransigeant*, bringing tears to his eyes. *L'Auto*, under a headline 'Studying the style of Vicente Trueba, king of the mountains', asserted: 'Never has a climber shown such incontestable superiority on the hills . . . With his very individual style, he can do anything he wants including puncture on the descents secure in the knowledge that he will finish the stage in the lead peloton . . .' The Spaniard pointed out himself that 'never has a solo rider managed to bridge up to me, neither on the descents nor on the flat'. It always needed a bigger group to bring him to heel.

Writing in *Paris-soir*, René de Latour, a celebrated Franco-American journalist who later worked for *L'Équipe* and British magazine *Sporting Cyclist*, described what set Trueba apart in the mountains and how he had revolutionized the art of climbing.

> There's something I want to explain to you, and it's the reason why his most direct rivals have such admiration for him. In short, it's this: Trueba is the only Tour rider who can change his speed on a pass, and do so in order to react to the circumstances of the race. This doesn't seem significant, but it is precisely because it's never been seen before. You'll quickly understand why. When a rider starts to climb a pass, he goes at a speed that suits him, a speed from which he will be able to slow, but which he'll never be able to increase. It's a particularity that's well known by the riders and also by those who follow them. Indeed, it's so true that it's virtually unknown to see a rider stick on a rival's wheel on a climb. But Trueba has changed everything. You see him start off slowly and poorly positioned. He's watching and observing. He looks 200 metres ahead. Suddenly he decides to go solo . . . and it's over. On the next bend you'll see him at the

front and nobody has been able to stay on his wheel given his frenetic pace. This doesn't prevent him, when he is well positioned, from dropping his pace as he's always ready to accelerate and literally 'sprint' if there's any sign of danger before the summit. Phenomenon is a term that's frequently used without rhyme or reason. Trueba is, without any shadow of a doubt, an authentic phenomenon.

De Latour doesn't say it, but the implication is evident: Trueba was the first modern-day climber. Although, in the Tour de France at least, he was restricted to just two gears, his ability to climb *accelerando*, starting slow and suddenly picking up pace, would quickly become the accepted method for racing in the mountains. It was adopted by Gino Bartali and Fausto Coppi at the end of that decade, and by many who came after them, including the great Spanish climbers following the Second World War, Belgium's Lucien Van Impe in the 1970s, Marco Pantani in the 1990s, and, much more recently, by Alberto Contador. They would tease their rivals, daring them to respond to this change of pace, a response that would break their tempo and, inexorably, their chances of catching the climber they were pursuing, who, on their best days, would always remain tantalizingly out of reach.

Soon after the 1933 Tour finished, Desgrange seemed to take on board criticism that the bonus time at stage finishes was penalizing the climbers, as it was announced that bonuses would be introduced the following year on the 15 climbs that counted towards the mountains competition, the first rider receiving a bonus equal to his advantage over the next rider up to a maximum of 2 minutes.

Trueba lined up in that race as the nominal leader of a mixed Hispano-Swiss team, but ended up being criticized widely for his lack of competitiveness. Prior to the stage over the Galibier, when he hoped to re-establish his pre-eminence on the climbs, he had said he was going to 'fill the road with corpses'. But he was outshone by his compatriot Federico Ezquerra, who beat his renowned team leader's 1933 time for the Galibier. Trueba insisted he'd climbed the mighty pass quicker than anyone, and he possibly did as the race organization only timed the first ten riders on the road as they climbed the Galibier and he reached the foot of it in sixteenth place that day. However, troubled by a stomach problem, he was never at his best and, sadly, he would never rediscover the form he had in 1933.

He lined up in the inaugural Vuelta a España in 1935 alongside his younger brothers Manuel and Fermín in BH colours, but quit on stage five, his stomach issues, which were diagnosed as colitis, steadily worsening. He started the Tour, but abandoned on stage five. It was then discovered he'd been further weakened by a tapeworm. He abandoned the 1936 Vuelta on stage five again and wasn't selected for the Tour, where Spain and Luxembourg combined to provide a ten-rider team. The outbreak of the Spanish Civil War soon afterwards effectively brought his career to an end. Like most of the Spanish racers, he was called up, in his case by the Republican forces.

His mantle as the sport's most exciting climber was picked up by René Vietto, who was the sensation of the 1934 Tour, the 20-year-old Frenchman winning four mountain stages on his debut in the race, while adding grace, beauty and flair to the technique showcased by Trueba. Philippe Bordas described Vietto as 'the first king of the mountains', a title that does a disservice to the Spaniard, but is to an extent well deserved, taking into account his backstory, his three flirtations with overall victory at the Tour, the panache with which he raced and, fundamentally, because of the way he epitomized the obsessive, difficult and slightly unhinged personality that we've come to associate with so many of the climbing greats.

Born into a poor family that lived in the hills directly above Cannes, Vietto started work at the age of 12, initially collecting jasmine blooms alongside his mother for local perfume-makers and, later, working as a bellboy at the swanky Majestic Hotel on the resort town's Promenade de la Croisette. He developed an interest in racing and a passion for Alfredo Binda and, inspired by the exploits of the Italian *campionissimo*, he put some of his wages towards a bike, venturing with his friends into the Estérel massif just inland from the Mediterranean and then joining the local bike club, where he quickly showed an aptitude for the sport and particularly for climbing.

By the early 1930s, it had become traditional for many professionals to start their season training and racing on the Côte d'Azur, and in the early weeks of 1932 Vietto began to test himself against them. He won the GP de Cannes, then finished eighth in the hilly GP Mont Faron at Toulon. The following season, he won in Cannes again and also on Mont Faron, which earned him an invite with the Italian Olympia team to race the Milan–Sanremo one-day Classic, where he finished thirteenth. He rode the Giro for them too that year, taking twenty-second place despite a string of crashes, as his hero Binda took the overall title for the fifth time.

Several Italian teams courted the young Frenchman, but he returned to France, racing as an individual at the start of the 1934 season until he finished sixth at Paris–Nice, when Helyett signed him. That spring he won the GP Wolber, a stage race for amateur and independent riders under the age of 25, the victory earning Vietto an unlikely spot on the French national team for the Tour de France. His selection was the focus of considerable debate, some journalists suggesting that he had the legs only for short climbs and wouldn't be able to support his leaders on the longest passes in the Alps and Pyrenees. Yet they were perhaps unaware of the precocious Vietto's training regime. At 17, he'd been doing return rides to Marseille, 175 kilometres to the west of Cannes. These outings steadily extended and reached well into the Alps, where he'd climb the Allos, Vars and Izoard passes before returning home, covering 500 kilometres in the process.

The doubters may have felt they had been justified in their criticism of Vietto when that Tour got under way. He finished 11 minutes off the pace on the opening day as defending champion Georges Speicher won the stage. Racing to Charleville on day two, he came in 33 minutes behind the front group that featured 1931 champion Antonin Magne, who took the yellow jersey from his French teammate. Yet as soon as the race reached the mountains, the Ballon d'Alsace to begin with on the stage to Belfort, it quickly became apparent that he was extraordinary, not only due to the speed with which he climbed, but in his presentation of the art.

Long in the leg but with a short torso, he was a complex and often difficult character. He often looked sombre and intense, and had a reputation for being taciturn and difficult, and for being compulsive when it came to training, often riding himself and his companions to complete exhaustion on long outings where he refused to stop to eat or drink. 'René practised a very hard training regime. He did a lot of kilometres and he didn't allow eating,' his domestique and long-time friend Apô Lazaridès said in a 1970s TV interview with Vietto sitting at his side. 'His discipline was something else. I remember putting in the kilometres with him once and I said, "René, I'm hungry, I can't go on." "Eat grass," he told me. And I ate grass that whole day.' But he was also known for acts of kindness and when he smiled, his dark eyes and features topped by thick black hair that tended to be slicked back, he resembled a matinée idol.

It was, however, the set-up of his bike and the style in which he rode it on the climbs that set him apart. His use of a track stem made it low at the front, with the handlebar narrow, the drops below it flaring to the sides. His saddle was narrow too and he perched on the point of it, apparently always ready to jump up on the pedals and climb *en danseuse*, the power in his sculpted legs delivered to the pedals through his toes, almost balletically. Unlike most of his peers, he didn't fit twin bottle-cages to his bars, preferring to carry bottles in his rear pocket or, later on in his career, in a cage fitted to the downtube in the modern fashion. 'A theorist of the garrigues, he invented hillside aerodynamics', wrote Philippe Bordas in his book *Forcenés*. 'René says he brakes on the bends when climbing. His black shoes are pierced with holes to better feel the wind. Vietto invents speed, alpinism, and fluidity. We owe him the first cycling approximation of grace.'

Add together the looks, the temperament, the innovative approach and the elegance of his style, and it was almost inevitable that Vietto would become the *chou-chou* of the French fans, especially once the extent of his brilliance in the mountains became apparent. The first glimmer arrived on the stage into Grenoble over the Télégraphe and Galibier. Federico Ezquerra of the Spain–Switzerland team led over both, but the Frenchman caught and dropped him on the descent from the Galibier and soloed for a hundred kilometres into the finish. Hailing Vietto as 'The little man from Cannes, as sweet, shy and cute as a first communicant', *L'Auto* said he underlined his potential as a racer, but urged him to be more exuberant at the French team's dinner table, where 'he only dares to open his mouth to eat and drink'.

Third on the next stage into Gap, he won again in Digne after leading over the towering Vars and Allos, the bonuses he gained on these passes and at the finish helping to lift him into sixth place overall, although still thirty-five minutes down on race leader Magne. Interviewed by *L'Auto*, Vietto admitted he'd gone into the stage determined not to break away, because of the physical toll it would extract, but had ended up on his own without actually intending to.

> I set a fast pace into the Col de Vars, with Antonin Magne on my wheel. I was saying to myself, 'If something happens to the yellow jersey, I'll be there for him.' However, two kilometres further on, I turned around and I couldn't see 'Tonin', so I kept going.

Approaching the finish, Vietto was in tears, it was assumed of joy. However, the pain was so bad in one of his knees that he had wondered if he would reach Digne. 'I only pedalled with one leg today,' he revealed after crossing the line, where he was more than six minutes clear of the rest. Just imagine . . .

There's no tactical logic to support Vietto's decision to push on rather than wait after dropping his team leader in the yellow jersey. In the modern era, he would have been rapidly called to order through his earpiece, as Chris Froome was when he opened a gap on Sky teammate and yellow jersey Bradley Wiggins in 2012. Bearing in mind the shockwaves that incident provoked, even after Froome had reined himself in, it would be fascinating to know what was said around the French dinner table in Digne that July evening. Perhaps Magne had given the youngster free rein, thinking that his teammate would bag the bonuses that otherwise might go to his rivals, knowing at the same time that his own advantage over Vietto was substantial. Never comfortable talking to the press, Magne was typically evasive at the finish. 'He was astonishing' was just about all he said of his young teammate.

L'Auto didn't care about the internal politics. Instead it heaped praise on 'the young hero', describing Vietto as 'the winged climber, the rider who's cherished by the fans . . . When he stands on his pedals, he seems to be possessed by a burning fire.'

He blazed again three days later on the roads into his home city, leading over the Braus, Castillon and Turbie passes, then outsprinting Italy's Giuseppe Martano, who was second overall and closing in on Magne, in a two-up sprint. His victory was the cue for chaos. Fans invaded the finishing straight and lifted Vietto off his bike and onto their shoulders, one punching Desgrange's assistant Jacques Goddet to the ground amid the mayhem. The organizing newspaper said that Cannes had never experienced a Tour day to compare with it, such was the extent of the euphoria, but few stage towns had. Vietto-mania was rampant.

Desgrange, though, offered a more critical analysis. 'He rode a bit like a child', he wrote of Vietto's decision to abandon his leader on the first climb in search of personal glory. Magne, always rather mournful and sparing with his words even in his moments of triumph, once again didn't say much, but was of the same mind as the Tour boss. 'What a terror the little guy is. Why did he go off so hard on the Braus? He made the race for the Italian,' he declared, *L'Auto* claiming rather incredibly that there was no sense of reproach intended.

Vietto hadn't so much ripped up the traditional script for Grand Tour racing as arrived at the race with his own version, with himself cast in what the French often describe as the 'free electron role', seemingly unconcerned with the objectives of his leaders, both past winners of the race, and of his team's strategy. It worked for him because he'd lost so much time in the opening days, because the French team was so strong (they won 19 of the 23 stages), because for a long time it didn't matter that one of their support riders was chasing his own goals, and because he was young and green and was simply competing in the unbridled, pressure-free, almost joyful way that he always had, helped, importantly, by immense popular support. Yet, with Martano now just two minutes behind Magne, he had to fall into line. No one, though, could have foreseen that doing so would elevate Vietto's status as France's favourite to even greater heights.

On the first stage into the heart of the Pyrenees, which took the riders to Ax-les-Thermes, Magne crashed on the descent of the Col de Puymorens, taking Vietto down with him. Although both were quickly back on their feet, they realized that the race leader's front wheel was broken. Vietto, 'now in possession of team spirit' wrote Desgrange, handed over his wheel and Magne continued on, saving his yellow jersey in the process. The next day, to Tarbes, a similar scenario occurred again, as Magne went down once more, his bike written off in the crash. Vietto, who was some distance ahead, turned around and rode back to the French leader to give him his bike. Goddet, who watched all this unfold, reported that the youngster wasn't at all happy about making this sacrifice. 'He doesn't know how to ride a bike, Antonin,' he raged. 'I'm not going to be a slave every day.' Fired up by this, he responded with one final extravagant flourish, leading over the Tourmalet and Aubisque to take a solo victory in Pau, securing the mountains competition in the process, before finishing fifth overall in Paris.

The legend that has built up around Vietto since his astounding Tour debut has it that he could have won that edition, that he was held back by the more experienced but physically weaker Magne. But it's a fabrication. His losses to his leader in the final 90-kilometre time trial at Nantes were slightly larger than the 9 minutes and 8 seconds he'd ceded following the older man's two crashes. Ultimately, the time he lost in the opening days cost him his yellow jersey hopes, but also opened up the way to his staggering run of success through the Alps, as had been the case for Trueba the previous year and would be so for innumerable climbers in the decades to come. The suggestion that he might have won, partly fostered by Vietto, was a product of the euphoria that he triggered during that Tour, an indication of the swell of feeling, of pure excitement that can be sparked when a climber is in full flight, especially one who is as compellingly graceful as the Frenchman.

Winner of two mountain stages and eighth overall a year later, his form and interest subsequently drifted, but he re-emerged as a contender in the final pre-war Tour in 1939 and the first post-war edition in 1947. He led the race in both editions, for 11 and 15 days respectively, and could – and probably should – have won both. However, his determination to ride everyone off his wheel whenever the opportunity presented itself, as if the Tour were nothing more than one of his ride-until-you-drop training expeditions with Apô Lazaridès, scuppered his chances on both occasions.

In 1939, the pressure of defending the lead at the head of a Sud-Est regional team comprising primarily younger riders gradually sapped his resistance, which was further weakened by a fever and his ebullience during the first half of the race. Climbing the Izoard pass in the Alps, where he should have shone, he couldn't hold the pace of Belgian rival Sylvère Maes and the title slipped from his grasp.

In 1947, riding for the French national team for the first time since 1935, having lost his best racing years to the war, he took the lead on the second stage, yielded it for a couple of days then regained it on the stage into Digne that crossed the Izoard, Vars and Allos passes. Troubled by an infected little toe, he held it until the final time trial, three days from the finish, when he fell from first to fourth. Ultimately, the title went to another French climber, Jean Robic. With squashed features, and protruding ears squeezed even more by the leather straps of his distinguishing 'hairnet'-style helmet, the Breton was a two-wheeled toby jug of a rider, the antithesis of the dashing Vietto. The stark difference between the pair extended to their racing style, Robic fighting with the bike as he climbed, forcing it forwards like a jockey spurring on a recalcitrant horse, while Vietto was the perfect stylist. As for that little toe, it went septic and had to be amputated and ended up pickled in a jar that for many years sat on a shelf behind the counter of a Marseille bar. It led to another legend: that he'd had it cut off to save weight – a story Vietto played up to. Once again, it was a myth, but another colourful one to add to a remarkable career, which in so many ways established the mould for the ideal of a climber – brilliant, graceful, flawed, unpredictable, and a law unto themselves.

Chapter 6

Bartali versus Coppi

Who is the greatest climber of all time? It's a question that is inevitably asked but not easily answered. While a poll ranking the greatest sprinters would result in more or less the same names – Mark Cavendish most likely at the top with Mario Cipollini, Freddy Maertens, André Darrigade and Charles Pélissier among the others likely to feature – and while a list of the best Classics riders – including such as Rik Van Looy, Eddy Merckx, Roger De Vlaeminck, Tom Boonen, Fabian Cancellara – would also be comparatively easy to compile, it's much more difficult to reach general agreement when debating the merits of the best climbers.

In the mountains, form is fleeting, opportunities present themselves far less frequently than for the sprinters, and the efforts and, consequently, strategy have to be judged according to the extent of a rider's physical resources and the situation of a race. Does a climber need to make a big effort on Climb A today when they believe they have more chance of gaining ground on Climb B in two days' time because the second ascent suits their qualities more? In theory, recorded times for climbs present the ability to compare, but they're not especially helpful in making an assessment given improvements in roads, bikes and equipment, training and nutritional advances, plus more immediate influences like the weather and wind direction.

There are, of course, some climbers who would gain unanimous selection, and high up on this list would be Gino Bartali and Fausto Coppi. At their best, the long-time rivals were peerless in the mountains, their styles contrasting but equally effective. Bartali, the pure climber who could accelerate again and again, was powerfully built, the devout Catholic who loved a cigarette, would subdue the opposition with repeated attacks, a cycling pugilist with a boxer's broken nose who pummelled his rivals into submission. Coppi, the archetypal *rouleur-grimpeur*, was an incongruous mix with his long legs tapered to perfection beneath a huge barrelled chest; the ultimate stylist, who was excommunicated by the Church for adultery, would test himself and the riders on his wheel with a first burst of speed, ease off, then breeze away with a more determined and sustained second surge.

The third of four children born to parents who were impoverished smallholders in Ponte a Ema, just to the south of Florence, Bartali worked in a bike shop from the age of 13 and soon took to racing. A frequent winner as he rose through the junior ranks, he first appeared in the Giro d'Italia in 1935, winning a stage and the mountains title. A year later, having joined the Legnano team with whom he would enjoy most of his success, he won his national tour for the first time. Exultation quickly turned to grief, however, his brother Giulio succumbing to injuries sustained when he crashed in an amateur race just a week after that 1936 *corsa rosa* victory. Bartali didn't touch his bike for two months and contemplated retirement, but returned to become the dominant force in Italian racing up to the outbreak of the Second World War, retaining the Giro crown in 1937.

He 'climbed as well as René Pottier', according to Géo Lefèvre, Henri Desgrange's one-time assistant who came up with the original idea for 'a tour of France', although the extent of his ability was initially hard to judge as a consequence of the political isolation imposed on the country's fascist regime, which made Italian races domestic affairs. Yet Bartali's performance on his Tour debut in 1937 confirmed his consummate talent in the mountains. 'Bartali spreads his wings' was *L'Auto*'s headline after he had scattered the opposition on the stage over the Télégraphe and Galibier into Grenoble, Desgrange describing how the Italian sized up rivals who included defending champion Sylvère Maes on the first pass, then delivered a knock-out blow on the second.

'He gave me the impression of perfection in his position and almost of complete ease despite the gradient. It's impossible to say when he's struggling and, at the hardest moments, he doesn't even think about standing on the pedals', wrote Desgrange. 'You should have seen how he went clear: without any visible effort.' Bartali finished alone, almost two minutes clear of the second-placed rider, his teammate Francesco Camusso. It put him in the yellow jersey, a staggering nine minutes ahead of his nearest challenger, Ward Vissers.

As the Italian was largely unknown both to the French press and fans, *L'Auto* turned to Bruno Roghi, director of *La Gazzetta dello Sport*, to give an insight into his strengths. Roghi said he was 'a mystic. He believes in forces beyond himself, and these forces give him absolute confidence,' alluding to his Christian beliefs. 'What's more, I think he's the greatest Italian rider of all time. Binda had perhaps a more harmonious and limpid style, but Bartali's muscular strength is incredible, especially around his lower back.'

Bartali's rivals suggested that he might have exerted himself too soon, but on the evidence of his performances before and after that Tour, the Italian would have won the race in Paris. Fate intervened, though, on the very next stage when, as the favourites descended on the muddy road into Briançon, his teammate Jules Rossi lost control of his bike as they crossed a bridge and slid into his leader, who tumbled over the parapet and dropped three metres into the water below. Although he remounted quickly, there was no question then of anyone waiting for the stricken yellow jersey as would be the etiquette in the modern era. The Belgians attacked immediately and Bartali's hopes of becoming just the second Italian Tour winner evaporated. Struggling with the injuries he had suffered in his fall, he abandoned a few days later.

Victory went instead to Frenchman Roger Lapébie, who was the first Tour champion to use a bike fitted with a derailleur, thanks to the ban on their use being lifted by newly installed race director Jacques Goddet, who had taken over from the ailing Desgrange. Equipped with the three- or four-speed Super Champion brand fitted on the bikes supplied by the organization, Tour riders were able to change gear on the move rather than stopping to flip their rear wheel when the terrain demanded. Desgrange had always feared that derailleurs would level the competitive field, offering an advantage to weaker riders. However, the evidence of that Tour suggested quite the opposite as the innovation resulted in a race that was faster – of the 46 riders that finished, 40 completed the Tour at an average speed quicker than 1936 winner Maes – and more selective – the gaps between the stage-winner and the last finishers widened compared to the previous edition. There were also fewer bunch finishes. The evidence that stronger riders drew greater advantage from derailleurs also won over naysayers such as Desgrange and Karel Steyaert, founder of the Tour of Flanders and manager of the Belgian national team.

In 1938, Bartali missed the Giro and built his season around the Tour, reportedly at Mussolini's insistence, the dictator hoping that he and his fascist government would be able to bask in the reflected glory that victory by an Italian would likely deliver. On the first key stage in the Pyrenees, everything went to plan for the Italians as their standard-bearer romped through the 'circle of death', leading over the Aubisque, Tourmalet and Aspin. However, descending the latter, his front wheel broke and he crashed, and once again the Belgians were quick to take advantage, their two climbers Félicien Vervaecke and Ward Vissers finishing first and second in Luchon, the former taking the overall lead, which he held until the first big day into the Alps, out of Digne to Briançon via the Allos, Vars and Izoard passes.

This was very much Bartali's terrain, and he took full advantage of it, as the first line of Desgrange's report on *L'Auto*'s front page made clear: 'Who could doubt, after the Digne–Briançon stage, won by Bartali, that Italian sport has in him, very probably, the greatest road cyclist who has ever lived?' He had turned his one-and-a-quarter-minute deficit on Vervaecke into an advantage of more than twenty-one minutes, Luxembourg's Mathias Clemens being between the pair in the GC standings, but still close to eighteen minutes behind the Italian. 'I don't think the history of the Tour de France has seen such a "re-establishment",' Desgrange added, describing how, high on the Izoard, Bartali had looked far down the climb and waved at 'two little ants' way down below. One of them was his teammate Mario Vicini, who, as the photo further down on the front page showed, had set up the initial attack, standing on the pedals as they climbed the Allos, his face creased with anguish, Bartali on his wheel in the saddle as always and showing not the least discomfort.

The performance produced an ecstatic response within the Italian camp, which had been instructed by Mussolini to return home victorious. 'You're a hero!' exclaimed General Antonelli, who had been appointed president of the Italian cycling federation without having any previous knowledge of the sport. He'd spent much of the race in visible torment, anguished and clueless, not understanding when the Italian team hadn't been leading on the flats, often sat on the bonnet of their team car on the climbs, urging his riders on. Team manager Costante Girardengo, Italy's first *campionissimo*, was often perched on the bonnet next to him. 'Fascism wanted a complete experience on the Tour de France. I received orders. I've executed them,' he confessed in Briançon, doubtless with a touch of relief.

Bartali's margin over Vervaecke in Paris was eighteen and a half minutes, all of it gained in the mountains, a substantial amount in time bonuses, but most of it by riding everyone off his wheel on almost every major col. Unlike Coppi, and indeed the majority of Grand Tour winners who would follow in his wake, he wasn't formidable in every area, losing four minutes over sixty-five kilometres of time trialling to Vervaecke in that race, for instance. Yet he was so incomparably strong in the mountains that these gaps in his racing make-up often didn't matter.

Racing in this manner captured the popular imagination, especially of the Italian fans. Although they'd already had a Tour winner in Ottavio Bottecchia, he'd ridden for French teams, enjoyed most of his success on French soil, and was an introverted, remote figure. Bartali, though, was undoubtedly one of their own and they adored him. Following the next stage into Aix-les-Bains, French radio commentator Georges Briquet described a mass of flag-waving *tifosi* mobbing him at the finish. 'These people had found a superman.

Outside Bartali's hotel at Aix-les-Bains, an Italian general was shouting, "Don't touch him – he's a god."'

The Italian is depicted quite beautifully in *Forcenés*, Philippe Bordas describing how

> Bartali rolls his broad mason's shoulders, advancing by jerks and jumps . . . Bartali invents the altitude sprint. He pushes a navvy's 48×23 gear, jumps from one bend to the next . . . God loves him in the high ranges and protects him from falling. In the descents where he brakes little, Bartali establishes his mystical proof. He believes in destiny, a destiny carved out of the hand of a canonized peasant . . . He is the first mountain genius to perform miracles on climbs, downhill and sprints.

That final phrase captures the Italian champion perfectly. Bartali soared and carried the popular imagination along with him. Was he the greatest of all time? It's not easy to say. However, what is certain is that this wasn't even his greatest exploit in the mountains at the Tour de France. That would come a decade later, after the Italian had lost what would probably have been his best racing years to the war, but had, although he never admitted it before his death in 2000, added to his legend in a wholly different way by helping Jews who were being persecuted by Mussolini's fascist government, sheltering one family in his cellar and, during his training rides around his home near Florence, ferrying documents that enabled hundreds more to evade capture.

Winner of the first post-war Giro in 1946, when he took the sixth of his seven mountains titles as well, Bartali returned to the Tour in 1948. By now 34 and struggling to maintain his pre-eminence over Fausto Coppi, who'd beaten him in the 1947 Giro, and Fiorenzo

Magni, who had just done the same in 1948, he began the race well, winning the opening stage to take the yellow jersey. But when the race reached the Pyrenees a week later he'd fallen more than twenty minutes behind the emerging star of French cycling, Louison Bobet. Consecutive victories in the mountains lifted him from the depths of the general classification to relative respectability in eighth place, but still eighteen minutes down on young Bobet.

Come the Alps, the Frenchman had gained another three minutes on the Italian leader, his buffer now twenty-one minutes as the thirteenth stage got under way in Cannes. Heading for Briançon, it was set to cross the Allos, Vars and Izoard passes, the scene of 1938's 're-establishment'. A decade on, it would be the first part of a trilogy that John Foot described in *Pedalare! Pedalare!* as 'quite simply the greatest three days of cycling in the history of the sport'. Bartali triumphed on all three, his performance so impressive that it has been credited, subsequently for the most part, with quelling the political turmoil that was raging in his home country following an assassination attempt on the leader of the Italian Communists, Palmiro Togliatti, who had been shot on the steps of the parliament building the day before, leading to mass strikes, clashes on the streets and more than a dozen deaths.

Act one began with Bartali and Bobet tracking each other on the Allos, where 1947 champion Jean Robic, his squashed features crumpled even further by his tightly tied leather helmet, attempted to turn around his fading fortunes. On the Vars, as icy rain began to fall and the unsealed road surface became glutinous and slippery, Bartali, 'the man of iron' who seemed impervious to any extreme in temperature, increased his pace, quickly dropping Bobet and closing on Robic by the crest of the pass. Sliding down to Guillestre, the village tucked in between the Vars and Izoard, the Italian, his chain jumping due to the grit thrown into it from the muddy road, distanced the fading Robic, while Bobet was still within four minutes of his Italian rival, until punctures and a broken pedal axle waylaid him.

Climbing the Izoard via its harder southern flank, Bartali powered on, never appearing to struggle. On this occasion, the inclement conditions meant that he couldn't look back and spy his rivals as he neared the summit as he had done ten years before. Yet, even if it had been clear, they would still likely have been invisible. Belgian Classics star Briek Schotte was nearest, but almost nine minutes back, Bobet was nineteen behind. By the finish, the veteran Italian had scythed the Frenchman's overall lead down to a single minute.

Act two, which featured the Galibier, Croix de Fer and Glandon passes early on and then three ascents in the rugged Chartreuse massif to reach Aix-les-Bains, ran to a similar pattern, with the conditions even worse than they had been twenty-four hours earlier, the temperature below freezing on the opening three climbs. Bartali bided his time, then made an initial sortie on the Croix de Fer, where the dogged Bobet was the only rider able to follow him, their duel captured in a famous image that shows them climbing what is nothing more than a rough and muddy track, both caked in so much grime that it's not easy to see where their shorts and short-sleeved jerseys give way to exposed skin.

On the approach to Grenoble, a group of ten came together at the front, only to be dynamited by Bartali's second attack. On this occasion, there would be no way back for his rivals as he crossed the Porte, Cucheron and Granier passes on his own to win by six minutes and take the yellow jersey after a swing of nine minutes on Bobet.

'I've never ridden a stage as tough as that,' the Italian confessed at the finish. Rarely in the Tour's history has a rest day been as well placed as the one that followed in Aix-les-Bains.

Act three provided confirmation that Bartali, on the climbs at least, was racing at a different level. He won in Lausanne after an attack on the climb above the Swiss city that no one else could follow, extending his lead over Bobet to almost 14 minutes. Another victory in Liège, his seventh of the race at the end of a stage over the short but steep hills of the Liège–Bastogne–Liège one-day race, added the final gloss. Bartali rode into Paris twenty-six minutes ahead of runner-up Briek Schotte, with France's Guy Lapébie in third and the courageous Bobet, picked out by the yellow jersey as a future Tour winner, thirty-three minutes back in fourth.

Writing in *La Gazzetta dello Sport*, Guido Giardini hailed Bartali's victory as 'an exceptional achievement', but qualified this by saying the Italian wasn't phenomenal, adding, 'I don't think there were many men of class in this Tour . . . it showed that world cycling is still looking for new names.' He pointed to the fact that third-placed Lapébie was a great rider, but one best known for his feats on the track. He could have added that Schotte was regarded as a Classics specialist and that young Bobet was making his Tour debut, and also that Coppi and Magni weren't in the field. In short, in a similar way to 2021 Tour victor Tadej Pogačar, whose victory, many said, was comprehensive but had come against a diminished field, Bartali was a fully deserved winner, but hadn't been thoroughly tested.

Yet he had beaten the defending champion Robic, the mercurial René Vietto, who had almost won the year before, and done so at a new record speed, his average of 33.404kph being a kilometre and a half faster than the previous quickest race won by Romain Maes in 1939. Moreover, at 4,922 kilometres, it had been the longest Tour since the 1931 edition. It seems, therefore, that 34-year-old Bartali had been faster and stronger than ever before. Like Pogačar, he appeared to have been well capable of beating any one of his peers, even those who hadn't been on the start line. Like the Slovenian, the youngest Tour winner since 1904, Bartali was a phenomenon, in his case because of his age and the fact that a decade had passed since his first victory in the race, a record that has yet to be matched.

Inevitably, analysis of Bartali's attributes as a climber demand comparison with those of Fausto Coppi, who, like his rival, was born into poverty in the Piedmontese hilltop village of Castellania, where his father was a subsistence farmer. He discovered his passion for riding on an old bike he found in his family's cellar, then put it to more practical use working as a delivery boy for a butcher in the neighbouring town of Novi Ligure. He started to race and, thanks to the money provided by his uncle and father that enabled him to buy a bespoke racing frame, to win. Fate also played a part, as his job in Novi Ligure placed him in exactly the right place at precisely the right time to further his chances of competitive success, because it was the home town of Biagio Cavanna, a former racer turned coach, who had already worked with Costante Girardengo, Italy's first *campionissimo*, and oversaw a stable of riders who adhered to the harsh training regime he set them. Although he lost his sight in 1937 as a consequence of getting dust in his eyes, this impediment only added to his guru-like status, Cavanna relying on his expertise as a masseur to assess the condition of his riders, as well as on an array of substances with which he fortified them. He took Coppi under his wing in 1938 and encouraged him to take on independent (semi-professional) status the following year, when he won a string of races in that category, often by large margins, which resulted in an offer to turn pro with Legnano later that same season.

Coppi's first significant clash with Bartali was as Legnano teammates at the 1940 Giro, which was won by the younger man. He announced himself to the cycling world on the stage into Modena when his leader had an issue with his bottom bracket and their *direttore sportivo* Eberardo Pavesi allowed Coppi the freedom to attack. Writing in *Corriere della Sera*, Orio Vergani declared that he had seen 'something new: an eagle, a swallow, I don't know what,' and described how the performance of this unknown rider silenced the astonished spectators at the roadside, who could do nothing more than applaud as Coppi swept by them.

Come the so-called Giro della Rinascita (Giro of Rebirth) of 1946, the pair were leaders of their own teams. Coppi, the winner of three stages despite being hampered by a broken rib sustained early in the race, was the stronger in the mountains and viewed as the moral victor by some, but Bartali, depicted as *'il vecchio'*, the old campaigner, drew on the full extent of his experience, attacking at the right moments, forging temporary alliances to prevail by forty-seven seconds in Milan.

A year later, with their rivalry at its height, the contest between the pair was just as tight, Coppi proving the victor on that occasion. In 1948, they marked each other so closely that Magni upstaged them both. From that year, however, Coppi almost always had the edge, especially in the Grand Tours. At his best, he was invincible, his climbing style quite different to Bartali's. In *Fallen Angel*, William Fotheringham's biography of Coppi, Alfredo Martini, who witnessed their rivalry in close-up as one of their closest competitors in post-war editions of the Giro, said,

Bartali had stamina, but Coppi had speed. Bartali's racing style was based on *grinta*, guts and strength. He used his stamina and sheer physical power, particularly in bad weather, to wear the opposition down with repeated attacks. Coppi, on the other hand, would wait until he could sense the right moment to make the single move that would get him clear off the pack. Once away, his ability to ride solo would ensure he could not be caught.

Whereas Bartali required a hilly course to profit from his qualities, Coppi could quickly transform a gap into a gulf on any terrain. He'd won the first post-war edition of Milan–Sanremo in 1946 with a 140-kilometre lone break after joining the early escapees soon after the 293-kilometre race had got under way. Three stages from the end of the 1949 Giro, he eclipsed even that performance on the 254-kilometre stage between Cuneo and Pinerolo that featured five long passes, the Maddalena (or Col de Larche), Vars, Izoard, Montgenèvre and Sestriere, his stage-winning ride 'the most legendary lone break in Italian cycling history', according to John Foot.

Coppi started that cold and wet June day forty-three seconds down on *maglia rosa* Adolfo Leoni, with Bartali more than ten minutes back in third. 'Coppi generally didn't attack Bartali in the mountains, but while riding at the back of the peloton as the Maddalena climb began, he noticed that Bartali was having trouble with his brake cables near the levers and was distracted. Coppi used that moment of inattention to attack,' Martini recalled. He sauntered up to lone leader Primo Volpi, as Bartali frantically chased, then stopped briefly to remedy an issue with his chain, which gave the other two the chance to ride clear. Once back in the saddle, Coppi cruised up to them and kept going. Pinerolo was 192 kilometres away.

In his wonderful account of that Giro, Dino Buzzati, watching this contest from a press car, was reminded of his classical studies three decades earlier and specifically the duel between Trojan prince Hector and Greek warrior Achilles in Homer's *Iliad*. He depicted Bartali in the Hector role of ill-destined hero. 'It's against a superhuman power that Bartali fought, and he could do nothing but lose: the evil power of age', wrote Buzzati.

The gap between the pair began to open, Buzzati saying of the two-wheeled Achilles: 'Victory took its place at Coppi's side right from the first moments of the duel. Anyone who saw him no longer had any doubts. His pace up those cursed climbs had irresistible power. Who could have stopped him?' Like Achilles, Coppi had been perfectly prepared for this contest. Awkward and ungainly on his feet, he was complete on the bike, his cadence perfectly smooth, back flat, arms relaxed, his effort best gauged by the distance he would gradually open up on the riders flailing in his wake. The muscles under the skin were visible, resembling extraordinarily young snakes about to shed their skins.

As Coppi pressed relentlessly on, few witnessed his epic ride, which took place mostly on near-deserted roads in France on what was the Giro's first incursion across that border. But his exploits were brought to life for the huge radio audience listening in Italy by Radiotelevisione italiana (RAI) commentator Mario Ferretti, who uttered the phrase that has become indelibly associated with Coppi in his white and celeste Bianchi jersey: '*Un uomo solo è al comando; la sua maglia è bianco-celeste; il suo nome è Fausto Coppi.*' (There's just one man on his own in the lead; his jersey is celeste and white; his name is Fausto Coppi.)

Like Hector, Bartali did not succumb easily, but he did yield. He finished close to a dozen minutes behind his rival, while the rest were in their own race, won by Martini nineteen minutes after Coppi had effectively wrapped up the title. Although the rivalry continued for some years, the balance of power had shifted to the younger man, who was initiating a paradigm change in the approach to bike racing. Guided by Cavanna, Coppi altered the precepts relating to race preparation and strategy, laying the foundation for the sport as we see it today. According to his French teammate Raphaël Geminiani, every advance in the sport can be traced back to the Italian and his perceptive guru, including diet, training, preparation, tactics and even doping. His influence was particularly apparent in the mountains.

Described by Philippe Bordas as 'the heraldic symbol of the climber', Coppi's impact was most apparent in what would prove to be his final appearance at the Tour de France, in 1952. It was the first edition to feature summit finishes, no fewer than three, at the Alpine ski resort of Alpe d'Huez, the Italian winter sports centre of Sestriere, and on the ancient volcano of the Puy de Dôme, which overlooks the city of Clermont-Ferrand in the Massif Central, their introduction designed to counter the monotony of the previous edition won at a canter by Switzerland's Hugo Koblet. Tour co-directors Jacques Goddet and Félix Lévitan believed they would add spice to a battle featuring the defending champion, his compatriot and predecessor Ferdi Kübler, French number one Louison Bobet, and 1949 winner Coppi. Ultimately, though, the Italian was the only one of the illustrious quartet who was on that year's start line in Brest, and the Italian soon demonstrated that the Tour organizers had overplayed their hand.

Coppi's strategy for the Grand Tours was to target two or three stages where he would focus most of his efforts, which became the method adopted by all stage-racing greats. Alpe d'Huez was the first of these. He didn't know the climb at all, and later confessed that he asked local pro Bernard Gauthier for advice on the gearing for his bike, which like those of his peers was fitted with a double chainring for the first time that season and when used in combination with the five-speed derailleur provided them with ten gears. Hearing what the Frenchman had to say about the steepness of parts of the new climb, Coppi was relishing the challenge, unlike most of his peers, who were concerned that the unprecedented uphill finale might result in many of them finishing outside the time limit. To guard against this possibility a number of older riders kept the peloton tightly corralled on the 250-kilometre approach to Alpe d'Huez from the start in Lausanne, shepherding any hopeful escapees back into the fold by brandishing their bike pumps.

As the bunch reached the foot of the climb towards the resort, Coppi was close to the front, waiting to see who would attack, aiming to use them as the hare that he would pursue. Frenchmen Geminiani and Jean Robic were the first to break the shackles on the steep ramp rising straight from the valley floor. 'Gem' was quickly defeated by the gradient, leaving the little Breton as the Italian's quarry. Coppi sped up gradually, caught Robic a third of the way up the 13-kilometre ascent, waited for the next difficult section, span his pedals a little faster coming out of a hairpin, then went hard again. 'I knew he wasn't there any longer because I couldn't hear him breathing,' he revealed afterwards. The stage was his, the yellow jersey too.

Following a rest day in Alpe d'Huez, the French team, and Geminiani in particular, attempted to unsettle the race leader on the stage to Sestriere over the Croix de Fer, Galibier and Montgenèvre passes, but only succeeded in 'stirring me up', as Coppi put it. Planning to hold back until the final ascent, he countered Geminiani's attack on the Galibier, Goddet describing him climbing as smoothly as 'a ski lift on its steel cable'. Relaxing in his room with a glass of yogurt after his post-stage massage, he told *L'Équipe*: 'As I felt very good, I kept on going.' He was eight minutes clear at the line and extended his overall lead to twenty minutes. The contest for the yellow jersey was over.

When Coppi won again on the Puy de Dôme, this time only by a few seconds, Goddet expressed his delight at the closeness of the contest, ending his review of the stage with the statement: 'We will come back to the Puy de Dôme again.' So why did it take seven years for the Tour to go back and six to feature another summit finish, atop Mont Ventoux in 1958? An answer lies further up in that same Goddet piece, where he describes the 'stupefying ease' of Coppi's overall victory, adding, 'that's always a detestable spectacle'. He and Lévitan had taken a bold step by introducing three summit finishes, too bold as it turned out, and had had their organizational fingers burned. As a consequence, they rowed back to the more traditional format, where riders crossed the major passes but raced to a finish that was often well beyond them, opening the way to the mob-handed pursuit of any lone climbing raider.

They couldn't have known, though, that they were basing this decision on the domination of one of the greatest stage racers and climbers in the sport's history, and for some the very best. According to Bordas:

> It's not one or two passes that Coppi crosses alone, but entire massifs. Coppi performs mountain escapes of one hundred and two hundred kilometres. Coppi becomes the new king,

the greatest climber of all time. He takes away from the chronicler the very idea of a comparison.

While equally valid claims can be made of others – Bartali, of course, but also Eddy Merckx and Bernard Hinault – what's more certain is that basing the decision to phase out summit finishes for some years, having witnessed Coppi's absolute hegemony, penalized the pure climbers who emerged in his wake, the likes of Federico Bahamontes, Charly Gaul and Julio Jiménez, while at the same time suiting *rouleurs-grimpeurs* in the mould of France's serial Tour winners Louison Bobet and Jacques Anquetil. Eleven years would pass before a Tour with two summit finishes, another nineteen before Goddet and Lévitan dared to include three. Having brought the climbers to centre stage, they immediately relegated them to bit-part roles.

Chapter 7

Duende in the mountains

In October 1933, Spanish poet and playwright Federico García Lorca presented a lecture in Buenos Aires entitled *Juego y teoría del duende* (Play and theory of the *duende*), the word deriving from *duen de casa*, the lord of the house, a kind of local spirit. For Lorca, this spirit emerged from within a person as a physical and emotional response to art, particularly to Spanish folk music and flamenco, where on certain occasions the singer or dancer and their audience could be drawn together by a visceral reaction to the performance. This might manifest itself in ecstasy, tears, goosebumps or by a kind of rapture or loss of control.

Duende was, said Lorca, distinctly Spanish in nature, bound up in a culture that had a strong focus on death as well as life and where poverty and hardship were endemic. He described it as an enigmatic force, often materializing in the presence of danger and especially when there was the threat of death, and as having cruel beauty. As well as *cante jondo*, the haunting songs that accompany flamenco, he linked it to bullfighting, to what he saw as the dance between toreador and bull, and it was in these domains that it became apparent in its purest form. But he said that it could be apparent in all of the arts, capable of producing what he defined as 'an almost religious enthusiasm', both in the artist or performer and in their audience.

In the period when Lorca defined *duende*, sport was only just beginning to gain the cultural pre-eminence that it has acquired over subsequent decades, but it has become the arena where we are most used to seeing reactions and emotions of this kind, where the gap between elation and despair is narrow and always apparent, where both the athlete and spectators are transformed by the nature of a performance. This exultation may not always be the result of the *duende* manifesting itself, but there are clear instances when this is the case. Among the most outstanding would be Diego Maradona's match-winning performance for Argentina in the quarter-final of the 1986 World Cup against England. Having risen from abject poverty in one of the roughest parts of Buenos Aires to become the world's greatest footballer, Maradona turned the course of that game with two moments that encapsulated *duende*. The first was the 'hand of God' goal that highlighted its impish aspect, his sly act of cheating inspired to a degree by his upbringing, where any opportunity to get ahead needed to be grabbed without immediate thought to the repercussions. The second was a match-winning goal of sheer brilliance, slaloming from his own half into the opposition's penalty area, leaving a string of English players floundering in his wake, then flicking the ball almost insolently into the net for a goal that remains the best scored in World Cup history.

In the same way that it can be apparent in any of the arts, this sense of *duende* can be seen in many other sports. Surfing, for instance, can offer that life or death element that results in very intense and particular emotions arising. Surfing writer Gibus de Soultrait highlights that sport's history, lifestyle and, above all, the imponderable uniqueness of the wave, its beauty, its power, its violence, its transparency, which concretize the singular song, the singular animal to which the *duende* resorts for its expression . . . Then to this is grafted the technical and aesthetic acuity of a body, in the conduct of a creative act, this elastic glide along slender tubes of water . . . that suddenly envelop the surfer in an oceanic movement that is a reminder of their existence.

However, there is arguably no sporting activity where *duende* is more apparent than on the mountain stages of the world's most prestigious and challenging road races. The setting is one of cruel beauty, the majesty of the scenery either heightened or compromised by the elements, the arena packed with fans to the extent that the riders are usually left with no more than a narrow, but fluctuating corridor of road to race on, the atmosphere loud, frenetic, unpredictable, and, it is important to stress, wholly addictive. Hearing riders speak about these moments, there's a clear sense of the presence of *duende*.

South Africa's Ashleigh Moolman Pasio, for instance, evokes a sensation that sounds very much like *duende* when talking about the difference in feeling between training and racing in the mountains.

In training, there's more of a mental battle with yourself. There'll be days when it's really hard and the pain feels particularly severe and then you have to say to yourself, 'Come on, you can do this.' You're trying to motivate yourself to keep going and to push the limits. But in a race, you get a kind of out-of-the-body feeling on the climbs. You do almost detach yourself from the pain, and the times you can manage to do that are when you produce your best performances, when you have that ability to be just completely in the moment, not really thinking about anything other than just riding your bike as hard as possible. There are other riders around you, there's the crowds, the closeness of them and the noise that they make, and combined with the effort you're making, you do end up in a place where you don't necessarily feel the pain.

Canada's Michael Woods offers a similar perspective on racing in these situations.

For me, it's always been weird, because when I've done my best climbs, when I've had the most success, it's been the most painless from a memory perspective. I know that I suffered, although suffer is not quite the right word – I know that I was hurting, that I was experiencing pain, but I don't remember that. I just remember having the presence of mind to know that I was going to have success.

When I'm on my best form, I'm able to really separate myself from my body and almost imagine myself watching from the helicopter above. I'm imagining myself watching from TV, where I can see the countdown to the finish line, the time gap to the breakaway, and I'm able to break the climb down into pieces. I have this incredible kind of perspective. That's when I'm at my best. When I'm at my worst, I'm there, I'm riding, I'm on the bike and I want to be anywhere but there, suffering and fighting and wishing that I had that same sensation I had on my best days.

These descriptions are imbued with a strong sense of *duende*, with the presence of an intangible essence that transforms elite athletic endeavour to the exceptional, lifting the racer above their rivals, even above themselves it seems. Its presence is further underlined by Woods when he evokes the change in mood that occurs within the peloton when the action shifts from the flat to the mountains.

> The peloton is such an angry and inhospitable place, with lots of noise. You're travelling prior to a climb at upwards of 60 kilometres per hour. People are fighting for position, it's sensory overload, especially when there's fans yelling at you, there's stimuli everywhere. There's traffic furniture, you're dodging guys, guys are pushing you. You can hear and smell brakes, it just feels wrong, it feels evil almost.
>
> And then, as a climber, when you hit a climb and start attacking all that goes away. And it's just silence. It's almost like there's a sink and the mayhem disappears down it, because all of a sudden you're going travelling at 15–20 kilometres an hour. You can hear guys breathing, no one's fighting anymore. No one's talking. And I really enjoy that because it's such a crazy change in feeling. You maybe hear the motorcycle up front, maybe the helicopter above, but you also hear the stream that's beside you that's carved itself into the side of the mountain and is the reason why you're riding up that part of the mountain.

Hearing these accounts, and at the same time accepting that there is a kind of transformative element at some moments of peak athletic intensity, be it *duende*, Zen or some other transmutative force, it becomes fascinating to reflect on the performances of climbers in the past who must have been stimulated and motivated in precisely this way. Just three months prior to Lorca's *duende* lecture in the South American spring of 1933, Vicente Trueba, a Spaniard from very much the kind of poor background that the dramatist suggested was the cradle for this spirit, lit up the Tour de France with his performances in the highlands, capturing the first King of the Mountains prize for his efforts. Though his was, according to Henri Desgrange and other journalists, a qualified success because he wasn't involved in the battle for cycling's grail that is the yellow jersey, Trueba's feat has endured, partly because he was the first winner of the mountains prize, but essentially because of the emotions and sensations triggered by his shows of climbing panache, a 'flea'-like figure bettering 'the giants of the road' in the most dramatic, beautiful and harshest arena in sport. At the time, fans responded to his feats for these same reasons, even though the stimulus for most of them came second-hand via reports in the press.

However, the essence of *duende* within bike racing is much easier to establish within the personalities and performances of Trueba's successors, because first radio and then TV coverage became more widespread, and many fans witnessed their exploits at the roadside. Like 'The Torrelavega Flea', they were Spanish and emerged in increasing numbers from the 1950s, as the country began to recover from the social, political and economic blockade imposed on Franco's fascist regime. They were led by Jesús Loroño and Federico Bahamontes, whose rivalry may not have the historic and sporting resonance of that between Gino Bartali and Fausto Coppi, but divided fans in Spain in the same way and was characterized by much more bitterness and hostility between its two protagonists. It then continued in the 1960s and 1970s with riders on the Faema and, particularly, Kas teams, notably Julio Jiménez and José Manuel Fuente, the latter almost certainly the best personification of *duende* because he raced according to the whims of an internal force that made him entirely unpredictable as an opponent, one capable of unparalleled brilliance, but equally of appalling setbacks that tended to be self-inflicted.

Spain's post-war isolation from the Tour de France ended in 1951. The following year, Bernardo Ruiz finished a very distant third overall to Coppi. Another season on, Loroño won a stage on his way to the mountains title. But it was Bahamontes who not only established the country as one of cycling's dominant powers, but also restored it to the sporting map almost singlehandedly. His successes over a decade from 1954 included Spain's first Tour victory and no fewer than six King of the Mountains titles, conferring emblematic status on him as a sporting personality within his home nation.

The eldest of four children born to a Toledo road-mender and his wife, Bahamontes was brought up in extreme poverty, like many in Spain during the post-civil war period. In a biography by Alasdair Fotheringham, *The Eagle of Toledo*, he reveals that his family was sometimes so short of food that he would catch cats, which his mother would gut and then fill with salt, pepper and vegetables. 'They tasted delicious. We called them "baby goats",' he says. He acquired his first bike at the age of 18, using it to boost his meagre earnings as a market labourer by more nefarious means. He would ride the brakeless second-hand machine to villages surrounding Toledo, where bread and other foodstuffs were in comparatively plentiful supply, and buy them on the black market for resale in the city, boosting his family's earnings.

After one trip, two fellow black marketeers told him they were off to a bike race and he decided to go along with them. He knew nothing about the sport, but plenty enough about wheeling and dealing to sort out a racing licence on the start line. When the race got under way, his ignorance of tactical niceties was highlighted when he attacked, but his ability shone through too as he managed to finish second despite his chain coming unshipped several times. He raced again the following weekend with the chain problem sorted, employed the same from-the-gun tactic, and on that occasion no one caught him.

Bahamontes began to travel to races with a friend, initially within the local region and then into other parts of Spain, the pair winning more often than they lost, making very good money from their success. He soon advanced to independent, or semi-professional, status, competing against many of Spain's leading riders and some from outside the country at the Tour of Asturias and the Volta a Catalunya in 1953, winning the mountains competition in the latter. Thanks to the patronage of Santiago Mostajo, a former Spanish road champion who'd become a successful Barcelona businessman, these successes led to him attending the Simplex pre-season training camp on France's Côte d'Azur that was run by former Tour legend Charles Pélissier and was designed to assess the potential of riders who might be able to step up into the pro ranks. Bahamontes stood out from the off. Towards the end of the camp he rode the hilly Nice–Mont Agel event against a field comprising primarily professional racers and won it. Six months later, he'd become one of their elite, finishing his first Tour as the winner of the mountains competition, his success leading to one French newspaper dubbing him 'The Eagle of Toledo'.

That race spawned the most famous tale about Bahamontes. According to many subsequent accounts, his gains on the climbs were so great that, on reaching the crest of the Col de Romeyère in the Vercors massif, he had so much time in hand on his rivals that he stopped for an ice cream while he waited for them to catch up. The truth, though, is more prosaic. According to the Spaniard, while he was climbing towards the top of the pass in the company of Frenchman Jean Le Guilly, a stone flicked up from a passing vehicle and broke two of his spokes. The halt at the summit, therefore, was unplanned and unwanted. He was simply killing time until the Spanish team car, stuck behind the bunch, could sort out his mechanical issue. He had, though, achieved his principal objective for the day, which was to lead over the Romeyère, that day's only categorized climb, enabling him to extend his lead in the mountains competition over second-placed Louison Bobet, the race leader.

They finished that way in Paris, Bahamontes the winner of the mountains title, Bobet the overall champion for the second year running. The Frenchman offered qualified praise for the Tour debutant. 'I've never seen such a great climber. Bahamontes can achieve a lot, if he stops clowning around,' he said. The incident atop the Romeyère illustrated this lack of seriousness. Other riders would have pressed on with some caution, hoping that the team car might arrive before Bobet's yellow jersey group swept them up. But the Spaniard sat tight, then compounded his misjudgement by filling his bottle with water and pouring the contents over riders as they crossed the summit, an action that earned him a fine from the race commissaires.

Bobet was more likely, though, to have been referring to the significant flaws in Bahamontes's make-up as a bike racer – his renowned lack of ability on descents, his lack of focus on time trialling as a discipline, and, above all, the fact that he was prepared to cede time early on in races in order to get more leeway when the mountain stages arrived, a shortcoming that *L'Équipe* and other papers also picked at regularly. This had long been and still remains a preferred strategy for some specialist climbers. There was another issue too that Bobet might not have been aware of, namely Bahamontes's constant desire to do things in his own way, even when this worked against his chances. Ruiz, says Fotheringham, 'depicts his former rival as a rider whose excessive individualism made him an isolated figure, incapable of asking for or receiving assistance at crucial times'. Like Bobet, Ruiz regarded Bahamontes as exceptional on the climbs, but adds that, 'he didn't know how to use his own strength; he was out of control. One day he'd beat you, then the next he'd do nothing. I couldn't work out what was going on inside his head.'

Fotheringham suggests that Bahamontes's individualism might have been down to the poverty he endured during his childhood, which led to a desire to accumulate money in the best way that he could, and that usually meant going for the mountains title. By the same token, he was reluctant to pay for loyalty when he needed it, especially within a Spanish team that was almost always riven by factions. His bitter relationship on and off the road with Loroño epitomized this totally. The two men loathed each other, that resentment initially stemming from their duel for the same perch as the leader of the Spanish national team, then fed by their difference as personalities. Bahamontes is often described as childlike and contradictory, ready to say one thing one day, then do something completely different the next. Loroño, on the other hand, was straight and uncomplicated, 'a bit too stiff-necked at times', according to his son Josu.

The two men's mutual antipathy wasn't concealed. Indeed, the press made hay with the pair's readiness to denigrate each other, building up the rivalry so that Spain divided between Bahamontistas on one side and Loroñistas on the other. It was fed too by political differences. While Bahamontes was from Castile in the heart of the country, from an area perceived as being conservative and pro-Franco, Loroño was from the independence-minded Basque

Country, one of the strongholds of the Republican regime that Franco had overthrown. It was like Barça versus Real on bikes.

The rivalry came to a head at the 1957 Vuelta a España, where they were partnered as leaders of a Spanish team from which Ruiz had been relegated to a regional outfit in order to make way for Bahamontes. However, the bulk of the riders in the line-up were drawn from the Faema trade team Ruiz led and that Bahamontes had left under a cloud at the end of the previous season. This was one of those moments when he should have rallied his teammates behind him by offering financial reward. Instead, he sat on his hands and paid the price for this late on the tenth of the sixteen stages to Tortosa. Holding a clear lead in general classification and given the full backing of the Spanish team by manager Luis Puig, who had instructed Loroño, by then more than a quarter of an hour in arrears, to focus on the mountains title, Bahamontes looked nailed on for overall victory.

In the first hour of that stage to Tortosa, Ruiz attacked with two others and was soon joined by Loroño and three more. In normal circumstances, Loroño would have protected his teammate's lead by refusing to collaborate, while, at the same time, the rest of the Spanish team would have set the pace in the bunch with a view to neutralizing the break or at least keeping it within close range. However, racing strategy was turned on its head. At Ruiz's urging, Loroño cooperated in the break while no one came to Bahamontes's assistance in the peloton, which eventually came in 22 minutes down. Loroño was the new leader and held the yellow jersey to the finish in Bilbao, where Bahamontes was second and Ruiz third.

There were unsubstantiated claims, backed by Bahamontes but also by several newspapers, that the race had been rigged on the government's orders to favour the victory of a Basque rider in that region, which had always been and would remain so difficult for Franco's regime to control. But no evidence has ever appeared of the telegram that was said to have been sent from Madrid with this request. Rather, it seems that either obstinacy, parsimoniousness, rank stupidity or a combination of all three had cost Bahamontes what would prove to be his best chance ever of winning his national tour.

Many comparisons can be made between the careers of the Tour's two six-time winners of the King of the Mountains prize: Bahamontes and Lucien Van Impe, who, by coincidence, was given a leg-up by the Spaniard into the pro ranks in the late spring of the 1969 season following his victory at the Vuelta a Navarra, where Bahamontes was managing a rival team. Aside from the obvious fact that they both had almost unparalleled talent in the mountains, they were also frequently criticized for taking the easy option by targeting the mountains prize over the yellow jersey, for being too individualistic and following their own path rather than listening to the sage advice of others or collaborating with teammates, and for being weak when it came to tactics and mental fortitude. What's more, when each of them did fulfil what many saw as their potential and win the Tour de France, each was indebted to a strong personality who managed to bend them to their will. For Van Impe, it was Cyrille Guimard, one of the sport's greatest strategists, who would guide three different riders to the yellow jersey. In the case of Bahamontes it was Fausto Coppi, while Dalmacio Langarica played a strong supporting role.

Coppi visited Bahamontes at his home in Toledo at the end of the 1958 season. He not only persuaded the Spaniard to sign for the Tricolfilina team, with which the Italian great was due to spend his last year as a pro, but also asserted that Bahamontes could win the Tour. 'He told Bahamontes to forget the King of the Mountains and stick with Anquetil and Rivière. He told him to switch strategy and he gained his trust. It's as simple as that. He transformed him,' said Coppi's former teammate Raphaël Geminiani.

Bahamontes's quest for yellow was helped by the comparative harmony within the Spanish team directed by Langarica, and the civil war that raged instead within the French ranks. Prior to the start, team boss Marcel Bidot had brokered the so-called 'Poigny pact' between 1957 Tour winner Jacques Anquetil, new French hope Roger Rivière, three-time champion Louison Bobet and 1958 runner-up Geminiani, but the enmity between the former pair, both immensely powerful *rouleurs* who regarded themselves as France's best chance of victory, would prove insurmountable.

Bahamontes waited until the mountains before he made his first decisive move, an attack on the Tourmalet where he and defending champion Charly Gaul gained two minutes on their rivals, but, oddly, didn't press home their advantage. Bahamontes later explained he was still biding his time. 'I'll go for it when it suits me,' he said. He knew he didn't have the team to control the race that early on, and that, as the race continued, the divisions within the French team would widen. Following that stage Bidot confessed, 'Our boat is still sailing, but it's leaking from all sides.' It foundered completely on the run through the Massif Central to Aurillac in blistering heat. With a break already away, Bahamontes attacked with 140 kilometres remaining, Anquetil one of the five riders that joined him. It seemed suicidal to their GC hopes, but when they reached the half-dozen riders at the front, it was clear that they might pull off a huge coup. Bobet attempted to bridge across to them on his own. Anquetil responded to this by raising the pace on the front of the break, which stayed clear to the finish. Bahamontes leapt to fifth and saw Gaul and Bobet eliminated from the GC contest, while Rivière was relegated to the periphery. 'At Aurillac, the time and the day had finally arrived that I was sure that I could win,' Bahamontes later said.

The mountain time trial on the Puy de Dôme provided his next stepping stone to overall victory. This kind of *montée sèche*, a climb that is tackled in isolation, was Bahamontes's speciality. He'd been second to Gaul when the organizers had included one for the first time the previous year on Mont Ventoux, and was using a bike fitted with lightweight silk tubular tyres and a six-speed rear cluster of sprockets, ranging from 14 to 23 teeth, coupled with a 51/44 double chainring that would give him the speed he needed on the flat approach to the climb. In a brief bit of footage from this time trial, Bahamontes, so beautifully rhythmic and effortless on the climbs normally, can be seen bobbing vigorously from side to side as he punches down on the pedals nearing the summit of the old volcano, clearly giving absolutely everything that he has, making the most of one of those days when his talent as a climber really stood out. 'When you're going well, you don't suffer, you enjoy it. Nothing can go wrong because you can see that it's not you that's suffering, it's the rest of the field,' he once said. 'Every turn of your pedals feels like a fresh round of applause a singer receives.'

He was flying. Fastest into the climb, he caught Rivière, who had started two minutes before him, two-thirds of the way up the Puy de Dôme and eventually finished one minute and twenty-six seconds up on second-placed Gaul, which moved him to just four seconds down on yellow jersey Jos Hoevenaers. With the Alps looming, the only strong climber close to the Spaniard was Frenchman Henry Anglade, who was 39 seconds behind Bahamontes.

The Spaniard's overall victory hinged on two Alpine stages. On the first into Grenoble, he found a willing ally in defending champion Gaul, who had endured a torrid defence of the yellow jersey, wilting in the oppressive heat where he always tended to struggle. Another lone ranger in the mountains, who raced according to his mood, brilliant at some key moments, invisible at others, the Luxembourg rider was the only one who pursued when Bahamontes attacked on the Romeyère, *L'Équipe* describing him, *duende*-like, as having 'the suppleness of a flamenco dancer and, what's more, his "cante jondo", the song rising from deep within him, is indeed the mountains, the stage where he can express himself with complete freedom'.

Gaul and Bahamontes joined forces on the subsequent rise to Villard-de-Lans, their collaboration briefly caught on some oversaturated black-and-white TV footage as they climbed up the dramatic Gorges de la Bourne. Sadly, this did not linger on them long enough to admire the beauty of their similar but subtly different styles, Gaul blessed with what sports writer Richard Williams described as a 'frictionless quality . . . particularly useful to a cyclist', pedalling smoothly in the high gears he favoured, dancing above his saddle for long stretches, Bahamontes, his shorts pushed high up his thighs in trademark fashion, seated more often but equally fluid. At the velodrome in Grenoble, Gaul was redeemed with the stage win, while Bahamontes moved into the lead, almost five minutes ahead of Anglade.

The stage to Valle d'Aosta highlighted the rifts within the French ranks, all of their riders being strong, but none of them willing to commit that strength to one of their compatriots. Bahamontes was dropped on the descent off the Iseran in an attack initiated by Geminiani, who had Anglade, Anquetil and Rivière with him. It should have resulted in Bahamontes losing yellow. Instead, the lack of collaboration enabled him to regain lost ground. When Anglade distanced him again on the treacherous, rain-swept descent of the Petit Saint-Bernard, Rivière and Anquetil rode on the front of the chase group, helping to limit Bahamontes's losses to 47 seconds. The home team had reached its nadir – it was Bastille Day, three-time winner Bobet had abandoned on the Iseran, his career ending at that moment, while two of the country's biggest stars had chased behind a compatriot from a regional team and in doing so had favoured a foreign rival.

Rivière defended himself by pointing out it was his Tour debut and argued that the Spaniard's victory had essentially been the consequence of a complete misjudgement of his qualities.

> The only times we thought about Bahamontes we remembered his eccentricities, which generally ended up wrecking his chances. So we let Bahamontes seem to lord it over the rest of us and then we expected Charly Gaul to wipe him out. But instead of that Gaul did nothing and Bahamontes, whom nobody rated, ended up taking the yellow all the way to Paris.

As had been the case the year before with Gaul – who'd won the Tour when the stars aligned for him in the final days of the race in the shape of the bad weather in which he often thrived, coupled with discord among his rivals – and would be the case in 1976 for Lucien Van Impe, Bahamontes had grabbed the best opportunity he would ever have to claim the yellow jersey. His defence of it emphasized the way in which he and Gaul could flip-flop between radiance and insipidness, the

Spaniard abandoning on the second stage complaining of stomach issues, despite the imprecations of his teammates and director. 'The Eagle of Toledo has become a corn-fed chicken and corn is all he has in his head,' was Tour director Jacques Goddet's condemnatory verdict.

Bahamontes could and perhaps should have won again in 1963, but was denied by Anquetil's grit and Geminiani's cunning as the Frenchman's team manager, substituting a light climbing bike for the ascent of the rough and steep Col de la Forclaz by the surreptitious cutting of a brake cable to enable the exchange to be made, thereby avoiding any infringement of the rule that then prevented the exchange of one fully functioning bike for another. He might also have prevailed in the 1964 race that's remembered purely for Anquetil's duel with Raymond Poulidor, but he was let down by his unwavering focus on the mountains title. Alasdair Fotheringham highlights a fascinating contradiction in this, pointing out,

> the less likely his attacks were to succeed in winning the biggest prize, the greater his reputation as cycling's best 'pure' climber, and as the dreamer who never gave up. Or, to use a very Castilian metaphor, the eternal tilter at windmills . . . Bahamontes lingers in the memory precisely because of his wayward eccentricity and love of seemingly pointless, impetuous, attacking. Unfulfilled potential is far more romantic than a series of brilliant results.

Chapter 8

Tilting at windmills

In France, the finale of the 1964 Tour stage to the summit of the Puy de Dôme is rated as the most iconic, the most legendary, of all time. It saw arch-rivals Jacques Anquetil and Raymond Poulidor going shoulder to shoulder on the distinctive conical peak that overlooks Clermont-Ferrand, the two French riders forced together by the narrowness of the road, the sheer numbers on the climb and the press motorbikes buzzing all around them, until 'Poupou' managed to gain ground, metre after painful metre, on the defending champion and race leader. At the line, he was 42 seconds clear, but still 14 short of taking the yellow jersey. Told that he had held on to the lead, Anquetil retorted, 'If Poulidor had taken the jersey from me, I'd have gone home this evening.'

What's often forgotten amid all the hoopla surrounding this defining moment in the enthralling Anquetil–Poulidor rivalry is that both riders were well beaten on the climb by a little-known and balding Tour debutant who was just three months shy of his thirtieth birthday – in fact, beaten by him for the second time in little more than a week. Born in Ávila, a hundred kilometres or so west of Madrid to a father who was an ambulance driver and a mother who was a domestic servant to a Spanish army general, Julio Jiménez arrived late on the professional scene, having already established a very different career as a watch-maker and -repairer in the shop of his cousin, Relojero Ángel, in Ávila. It was his cousin who encouraged Jiménez to train and make the best use of his racing talent, which became particularly evident when roads started to climb.

Like his racing style, Jiménez's professional career progressed in fits and starts. He made his Vuelta debut in 1961 for the small Catigene team, finishing second in the mountains competition. That performance helped to earn him a contract with one of the peloton's best-funded squads, Faema, for the following season. It resulted in a better salary and a more challenging race calendar, but with a significant restriction because the team backed by this Italian coffee-machine manufacturer had two contingents of riders, one mainly Belgian, the other Spanish. Unfortunately, for the second group, it was the first cohort led by Classics star Rik Van Looy that dominated the line-up for the Tour. Consequently, barring occasional outings outside Spain, including the 1962 Dauphiné Libéré where Jiménez won a stage after a long break through the Chartreuse massif, Faema's Spanish wing was largely restricted to a domestic calendar.

Nevertheless, the Ávila climber continued to receive good reviews, notably in winning the mountains title in his national tour in 1963, and his performances captured the interest of another Spanish outfit, Kas. After a mediocre debut at the Tour in 1963, the team backed by the Basque soft-drinks manufacturer lured Jiménez with a promise of a start in the sport's biggest race. He was in great form approaching it, winning two stages at the Vuelta and defending the King of the Mountains crown as he finished fifth overall.

In its Tour preview, *L'Équipe* picked him out as a rider to watch, saying,

Undoubtedly, Jiménez is a climber of great quality who's both audacious and courageous, but he's a bit too much of a specialist, focusing most of his efforts on the cols and only participating very occasionally in the overall contest if he finds himself on terrain that doesn't suit him. There's one good reason for that: Jiménez is slightly built and doesn't seem to possess sufficient reserves to last the pace for three weeks.

This prediction proved half-right, as the Spaniard shone on the climbs, but he also stayed the pace as he engaged in an extended contest with Federico Bahamontes for the climbers' title, the pair offering a contrast in styles, the 1959 Tour winner staying in the saddle for the most part, while Jiménez 'attacked them *en danseuse*, his toes pointed down, turning the art of climbing into wonderful choreography', according to *L'Équipe*'s Philippe Brunel.

Jiménez's style was described as *sautillant*, leaping forwards like a grasshopper, a quick flight of speed followed by a pause, then another jump. He employed this darting approach to good effect on the stage from Perpignan to Andorra, breaking away on the Col de la Perche, then riding over the Puymorens and Envalira to win in Andorra by almost nine minutes as the favourites watched each other.

His was the kind of solo exploit that would likely garner rave reviews in the modern era if a Tour debutant won a big mountain stage by such a substantial margin. But the Spaniard's feat received only qualified praise from Jacques Goddet, the Tour director bemoaning the lack of action between the favourites and saying the stage 'served only as a celebration of an exploit of an anecdotal nature, a flea-like leap achieved by Jiménez, the little Spaniard with the sad features, thinning hair, who jumped to eighth in the general classification'. In the face of this and other criticism, race leader Anquetil said, dismissively, of his decision to mark Bahamontes: 'I'm hunting the eagle. So we let the little sparrows fly away!'

Lauded by *But et Club* for 'his incredible fluency', the sports paper describing how he 'never grimaced, remained relaxed, constantly increased his tempo and with it his advantage', Jiménez continued to harry Bahamontes in the mountains. Wearing Kas's reversed colours of blue jersey with yellow sleeves and collar to avoid a clash with the *maillot jaune*, he got the better of his older and much more experienced compatriot once again on the long stage through the Massif Central to the Puy de Dôme. Part of a ten-strong group that included all of the GC favourites, Jiménez vaulted away 4.5 kilometres from the finish, Bahamontes chasing him in vain. The two French rivals for the yellow jersey left the pair of Spaniards to their duel, Poulidor saying of Jiménez just after he'd finished: 'When he dropped us, he was pushing an incredible gear. If I'd gone with him, it would have killed me!'

Having claimed a second stage win on his debut, a startling debut by any standards, Jiménez paid tribute for the success to his team director, Dalmacio Langarica, who had, of course, been behind Bahamontes's time trial success on the long-extinct volcano in 1959. 'I just listened to him and attacked at the ideal place four kilometres from the summit. I knew that Bahamontes wouldn't be able to get back up to me. Federico is superior on a big col, but on a short and steep slope he'll never beat me,' the Spaniard told *L'Équipe*.

Knock-kneed, wafer thin and appearing rather incongruous standing alongside his teammates in Kas's pre-Tour picture the following season, looking every inch 'The Watch-maker of Ávila' that he was now nicknamed rather than one of the peloton's most devastating climbers, Jiménez turned the tables on Bahamontes, denying him a seventh mountains title by claiming the Trophée Poulain, as the competition was now known thanks to its chocolate-making sponsor. He won another two stages as well, but his focus on the climbs also drew significant criticism. Writing in *L'Équipe*, ex-pro-turned-journalist Jean Bobet was scathing in his assessment, declaring:

> Julio Jiménez's exploits were only monologues. Nobody needed to respond to this oddball, who's adorned with such gifts in the mountains, because he doesn't have a place in the final discussion. Gaul and Bahamontes took on the others in the mountains. All he did was to conquer the mountains. Gaul and Bahamontes were valued contributors to the overall debate. Jiménez is only an entertainer. He's not even a trouble-maker.

Another story in *L'Équipe* revealed that his jumpy style, his tendency to ride at the back of the peloton and his red-and-yellow Spanish champion's jersey, which apparently made him look like a cooked crustacean that had been dressed with saffron, had resulted in Jiménez being nicknamed 'the crayfish' within the Tour caravan. *Miroir-Sprint*, meanwhile, described him as,

> a specialist climber and no more than that . . . In fact, Julio Jiménez offered us an interlude, a kind of race within a race, but he took advantage of conditions that were so favourable that it's impossible for us to establish a serious comparison with his predecessors: Coppi, Bartali, Geminiani, Bobet, Gaul and even Bahamontes, who all harboured ambitions that were more complete.

Jiménez even offered some support to these arguments, often insisting that he would never win the Tour because he was afraid of being in the peloton, especially when the wind started to blow and there was constant movement within it.

Yet the Spaniard typified the pure climbers who were hamstrung by the continued reluctance of race organizers, including those of all three Grand Tours, to include summit finishes. It now seems odd to think that they remained so afraid of a rider dominating high-altitude finales in the way that Fausto Coppi had in the 1952 Tour, but were, at the same time, very happy to pepper their routes with time trials. The *parcours* of the epic 1964 Tour is a perfect example of this kind of lopsided thinking. The Puy de Dôme, not an especially long climb, was the only mountain-summit finish, while there were three individual time trials, all of them won by Anquetil. This imbalance, which favoured *rouleurs-grimpeurs* like the Frenchman, continued into the 1970s when television coverage of racing increased dramatically and event organizers realized that the need to hold the attention of the TV audience could be achieved in part by introducing more summit finishes.

Sadly for Jiménez and other *grimpeurs purs*, this change of direction came too late to benefit them. In retirement, the Spaniard has frequently reflected that his *palmarès* would have looked very different if there had been more summit finishes in the 1960s. His claim is further supported by him responding in the best way to criticism of being one-dimensional, by demonstrating that he wasn't. After the disparagement of his tactics and the hints of xenophobia in the jokes and sniping about his national champion's jersey, Jiménez would have the last laugh.

In 1966, he left Kas and its many cliques, each with a climber at its epicentre, for the Ford France team led by Anquetil and managed by Raphaël Geminiani. He'd been signed to support the Frenchman at the Giro and Tour, but ended up in very different roles at both events. 'Gem' took the Spaniard under his wing, setting him up in a house near his own home close to Saint-Étienne, where he could direct his training and work on other aspects of his competitive make-up. He described Jiménez as being in 'a raw state' and having 'a minimum of ambition' when he arrived at Ford. 'Now he's looked after like a leader and his metamorphosis has occurred naturally.'

At the Giro, Jiménez held the leader's pink jersey for eleven days before slipping to fourth, a place behind Anquetil. At the Tour, he retained the Trophée Poulain and, more significantly, played a crucial role in the overall victory of his Ford teammate Lucien Aimar. Highlighting the fundamental role that the Spaniard had played in the Frenchman's success, *L'Équipe* first pointed out the slightness of his stature, describing how, 'When resting, he seems even smaller and frailer than he does on the road, where he nevertheless gives the impression that he's stolen his big brother's bike.' It then added that the Spaniard had performed wonders on that bike, chasing down attack after attack in the Alps and by setting a fast pace that Aimar could follow but making it difficult for the yellow jersey's rivals to break clear, a tactic more usually associated with Miguel Induráin's all-conquering Banesto team of the early 1990s or with the Sky team fashioned by Dave Brailsford in the second decade of the twenty-first century, but employed by Ford France when the Spanish five-time Tour winner and the highly successful British manager were still toddlers.

Jiménez agreed that he'd made huge strides having swapped the almost lackadaisical approach to racing within Spanish squads for the rigour of Geminiani's team, his learning experience cemented by his long stint in the lead at the Giro. 'Until this year, I've not had a great deal of knowledge about teamwork; in Spain, it's a lot less systematic, it depends a bit on inspiration,' he said at the end of that Tour. It took some years for the Spanish ethos to change, arguably until the appearance of the ONCE team managed by Manolo Saiz in the late 1980s.

When the Tour reverted to national team format in 1967, co-directors Jacques Goddet and Félix Lévitan served up the most mountainous route since the Coppi-dominated race of 1952, and Jiménez went into it as the undisputed leader of the Spanish team, targeting the yellow jersey rather than the mountains title. However, a dispute between Kas directeur sportif (DS) Langarica and the Spanish federation resulted in the pick of that team's riders focusing on the Vuelta and Giro, undermining Jiménez's prospects before the race had even got under way. Nevertheless, he began it very well, losing a mere nine seconds on the stage over the cobbles into Roubaix, Goddet describing him as 'an angel who became a devil' for his exploit.

The Tour boss was very taken by what he described as the 'complete transformation' of the race's best climber, detailing how,

> Those of us who drive just behind the peloton had got used to seeing him as a follower swinging on and off the back of the bunch, seemingly indifferent to contesting the race during the flat stages. His was, for us, the most familiar backside, and seeing it was the signal that we'd reached our correct position. The Tour was for him, once he'd carefully negotiated a stage to finish within the time limit, a super mountains championship in which he would certainly turn out to be the

winner, since he devoted all of his energy, all of his ambition
and his unparalleled talent to it.

Jacques Anquetil, who wasn't racing but watched the finish at
Roubaix, was also hugely impressed. As he congratulated his
teammate on his exploit, he told him, 'Julio, you've perhaps won the
Tour de France today. I confess that yesterday evening I didn't give
you much of a chance.'

Yet Anquetil, Jiménez and just about everyone else on the race
was caught out by Roger Pingeon. The very next day, the Frenchman
got into a long-range break on the stage to Jambes and finished more
than six minutes up on his rivals. In a field that lacked an obvious
favourite, Pingeon had installed himself as that rider thanks to one
daring coup.

From then on, Jiménez was playing catch-up. Almost eight
minutes behind the unexpected holder of the yellow jersey going
into the Alps, he cut three from that deficit on the stage over the
Télégraphe and Galibier into Briançon, moving to third overall.
Despite this impressive gain, he admitted that riding for GC and, as
a consequence, having to follow the pace of his rivals on the flatter
stages, had cost him some of his edge on the climbs, a dichotomy
that has affected countless mountain specialists. 'I've never used
such small gears on the Galibier as I did this year. I went down to
42×22 and even 42×24,' he revealed. Three years earlier, he'd used
a 45×22 gear on the same climb, a very significant difference. 'But
that was another era. I could still push a pretty big gear and open
up an advantage. But now . . . It's simple, I can push a very big gear
on the flat, but on the climbs I'm forced to . . . rein myself in. I'm
undoubtedly more complete as a rider: more consistent on the

flat, less effective in the mountains,' he acknowledged, while also highlighting another factor: he was three years older.

A solo attack on the stage into Luchon – during which he was chased frantically by Pingeon and his teammates Raymond Poulidor and Lucien Aimar, like 'three moles chasing a grasshopper' wrote L'Équipe's Pierre Chany – enabled Spain's leader to gain three more minutes on the yellow jersey, moving him up to second on GC. He tried again on the stage into Pau over the Tourmalet and Aubisque, but, with more distance to cover on the flat to reach the finish, he couldn't hold off the return of Pingeon and his sentinels and remained two minutes behind Pingeon as the Tour began to head north towards Paris.

The respective strength of the French and Spanish teams, Jiménez said as the race left the Pyrenees, was the principal difference between him and Pingeon. 'I can assure you that with the Kas team I would have won this Tour,' he told Le Parisien Libéré.

> I'll go even further than that: I could have managed it with only three or four members of that team, [Francisco] Gabica, [Aurelio] González and [Gregorio] San Miguel for instance, who are all very close to me in the mountains. They would have attacked in waves, fired the warning shots that would have prepared the ground for me. I would only have had to deal the final blow.

Hoping to at least take the yellow jersey on the Puy de Dôme, Jiménez only gained 24 seconds on Pingeon, who was shepherded to the finish by Poulidor. Witnessing his disappointment as he crossed the line, Goddet described him, in a clear tribute to the qualities he shared with his illustrious compatriot Bahamontes, as 'an eagle no longer

British writer, philosopher and polymath John Ruskin's descriptions and paintings, like this one of the Mer de Glace at Chamonix, raised the profile of the mountains as a travel destination from the middle of the nineteenth century.

Henri Desgrange, pictured in 1895, had an illustrious racing career before becoming editor-in-chief of *L'Auto* and Tour de France founder, which included setting the first recognized mark for the hour record.

1910: a lone rider climbing in what became known as 'the circle of death', comprising the Aspin, Peyresourde, Tourmalet and Aubisque passes.

Alphonse Steinès appears to be holding up Octave Lapize after the Frenchman had won the 1910 Tour, the first to enter the high mountains. On the right is *L'Auto* journalist and Tour starter Georges Abran.

Italy's two-time Tour winner Ottavio Bottecchia approaches the top of the
Col d'Izoard in 1925.

Nicknamed 'the Mouse', Frenchman Benoît Faure, seen climbing the Tourmalet in 1930,
was one of the great climbers of the interwar years.

Dubbed 'The Torrelavega Flea' by Henri Desgrange due to his frequent accelerations in the mountains that enabled him to jump ahead of his rivals, Vicente Trueba was the winner of the Tour's first mountains competition in 1933. He's seen leading the race towards the summit of the Tourmalet on a day he also led over the Aubisque.

A maverick climber renowned for the beauty of his style, René Vietto won four stages and the mountains title during his Tour debut in 1934. Note the then unusual placement of a water bottle on his downtube during the Briançon stage of Monaco–Paris in 1946.

For many the greatest climber the sport has ever seen, Gino Bartali's exploits in the mountains at the Tour and Giro were legendary. He's seen after winning his third Giro crown in 1946, when he also clinched the sixth of his seven mountains titles.

Fausto Coppi leads Jean Robic towards the Tour de France's first-ever summit finish at Alpe d'Huez in 1952. The Italian took the stage and the yellow jersey.

The long-term and bitter rival of Federico Bahamontes, Jesús Loroño, pictured on the Tour stage to Cauterets in 1953, which he won. He also clinched the mountains title that year.

Two climbing greats, 1958 Tour winner Charly Gaul and six-time King of the Mountains Federico Bahamontes, resplendent in the yellow jersey he won in 1959.

Julio Jiménez does a lap of honour after winning the 1965 Tour de France stage into Bagnères-de-Bigorre.

Julio Jiménez (centre) is all smiles after finishing second in the 1967 Tour. He's picture alongside overall winner Roger Pingeon (left) and third-placed Franco Balmamion (right) at the finish in Paris's Parc des Princes.

Wearing the white jersey of best young rider, Eddy Merckx displays his racing philosophy of *la course en tête*, racing at the front, on the climb of the Ballon d'Alsace in the 1969 Tour.

José Manuel Fuente pictured during his race-winning solo raid through the Alps at the 1973 Tour of Switzerland. Note the unusual fitting of bar-end shifters, much more frequently seen in cyclo-cross.

capable of long flights'. Caught by Pingeon in the final time trial, as a result yielding two minutes to his rival, 'The Watch-maker of Ávila' finished second on GC, winner of the mountains title for the third year in a row, and, significantly from an historical perspective, as the last rider to race on the old Parc des Princes track that had hitherto hosted the finale of every Tour and was torn down later that year in a redevelopment that led to it becoming the permanent home of the Paris Saint-Germain football team.

Tenth at the Giro the following year, where he won two stages, he again led the Spanish team at the Tour, this time managed by Langarica and with nine Kas riders alongside Jiménez. It looked promising but proved frustrating. Hampered by cold and wet weather, he slipped into a domestique's role for Gregorio San Miguel, who took the yellow jersey in the closing days but eventually finished one place shy of the podium. Although Jiménez signed for one more season with the new and modestly funded Eliolona team, whose figurehead was Gino Bartali, the Giro ended up being the final swansong for both the Italian squad and its Spanish team leader, who retired to focus on his business interests, which included two dance bars in Ávila and, later, a string of hair salons in the Canary Islands.

Among the many tributes as the Spaniard stepped away from racing, he was perhaps encapsulated best by his team manager at Ford and Bic, Geminiani.

> He was one of those natural climbers, capable of opening a gap in the same way as Ocaña, who succeeded him. Jiménez used to 'windmill' to start with, using small gears; but then he would get into the big ring and open up gaps in the purest style of Spanish climbers.

Like Bahamontes, Jiménez had learned to make the most of his ability in the mountains, while adapting to the demands imposed on pure climbers by rivals who would bully them in time trials and on the flat, and race organizers who essentially didn't want to see them win, or were at the very least reluctant to serve up the kind of terrain where they were likely to have more chance of success. He was, said his fellow professional Jean-Marie Leblanc, who would ultimately go on to become the Tour director, 'warmth, serenity and a smile. The profile of the perfect gentleman.'

As he bowed out, his successors were waiting in the wings, broiling rather than serene, tempestuous and unpredictable, and ready to kick arse in the mountains, anyone's, even Eddy Merckx's whenever they got the chance. Windmill-tilting was out. The conquistadors were coming.

Chapter 9

The essence of *duende*

Working on this book, I often found myself daydreaming, sometimes about the mountains, wishing I was riding in them rather than writing about them, but more often about climbers' characteristics and qualities, and the inevitable question of who's the best of all time. My preference changed regularly, depending on who I was writing about. I'd always been captivated by Lucien Van Impe, the first rider to make the Tour's red polka-dot jersey their own, whose smile, speed off the mark, King of the Mountains titles, tight perm poking through the straps of his leather 'hair-net' headgear and even his name typified the attributes required to be a member of climbing's royalty. He'd even named his house in the Flemish town of Erpe-Mere (a handful of kilometres south of the village of Impe, hence Van Impe) Alpe d'Huez. It was there, in 1976, that he took his first stride towards a Tour de France title that remains, five decades later, the last won by a Belgian racer, and it was also the setting for his biggest disappointment, just one year later, when he appeared to have the yellow jersey in his grasp again only to be thwarted by hunger 'knock' and *de val* (the fall), to use the title of a Belgian documentary made about his crash into the roadside ditch close to the top of the Alpe when he was hit by a passing race vehicle.

Then I read about the career and tragically shortened life of René Pottier, who had previously been little more than a name in the exclusive list of Tour champions about whom I knew next to nothing. The sport's first great climber, how many titles would he have won if he hadn't taken his own life? After Pottier, I had my head turned by the stylish and, when it most mattered, ill-fated René Vietto, with his 1930s matinee-idol looks. Then by Gino Bartali and Fausto Coppi. Ultimately, though, one name stood out: that of a rider who I'd never seen race, whose career had ended before I'd even got interested in bike racing.

José Manuel Fuente was the essence of *duende*. He could be exceptional and dreadful on the very same day. He terrified his rivals, mystified his teammates and thrilled fans in the first half of the 1970s. Describing him as extraordinary barely does him justice. He was a one-off, arguably the incarnation of the perfect climber, not in style perhaps, but almost peerless when it came to every other quality that would be ascribed to the archetypal king of the mountains. He constantly harried and sometimes defeated Eddy Merckx, who described him as 'the greatest climber in the modern history of cycling'. Across the span of three seasons, he also engaged in an enthralling duel with compatriot Luis Ocaña, another rider who seemed to race according to the whims of some internal spirit, neither of them able to completely dominate the other, their antipathy and brilliance encapsulated in one of the Tour's greatest mountain contests – one that, oddly, is almost forgotten.

Fuente was born in Limanes, just to the east of Oviedo in Spain's northern province of Asturias, in 1945, the same year as Merckx and Ocaña, but didn't have such an easy passage into the pro ranks as his two future rivals. 'I never had a real childhood, nor a real youth,' he wrote in his autobiography. When he left school at 14 to start a metalworking apprenticeship, his future seemed mapped out:

minimal wages and long hours for the rest of his life. He'd seen his parents wearing themselves out, labouring from dawn till dusk, and was desperate to escape the same impoverished fate . . .

Cycling was his escape route. A self-taught racer with short arms and disproportionately long and thin legs, his style was ungainly, but effective. 'From the start I was a fighter,' he said. Attacking was his weapon. This was instinctive, often recklessly so, but it often paid dividends. His initial breakthrough occurred in 1969 when he was picked up by Werner, one of Spain's leading amateur teams, who provided an eightfold boost to the 650-peseta-a-month wage he was earning in the workshop. By then 23, Fuente was finally able to focus on racing full-time, although his quirky approach to the sport continued. He prepared for the season by delivering butane gas bottles, asserting that carrying them up several flights of stairs helped to strengthen his legs as well as earn him some useful extra cash.

Nicknamed 'El Tarangu', an Asturian word describing a man reputed for his strength and character, Fuente ended that season as Spain's best amateur, his successes including a stage victory at the Vuelta a Navarra, where Van Impe, a year the Spaniard's junior, took the overall title. Yet, just as this pair's careers seemed to be coming together, their fortunes diverged. While the Belgian quickly went on to make his Tour debut a few weeks later in a race that was completely dominated by Merckx, finishing twelfth on GC and earning great reviews, the Spaniard found himself without a team, thanks to a wage dispute. After Werner stepped up into the pro ranks, Fuente and his colleagues asked for a pay rise. The team responded by approaching each of them in turn in order to break their united front. They spoke to Fuente last, and he was the only one to reject their lower offer.

His refusal to bend highlighted his principled attitude, which is best encapsulated in the no-nonsense phrase that he would often use when explaining why he didn't get involved in financial wheeling and dealing at races: 'An Asturian never sells himself, but fights until the death.' He wasn't done yet.

Fuente continued to train through the winter, riding cyclo-cross to maintain his race fitness, and eventually got an offer to turn professional from the Karpy team, which resulted in him making his debut at the Vuelta a España in 1970. That year, the race introduced a new competition for the best-placed new professional, who would wear what was dubbed the tiger jersey despite its blue and yellow hoops. There was some surprise when Fuente took it in the prologue time trial on the opening day, but even more so as he held it through to the finish, where he placed sixteenth, five minutes down on overall winner Luis Ocaña.

As well as impressing with his talent, Fuente stood out for other reasons at the Vuelta. He refused to shave his legs during the race, for instance, in the Samson-like belief that he would lose his strength on the climbs if he did. Another idiosyncrasy was the cyclo-cross-style fitting of his gear levers on the ends of his drop handlebars rather than on the bike's downtube, a choice he stuck with for the duration of his racing career. His distinctive posture also made him easy to pick out, his back ramrod-straight and more upright than other riders, his neck following the same line rather than being tilted forward, so that he gave the impression that he was peering at something in the distance, the next chance for an attack perhaps.

Fuente's success in 1970 led to a move to the much bigger Kas team. As he prepared for the new season, he once again supplemented his income, swapping gas bottle deliveries for the garlic trade. He and a teammate would drive to Navarra in north-east Spain, fill their cars with garlic bulbs bought from producers, and then sell them in markets all over Asturias for a higher price. Perhaps he devoted too much time to it, for when racing got under way, his results were mediocre, his lack of form emphasized at the Vuelta where he finished fifty-fourth out of sixty-eight finishers, almost an hour down on winner Ferdinand Bracke. A teammate described his performance as 'catastrophic', while the team doctor said he'd ridden like 'a truck driver'. Dismayed by Fuente's lack of competitiveness, Kas's management pulled him from the Giro line-up, making it clear that he was on his way out of the team, only to backpedal on that decision when one of their Giro selection got injured. Fuente was the substitute, although team boss Dalmacio Langarica made it clear that they weren't expecting anything from him, telling the press that Kas would be starting with 'nine cyclists and a cycle-tourist'.

Fuente began the race by fully living up to his team director's pessimistic assessment, losing 57 minutes in the opening 4 days to be the *lanterne rouge*, the last rider in the overall standings. He finished outside the time limit on stage two, when the experienced and well-regarded Langarica had to use his considerable influence on the organizers to get him reinstated. This pressure paid off. A week later, he won at Pian del Falco ski resort at Sestola. According to his teammate José Antonio González Linares, 'He always used to attack in his 54-tooth big ring, even when the road was uphill.' Part of a large breakaway that reached the final climb together, he attacked repeatedly in that 54 ring, spinning it rapidly in repeated attacks, which 'was like using a garrotte on a rival', said another Kas teammate Francisco Galdós.

As he had led over all three climbs that day, Fuente also pulled on the green mountains jersey, which he kept for more than a week, his reign including a Bahamontes-like flourish on the thirteenth stage that featured the ascent of the Pian delle Fugazze. Topping it, he was so far ahead of the peloton that he stopped and had a can of soft drink at the summit. He lost the jersey to Pierfranco Vianelli, winner on Austria's fabled Grossglockner pass in the middle of the Giro's final week, but struck back on the two big stages in the Dolomites that followed to claim the first of what would be four consecutive victories in the race's mountains competition. Not only had Fuente's form turned around, but so too had Langarica's opinion of him, shifting from disappointment to delight during the second half of the Giro. Wanting to make the most of the climber's purple patch, the Kas DS selected him for his third Grand Tour in four months.

Although the 1971 Tour would end anticlimactically as a consequence of the crash that led to yellow jersey Luis Ocaña abandoning the race in the midst of a raging battle for the title with defending champion Merckx, the race still stands as one of the all-time greats in terms of the action and drama served up on the climbs. The dashing Spaniard was at the heart of most of it until his tragic exit on the descent off the Col de Menté in the Pyrenees, but with a stellar supporting cast that included Merckx of course, Fuente, Van Impe, Bernard Thévenet and Joop Zoetemelk, the Kas rider being the only one of them who wouldn't end up riding into Paris in yellow during his career.

In common with Fuente, Bahamontes and so many other racers within the peloton in that era, Ocaña's childhood had been defined by poverty. He was born near Cuenca in central Spain, but the family moved regularly as his father shifted from job to job until they settled in the small French town of Magnan, in the south-west of the country near Mont-de-Marsan, when Luis was 12. Like Fuente, he also left school at 14 to take up an apprenticeship, in his case as a carpenter, and it was his boss there who initially supported the teenager's early interest in racing, paying for licences and his first proper racing bike, an investment that Ocaña paid off in instalments. Renowned for what the president of his club in Mont-de-Marsan described as 'mad dog attacks', he scorched through the regional amateur scene and impressed at national level, winning the amateur Grand Prix des Nations time trial in 1967.

Due to his Spanish nationality and background, French teams overlooked him, and he turned to his home country for his first pro contract with Fagor in 1968. National champion that year, second in the Vuelta the season after, Ocaña's meteoric rise continued, his flamboyant, attacking style making him a fan favourite and finally drawing the attention of squads in France. In 1970, Bic, the former team of Jacques Anquetil and Julio Jiménez that was still managed by Raphaël Geminiani, signed him to replace Lucien Aimar as its leader. Winner of the Vuelta, where debutant Fuente took that tiger jersey, and the Dauphiné Libéré, he talked up his chances of beating Merckx at the Tour, but failed to live up to his promise of 'a war' with the Belgian, who remained peerless in his defence of the yellow jersey.

With Merckx in his pomp, Ocaña, like most of his contemporaries, often found himself riding for second place. Beaten by the Belgian at Paris–Nice and the Dauphiné in 1971, he became obsessed with the idea of not only vanquishing the Belgian but stepping right out of his shadow. According to Thévenet, who would go on to win the Tour on two occasions, 'it got to the point where he called his dog Merckx just so that he could have the pleasure of saying, "Heel, Merckx!"'

Blessed with the chiselled, dark looks of a movie star, Ocaña finally achieved his box office moment at Orcières-Merlette, where he had 'The Cannibal' on a plate. It had been apparent the day before when the riders raced through the Chartreuse massif that Merckx wasn't in peak condition, as he had lost the yellow jersey to Joop Zoetemelk. Ocaña had been the instigator then, attacking when Merckx had punctured – they were less concerned with unwritten rules of etiquette then – and he was quick to move again when Joaquim Agostinho attacked on the Côte de Laffrey, the climb almost straight out of Grenoble heading for Orcières-Merlette. Zoetemelk and Van Impe followed. By the summit, they had two minutes on Merckx's group, which had thinned down so much in the frenzy that resulted from this early attack that it barely qualified as a peloton.

In Daniel Friebe's *Eddy Merckx: The Cannibal*, Ocaña's roommate, Johny Schleck, knocks back the Spaniard's post-stage claim that his offensive was pre-planned. 'Luis wasn't Merckx. He never calculated or thought about the long-term consequences. If he felt good, he'd attack, simple as that,' said Schleck. Whatever impulse or spirit triggered Ocaña's attack, it stayed with him. He dropped his three companions approaching the second climb, the Col du Noyer, steadily extending his advantage over the Merckx group all the time, much to Thévenet's astonishment. 'I remember the blackboard motorbike coming and going between us and him on the Noyer. Each time he came back to show us the time gap, Luis had gained another minute on us. I was saying to myself: this can't be right! How's it possible?'

At the line, Ocaña was close to six minutes ahead of lone chaser Van Impe and almost nine up on Merckx and the other GC contenders. Speaking in 2020 to *L'Équipe* about that stage, where he was one of the victims, Frenchman Cyrille Guimard hailed the Spaniard's exploit, the inference of a *duende*-like influence impossible to miss.

> He was like a guy in the arena, the matador who's about to make the kill. His engine was the bull. It was because of his character that he did things that weren't expected in races. Luis also had such good looks, he was beautiful. He should have been a film star.

Just 38 riders, one-third of the field, finished inside the time limit that day, which the organizers adjusted outwards so that the bunch and a few stragglers – including Fuente who was the penultimate finisher – could stay in the race. During the rest day in Orcières-Merlette, Merckx was already making plans to strike back at Ocaña. According to Kas's Andrés Gandarias, he even approached the Spanish team to ask for their help on the next stage to Marseille, but his request was turned down because this would have meant stabbing a compatriot and, to some, a friend in the back. Gandarias tipped Ocaña off about this request.

When the riders lined up in Orcières-Merlette for the 251 kilometre stage to Marseille, it was evident that the new race leader hadn't heeded this warning. He lined up towards the rear of the peloton, delayed he said later by a radio interviewer, and therefore completely out of position to respond to an immediate attack by Merckx's teammate Rini Wagtmans on the descent from the resort back to the valley. The peloton split, eight riders including Merckx joining Wagtmans in the vanguard. Their assault triggered a stage-long battle conducted at a ripping pace. Ultimately, Ocaña's losses were limited to two minutes. Kas's riders, though, were almost wiped from the race. When Luis Zubero crashed on the descent from

Orcières – the incident hampering the peloton's pursuit of the Merckx group – seven of his teammates stopped to pace him back, expecting the tempo to lull at some point. Like Ocaña at the start, they soon realized that their assumption was wrong. They spent the whole day chasing, Fuente suffering hunger 'knock' so badly that at one point he stopped to abandon. Following physical threats from his strapping teammate Nemesio Jiménez, he continued, shepherded to the finish, although it seemed their efforts had been in vain, as the eight Kas riders were among thirteen who finished outside the time limit. Once again, though, the race jury stepped in, citing the exceptional nature of the stage – completed at an average of more than 46kph! – as the reason for reinstating them.

Two days later, after Merckx had won a short time trial at Albi, where Ocaña ceded just eleven seconds, Fuente decided he would try to repay Jiménez and restore the honour of his team by going for the stage win on the long Pyrenean stage over three middling passes to Luchon, attacking with four others after 50 kilometres. On the Portet d'Aspet, the first of the trio of climbs, with 70 kilometres left, he pressed on alone. He crossed that summit with a lead of two minutes and had increased this to almost five going over the Col de Menté, when a violent mountain storm broke over the race, the Spaniard the first to feel its force. The top section of the descent, through a run of tightly stacked hairpins, became a river of mud, water and rubble that Fuente struggled to negotiate, the Spaniard crashing more than once. Minutes behind him, Merckx, sensing an opportunity to apply pressure on the race leader, also hit the deck briefly. Moments later, on the last hairpin before the climb runs straight down into the Haute-Garonne valley, Ocaña slid off into the verge. He began to get up, only to find Zoetemelk careening towards him, still in the saddle. The Dutchman hit him a glancing blow that sent Ocaña to the ground. He'd just got back on his feet when Joaquim Agostinho hurtled into him like a linebacker flooring a quarterback, leaving the Spaniard unable to continue. Merckx, it's worth noting again, didn't wait to see if the yellow jersey was okay.

As this drama played out, Fuente emerged from the deluge and increased his lead going over the Portillon pass, eventually finishing more than six minutes ahead of a small group led in by Merckx. He'd ridden 70 kilometres alone and gained ground throughout, despite crashes, a puncture and leg cramps, which were a regular issue for him. He won again the next day on the very short 19-kilometre stage from Luchon to Superbagnères that effectively served as an unofficial world climbing championship, with the hospitalized Ocaña the obvious absentee. The weather was still poor, the riders cloaked in rain gear as they set off. Merckx's Molteni team soon provided some heat, though, barrelling up the road that bumps upwards alongside the River Pique to reach the sharp right turn that leads up to the ski resort.

There were little more than twenty riders in the front group going onto the climb. Fuente was the first to attack, Merckx, Van Impe and Thévenet tracking him. The Spaniard went again, Van Impe closing him down, the pace easing until, with six kilometres remaining, Fuente stomped hard in his 54 ring and forged the winning gap. He wasn't, of course, weighed down by concerns about the overall classification like his rivals, his only interest being the stage win, but it was still a hugely impressive performance, with Van Impe and Thévenet the only riders to finish within a minute of him on what remains the shortest road stage in Tour history.

Although these back-to-back victories would prove to be Fuente's only successes at the Tour, his level of performance and, above all, his consistency continued to rise over the next three seasons. Were his sights lifted by Ocaña's bravura performance at Orcières-Merlette, by the fact that his compatriot showed that it was possible to go toe to toe with Merckx and emerge triumphant? There's no evidence to support this, but during these three seasons, the two Spaniards reached the greatest heights of their careers, appearing to spur each other on in a very similar way to bullfighting greats Luis Miguel Dominguín and Antonio Ordóñez during their series of contests in the summer of 1959 that were the focus of Ernest Hemingway's *duende*-tinged book *The Dangerous Summer*, with Merckx the taurine presence that they both sought to subdue even as they pushed each other to more spectacular heights.

Langarica said in the wake of that 1971 Tour that he believed Fuente would be able to challenge for victory in the Grand Tours once he had more experience. Yet that breakthrough success came even quicker than the Kas DS imagined. The Spaniard lined up at the Vuelta in the spring of 1972 with the aim of supporting team leader Miguel María Lasa's overall pretensions and with the mountains prize as a secondary objective. Going into the key mountain stage to the Pyrenean ski resort of Formigal, Fuente, already leading the mountains classification, was two minutes behind the yellow jersey, his teammate Txomin Perurena, while Kas also held second and third place thanks to Lasa and Jesús Manzaneque, respectively. He was given the job of defending the positions of the top three by following any attacks early in the stage.

Recalling that day in Oscar Cudeiro's biography of Fuente, *El Tarangu*, Perurena said that he sensed that something extraordinary was brewing.

The moon had an effect on him, although I don't know whether it was when it waxed or waned. That's something that I say in complete seriousness. On the morning of the Formigal stage, he smoked six cigarettes, although he didn't call that smoking. That morning he was affected by the moon, very nervous.

Fuente followed an attack by José Grande before the first climb, the first-category Alto de Monrepós, went clear climbing it to increase his advantage in the mountains competition, then kept on going, looking for the stage win and more King of the Mountains points at Formigal. To his credit, Perurena sanctioned this attack, but he and no one else in the peloton could have expected one rider to keep gaining ground on them heading towards a summit finish when the bunch was sure to be going full bore. Fuente, though, barely wavered, crossing the line six and a half minutes up on the second rider, Antonio Menéndez, and two more clear of Perurena and other GC contenders. With half a dozen stages remaining, Fuente had the title sewn up. Naturally, though, he didn't ease off.

He finished a close second the next day on a tough stage through the Basque Country to the Arrate summit finish, then showed his brilliance on the climbs on the penultimate day. Reaching the foot of the final ascent, the Orduña, the peloton was two and a half minutes down on the six escapees, none of whom were a GC threat. Nevertheless, Ocaña attacked at the foot of the eight-kilometre climb. Four riders initially followed, Fuente accelerated again and was soon out of sight. 'Climbing of this kind hadn't been seen in Spain since the era of Bahamontes and Julio Jiménez, showing such elegance and skill that he seemed to be floating on the pedals,' says

Cudeiro. Fuente caught each of the breakaways, the last of them 800 metres from the top, to which he continued alone. There, he eased off, his point proved. His win was no fluke, based on his breakaway success at Formigal. He was the strongest.

For *L'Équipe*'s Pierre Chany, these performances compared with those of the best climbers in recent history. He wrote:

> José Manuel Fuente is an irresistible rider. He impressed me at Formigal, but much more on the Orduña, where he was sublime. He's a born fighter and the way in which he climbed the Orduña bears comparison to the most glorious feats in international cycling, to those achieved by Bahamontes and Gaul. In short, Fuente is an authentic champion.

As for Fuente himself, he acknowledged that he'd done it because so many had written and said that his Formigal victory had come with the consent of the peloton: 'I really wanted to do what I did on the Orduña, and I wanted to do it because I felt like I'd been stabbed in the back when it was said that I was a lucky winner.'

A week after securing his first Grand Tour title, he lined up at the Giro to have his first real crack at Merckx as a rival, although the Belgian said going into the race that he regarded Lasa as the bigger danger on the Kas team. By the end of stage four, Fuente had corrected him on that. Similar to the Superbagnères stage, this was a short test, just 48 kilometres, starting on the Adriatic coast and finishing at 1,700 metres up on the demanding Blockhaus pass in the Abruzzo mountains. Kas had a simple plan for it: set the pace into the bottom of the climb, where Fuente would attack and see how Merckx responded.

It worked better than they could have dared to hope. Fuente

made his move with 18 kilometres remaining, while no fewer than 6 Kas riders sat on Merckx's wheel as he led the chase behind the lone leader. With four kilometres to the line, Lasa could see Merckx was wilting and skipped away from him to take second place, one minute and thirty-five seconds behind his teammate. Merckx came in another minute later, those gaps the same on GC, as Fuente pulled on the *maglia rosa*.

'We'd warmed up before the stage, very early, not long after dawn, so that we were sweating and had some kilometres in our legs at the start,' Lasa recalled in an interview with *El Diario Vasco*.

> We'd arrived at the Giro going like motorbikes. We'd come from the Vuelta a España and caused havoc on the Blockhaus. The road was bad, a real mountain road, with almost no asphalt on the surface at all and the climb was hard, primarily because it was long. There weren't any steep ramps, but it went on for an eternity.

Just as he had when Ocaña had knocked him down at Orcières-Merlette, Merckx struck back quickly, attacking three days later on Monte Scuro with Gösta Pettersson, the Swede winning the stage as Merckx moved into the pink jersey. Fuente was far from done, though. On the third weekend, he and Kas almost managed to turn the situation around on the Jafferau stage in the Alps, the Spaniard dropping Merckx on the climb to Sestriere and bridging up to teammates Vicente López Carril and Francisco Galdós, only for the Belgian to reel the trio in on the unpaved climb to the finish, drop Fuente in the final kilometre and go on to win the stage.

Fuente's tactical ability was severely questioned, having attacked Merckx from so far out, but at the same time he was lauded for having the courage to take on the all-conquering Belgian, which few riders did in such a brazen way. 'José Manuel is a temperamental rider, I believe that his best quality is that he never sees himself as beaten. And he always attacks; sometimes this means he wins, although on other occasions it ends the opposite way,' said López Carril after the stage.

Two stages later, Fuente was on the move again, escaping on the long and lofty Foscagno pass. He kept a narrow lead over Merckx crossing the Passo d'Eira, but punctured on the descent into Livigno, which enabled the Belgian to take the stage win. There was some consolation, though, as the Spanish climber rose to second on GC. The next day, an 88-kilometre gallop to the summit of the towering Stelvio via the Fuorn pass in neighbouring Switzerland, Kas produced another show of collective force. Santiago Lazcano attacked first and, when he was reeled in, Fuente accelerated with a dozen kilometres to the top, heavy rain gradually turning to thick snow as he approached the finish, where Merckx yielded two minutes to his Spanish rival. By then, though, Fuente and his teammates had run out of climbs to play with. The mountains winner once again, he finished five minutes down on Merckx in Milan, with Galdós third, López Carril fourth, Lasa ninth and Lazcano tenth, a staggering feat for a foreign team in a Grand Tour.

The Italian press was in raptures, calling Fuente 'the earthquake' and 'the cyclone'. Merckx too was impressed, confessing that he was glad that he'd taken that time back after the Blockhaus as he would never have regained it in the final week. 'Fuente is the greatest climber in the modern history of cycling,' he declared. 'He's the climber that world cycling has needed since the departures of Bahamontes and Gaul and, as far as I'm concerned, he's one of the legendary true climbers, of the same stature as the greatest we've ever seen.'

Fuente arrived at the 1973 Tour with another Giro mountains title to his credit and as the winner of the Tour of Switzerland. During the *corsa rosa*, he'd been hampered by leg cramps thought to be linked to the prominent tangle of varicose veins in his left calf, but he still stuck to his standard tactic of all-out attack whenever an opportunity presented itself and defended his approach by saying,

> I'm not ashamed of taking up the fight and falling to a dignified defeat. It would be worse to sit in the wheels. If I'd done that I could have been second in the Giro. But I prefer to give everything, to attack and it either pays off or I lose. To do anything except sit in the wheels.

His Swiss win contained two moments that highlighted his extraordinariness. The first occurred on the evening before the mountain time trial at Siebnen, when a group of Kas riders went out to recon the course. 'Suddenly Fuente wasn't with us and looking back we saw him stretched out on the road with his head on the tarmac,' recalled Francisco Galdós. They assumed that he'd fallen and was lying injured, but as they hurried back to check on him he sat up. He had, he told them, been checking the road's gradient and he continued with his peculiar method up the remainder of the climb.

> I rode quickly towards him as he wasn't moving, but when I reached him he told me to relax, that he was just working out the gradient of the road. A kilometre later, he did the same thing. Perhaps he was just ahead of his time and was

focusing on details that the rest of us didn't put value on. What's certain is that he did extravagant things that weren't at all normal.

The second event that underlined his singular approach and ability took place on the 'queen' stage over the Nufenen, Saint Gotthard, Furka and Grimsel passes, where Kas put on a spectacular show, first putting two riders in the break, then having them wait for Fuente when he attacked from the peloton in order to pace him up to the other escapees. He attacked on the Saint Gotthardpass, shook off his final rivals on the Furka and finished more than five minutes clear. It was a classic demonstration of team riding on a mountain stage, as well as of Kas's belief in Fuente and their loyalty towards him, which could also be seen two decades later in the same unhesitating commitment to Marco Pantani by his Mercatone Uno team.

Having already ridden and won both the Vuelta and Giro, Merckx sat out the Tour, which presented his rivals with an opportunity. It promised to be thrilling, but ended up as a romp for Ocaña, who won six stages and arrived in Paris with a Cannibal-like buffer of sixteen minutes on runner-up Thévenet, with Fuente just behind the Frenchman in third. As there had been in Switzerland, there were moments that highlighted El Tarangu's brilliance, but also key incidents that emphasized how his unwillingness to compromise his principles could work against him when it came to the critical issue of deal-making.

As untouchable as he had been two years earlier, Ocaña took the yellow jersey at the end of the first week at Gaillard in the Alps, with Fuente already more than eight minutes back and outside the top ten. According to Antonio Menéndez, Ocaña went to the Kas hotel that evening and offered each of the riders 500,000 pesetas if they would back him in his quest for the title, adding that he would allow Kas to go for stage wins, the mountains jersey and second place in Paris. Fuente offered a short response: 'No! No! And no!' Turned down by Kas, Ocaña turned to three or four other teams, 'and they made mincemeat of us', said Menéndez.

The fall-out between the two Spanish team leaders became apparent on the marathon mountain stage to Les Orres, one of the most enthralling in the race's history although it's seldom remembered as such. It crossed the Madeleine, Télégraphe, Galibier and Izoard passes, for a total of 5,200 metres of vertical gain, and remains the only occasion on which the Tour has tackled both the Galibier and the Izoard via their more severe northern flank. The antagonism began when Fuente stopped in the valley after the Madeleine to change into dry clothes. As his team waited for him, Ocaña's Bic team went to the front, forcing Kas to chase flat out to regain contact with the peloton before reaching the foot of the Télégraphe.

Cue Fuente's response. As soon as the road began to rise from Saint-Michel-de-Maurienne, he attacked, and kept on doing so, Ocaña countering each time. One report said he'd accelerated 21 times. Thévenet and Zoetemelk managed to catch the Spaniards with three other riders on the short descent to the foot of the Galibier, only for Fuente to scatter everyone bar the yellow jersey when they began to climb again. As they rode away together, Ocaña asked Fuente to collaborate rather than keep attacking, a request that was again rebuffed. Approaching the summit, Ocaña uttered the biting phrase, 'Follow me if you can.' Fuente did, sticking to his compatriot's wheel for the most part. With 30 kilometres left, Fuente punctured and, naturally, Ocaña didn't wait for him, riding solo to finish a minute clear. There was a gulf behind the Spanish pair, Thévenet losing seven minutes, Joop Zoetemelk twenty minutes despite finishing sixth in Les Orres.

Jacques Anquetil described the Spaniards' duel as, 'One of the greatest exploits in cycling history.' Meanwhile, according to Menéndez and Fuente, Bic offered another deal: El Tarangu would be guaranteed the second place he now held and the mountains jersey if he backed his rival. Once more he refused, and eventually lost both prizes as Ocaña's team, helped by alliances with other squads, thwarted his every move.

The contest underlined the differences between the two riders. Ocaña was the better all-rounder, untypically Spanish in that he could compete with the best in time trials, while also more cunning in the use of strategy, both on the road and, vitally, away from it in his deal-making. Fuente was the slightly better climber, able to rally his team around him but, due to his principles, only interested in an unadulterated test of racing ability. More than that, though, it emphasized how unbridled they could both be, slugging it out on the most historic and challenging passes in road cycling without a thought of sitting in behind their teammates and waiting, or of evaluating the consequences these solo efforts might extract from them. Unlike more calculating GC riders, such as Zoetemelk and Van Impe, who would wait and watch, often not attacking at all, it was win or die trying for Ocaña and Fuente. There was no glory in being an also-ran.

Chapter 10

The best of all time

José Manuel Fuente and Luis Ocaña went head to head again at the Vuelta the following spring, the battle between them just as enthralling as it had been at the Tour nine months before. Fuente claimed first blood with an attack on the Leones pass near Madrid that no one could follow and then took the yellow jersey from teammate Perurena in the next day's short uphill time trial. It meant that he would be leading the race when it went into his home region of Asturias for a stage finish on his home climb, the Alto del Naranco above Oviedo. 'Today I'm going to break the race apart,' he asserted at the start of it. He was as good as his word, bridging up to the break with his teammate Lazcano, then attacking with two more, Lasa and fellow Asturian Menéndez, to whom Fuente wanted to gift the stage. But his faithful domestiques couldn't hold his wheel as Fuente pressed hard on the final ascent, crossing the line with his left leg raised in the air, a gesture not appreciated by some of his rivals who took it as meaning that he could have won with one leg, but that was actually his way of paying tribute to the local surgeon who had operated on his varicose veins that winter, helping to resolve the issue with cramping that had long affected him.

Bic's Ocaña and Joaquim Agostinho struck back, the pair of them attacking on the stage to Cangas de Onís at the moment when Fuente was struggling at the back of the peloton with a chain issue – TV images back up the fact that there was no question of them waiting for the yellow jersey. The race leader took up the chase, passing the whole field on the Mirador del Fito climb and getting back on terms with his two rivals just before the summit, snuffing out the threat to his leadership of the race.

On the final mountain stage through the Basque Country to the summit of the Arrate, Fuente suffered his worst moment, sustaining a head wound in a crash in which Ocaña also went down. He managed to limit his losses to a few seconds, which gave him just enough of a cushion to fend off Agostinho in the final-day time trial, when his lead was cut to just eleven seconds by the Portuguese, Lasa taking third place ahead of Ocaña in fourth.

There was barely a chance to celebrate that second Grand Tour success, however. Four days later, Fuente started the Giro, with Merckx again in his sights. Over the following three weeks, the Asturian served up what was arguably the most consistently brilliant display of climbing in the history of road cycling. Victory in the first mountain stage at Sorrento put him in the *maglia rosa* as race leader. A week later, he extended his advantage by winning the next mountain test on Monte Carpegna, where Merckx was just over a minute behind in second. Two days after that, he won the third mountain stage, the Belgian again the runner-up, forty-one seconds back. Merckx trimmed the Spaniard's lead in a long time trial at Forte dei Marmi, but the Kas leader was still in pink with the most challenging mountain stages yet to come, apparently destined to become the first rider to defeat 'The Cannibal' in a Grand Tour, more than a year before Bernard Thévenet achieved that feat.

His hopes fell apart, though, on a cold and wet medium mountain stage to Sanremo, when, said teammate José Antonio González

Linares, he became 'moonstruck'. His grasp of cycling common sense deserted him, opening him up to attack. This dramatic tidal change occurred suddenly, at a point when Kas were controlling the stage. They had two riders in the four-man break, but Fuente became nervy, wanting his teammates to pull on the front of the peloton rather than let other teams do the work. They advised him against this, so he went back to the team car to speak to Kas DS Antón Barrutia. When Fuente returned, he started pulling the bunch along himself.

'Antón had ordered him to stop, but when he became "moonstruck", as we used to say, he didn't listen to anybody. He pulled flat out for 10km. The Italians, like Felice Gimondi, couldn't believe what they were seeing,' explained González Linares. 'When the other teams started to pull, the first to be dropped was El Tarangu.' It was and arguably remains the most obvious demonstration of a race leader scuttling their chances of overall victory in Grand Tour history.

No sooner had Fuente's fortunes ebbed than they flowed back again. He rebounded from this catastrophic lapse with victory at Monte Generoso above Mendrisio. After that, his fourth win, Barrutia made the point that was fundamental to understanding the way Fuente raced. 'He's one of those people for whom there is no middle way: it's either all or nothing. You have to accept him as he is, because I don't think he's ever going to change,' the Kas director asserted. The next day, Kas dominated once again on the lumpy road into Iseo, Fuente catching teammate Lazcano on the final climb of the San Fermo, the pair of them riding in together, Fuente allowing his teammate the win and in the process losing out on the time bonus. 'We're 10 brothers in this team and my teammate's victory is worth more to me than a minute's bonus and even the Giro title itself,' he said, underlining once again that he had his own very particular sporting code, underpinned by a strong attachment to fairness and loyalty, which no doubt explains why his teammates were always so committed to him despite his idiosyncrasies.

Then came a memorable stage to the famous Tre Cime di Lavaredo summit in the Dolomites. It didn't start well for the Spaniard, who got only three hours' sleep after deciding in the early morning that he wanted to call his wife and then became worried when she didn't answer – she was, it turned out, staying with her parents. He was so tired the next morning, his team felt he would likely abandon. Instead, he won the stage. He attacked on the first difficult section of the final climb, with ten kilometres left, gaining time on Merckx steadily all of the way to the finish, but was ultimately disappointed at only recouping a minute and forty-seven seconds on the Belgian, which left him more than three minutes behind on GC. 'It's a shame because I'd been told the final part was very hard, so I saved something for it . . . I still had three sprockets left to use,' he revealed. He'd not ridden flat out, but had still beaten Merckx for the fifth time, a feat no other rider ever got close to matching.

The final mountain stage was another epic through the Dolomites. Kas were on the offensive throughout, their riders attacking on the Falzarego, the Valles and the Rolle passes, before Fuente made his move on Monte Grappa, where he gained almost three minutes on Merckx. At this point, with the Spaniard close to being the race leader on the road, the Belgian reacted, closing this gap in extremely rapid fashion. Fuente subsequently accused the race organization of sending him the wrong way, although Giro runner-up Gianbattista Baronchelli offered a more colourful explanation, saying that after the Belgian had found out the extent of Fuente's lead he rode so hard on the dirt road to the summit of Monte Grappa, 'that his bike seemed to be ploughing a furrow'.

The race was done, but Fuente wasn't. On the final day, a very flat 257 kilometres from Bassano del Grappa to Milan, he told his teammates he was going to attack and went with just 35 kilometres covered, gaining more than two minutes before being chased down. After the peloton had passed through the feed zone, he attacked again. In order to defend his lead, Merckx made the decision to bridge up to him, the pair of them opening up a minute's lead until the Belgian refused to collaborate in the escapade.

Ultimately, Merckx won his fifth Giro, but Fuente won the popular vote. He'd triumphed in five of the eight mountain stages, gifted a sixth to a teammate, and finished in the same time as the winner on the other two. His capture of the mountains classification for the fourth year in succession was an unprecedented feat. 'This Giro will go down in history as Fuente's Giro,' said Jollj Ceramica DS Marino Fontana. 'Fuente deserved to win. He made some mistakes, but all of the others, absolutely all of them, raced defensively. He's the only one who's had a spectacular Giro.'

Sadly, it would prove to be El Tarangu's final show-stopper. Fuente struggled through the early part of the 1975 season, then lined up at the Tour only to finish outside the time limit on a 'half-stage to Roubaix'. Medical tests subsequently revealed he had hepatitis and kidney disease, the latter probably stemming from illness when he was a child. He was checked again in Italy, with the same diagnosis, acute nephropathy, and was recommended complete rest. Kas initially said they would respect his contract through the rest of that season and to the end of the next, but then rescinded it in early 1976. He made a brief return to racing at the Tour of the Mining Valleys in

Asturias, winning a half-stage summit finish at Valgrande Pajares, racing in Bianchi colours, then retired for good.

Fuente died in July 1996, aged fifty, two months after receiving a kidney transplant. In a Spanish documentary about his life and career, highly experienced DS Javier Mínguez recalled how in conversation with Eddy Merckx, the Belgian had picked out El Tarangu as the rider who made him suffer the most on the bike. 'I think he was the typical Spaniard with that trait that characterises us: he had no pause button.' All or nothing. Always captivating.

His record over four seasons between 1971 and 1974 was astonishing. He won two editions of the Vuelta, finished runner-up at the Giro and third at the Tour, winning fourteen stages and five mountains titles in the process. He rivalled Ocaña and Merckx, the two pre-eminent Grand Tour racers of that period, and was able to do so purely as a result of his outrageous talent on the climbs. His only shortfall was in tactical sangfroid, but that deficit was also fundamental to his virtuosity.

In weighing up whether he was the best of all time, it's useful to make a comparison with Lucien Van Impe, who was one of his direct contemporaries. When I met the Belgian in 2014 at Alpe d'Huez, his home in Erpe-Mere rather than the mountain where he first wore yellow, he was unequivocal in picking out Fuente as the best climber he ever raced against. 'He was so strong. When he attacked I knew that there was no way that I could try to stay on his wheel,' Van Impe confessed. The only way to respond to the Spaniard's attacks, he explained, was to claw your way gradually back up to his wheel. 'He wasn't so good with his tactics,' he added, laughing.

Van Impe told me that during the course of their first competitive encounter, racing as amateurs at the Vuelta a Navarra in 1969,

Van Impe got friendly with another Spanish climber, Pedro Torres, their relationship stemming from a stage when the Spaniard had paced the Belgian back up to the peloton after he had crashed. At the finish, he'd asked Torres why he'd helped him out and had been told that their positions might be reversed at some point in the future and Van Impe would then be able to return the favour. That moment arrived at the 1973 Tour de France, when Fuente, Van Impe and Torres all targeted the mountains jersey.

'I admit that I was a bit jealous of Fuente because he was stronger than me,' Van Impe confessed. 'I was ready to take him on but I knew that I couldn't beat him all that often, so I spoke with Pedro Torres.' The pair reached an agreement whereby the Belgian would sit tight with Fuente in the mountains while Torres went on the attack. The ruse worked, playing a part in the Spaniard's victory in the mountains competition, although Luis Ocaña's determination that Kas would take as little as possible away from the race because of Fuente's refusal to collaborate with him was probably more significant in ensuring Torres's success. The tale says a good deal about Fuente's qualities and how he was viewed by his rivals, but also about Van Impe, who was clever in his race management, but not perhaps to the extent that he thought he was.

Fuente's final afternoon as a Tour de France rider, in 1975, was also the first to feature a rider wearing the red polka-dot jersey as the leader of the King of the Mountains competition. Unusually for a race that has tended to set trends rather than follow them, the Tour was the last of the Grand Tours to introduce a distinctive jersey for its best climber, the Vuelta highlighting this rider with a green version in its first edition in 1935, while the Giro had opted for the same colour in 1974. Described as 'clownish' by the Tour's co-director Jacques Goddet, the bizarre-looking design was the idea of the race's other co-director Félix Lévitan, who based it on a red polka-dot jersey that had been worn by Henri Lemoine, a French track star of the 1930s who had been one of Lévitan's first cycling heroes.

Joop Zoetemelk was the first rider to be adorned in this *maillot à pois*, the dotted jersey. The race had begun with Francesco Moser clinching victory in the prologue time trial in Charleroi on the opening day. In the next morning's half-stage to Molenbeek, Zoetemelk led over the Côte de Bomerée to claim a small place in Tour history as the first racer to wear polka dots, then hung on to it in the afternoon's half-stage to Roubaix, during which Van Impe closed to within a point of him after he led the race over the Muur at Geraardsbergen, a climb with particular significance for him as he had climbed it hundreds of times as a youngster. Second place the next day on the Côte de Petit-Wimy, near Arras, put Van Impe into the climber's jersey, which remained on his shoulders all the way to Paris.

It was the third time he had won the mountains title, but was more significant because his victory in the final time trial at Châtel, which helped to secure third place in the overall classification behind Bernard Thévenet and Eddy Merckx, demonstrated both to Van Impe and his long-standing team manager Jean Stablinski that the Belgian could challenge for the yellow jersey. Although he'd been third before, in 1971, and had three other top-six finishes on his *palmarès*, he'd always been on the fringes of the yellow jersey contest. Finally, on his seventh appearance in the race, he'd been at the centre of it.

Despite his brilliance as a climber, there was always a sense of reluctance about Van Impe. When we'd sat at his dining table discussing his career along with his wife, Rita, and daughter, Suzy, he admitted that he'd never really enjoyed racing. 'I did like working on bikes, but I only raced because my father insisted on it and because I got paid for it,' he said – quite an admission for a rider whose career spanned 18 seasons, beginning in 1969 when Jacques Anquetil was still among the peloton's star names and concluding in 1987 when Miguel Induráin was starting to work his way up the Grand Tour hierarchy. This made Van Impe the only rider who raced with all four five-time Tour de France champions and one of a handful who competed directly with Eddy Merckx and Bernard Hinault when they were at their all-dominating peak. It's surprising too because the elfin Belgian has such an impressive *palmarès* of his own, including victory in the 1976 Tour, six King of the Mountains titles in that race and another two at the Giro, as well as eleven Grand Tour stage wins.

On the road, this reluctance was apparent in Van Impe's tendency to follow rather than instigate attacks. He was happier staying in the shadow of his biggest rivals, Merckx above all, so unwilling to provoke 'The Cannibal' by taking him on directly that one writer described his style as 'parasitical'. By the time Fuente made his Tour debut in 1971, Van Impe already had a reputation as a *'profiteur'*, a rider who took advantage of the work done by others, with Dutchman Zoetemelk being another branded with this label not least by Merckx, who castigated him for being a *'ratagasse'* or 'wheel sucker' during one Tour de Romandie. In *Eddy Merckx: The Cannibal*, Daniel Friebe describes how, after Ocaña had abandoned following his crash on the Col de Menté, the Belgian considered quitting the race, not wanting to take what might be seen as a hollow victory, but was persuaded to continue by his team director, Lomme Driessens, because Van Impe and Zoetemelk would have been the principal beneficiaries. What's more, on the stage through the 'circle of death' to Eaux-Bonnes, which followed Ocaña's departure and Fuente's back-to-back Pyrenean wins, Merckx chased down Van Impe after his compatriot had sat on his wheel most of the way up the Col du Tourmalet and then attacked, 'jumping away under my nose'.

When Van Impe did emerge, flitting and darting with Peter Pan-like vitality in the mountains, he was magically captivating. In *The Yellow Jersey Club*, Ed Pickering describes his riding style as 'a harrying, restless, nagging *agitato*. He punched and jabbed at the pedals, his rhythm erratic – standing on the pedals, sitting down, immediately standing up again.' This was the result of the training method imposed by his father, Josef, one of eight children who were all cyclists, who encouraged his own seven children into the sport as well, Lucien being the third of them. Josef wanted Lucien to be a climber, and pushed him hard towards that objective, making him train and race on a bike with a fixed gear so that he had to pedal all the time, and sprint *en danseuse* up steep Flemish climbs such as the Muur as many as three dozen times in one session, 'to boost my *souplesse*' said Van Impe.

After leaving school at 14, he worked for a company that made coffins and then took on newspaper deliveries on a round that covered up to 40 kilometres, his bike weighing between 60 and a 100kg with all the printed matter loaded onto it. He won the mountains title at the 1968 Tour de l'Avenir, a perennial indicator of the best upcoming talent, and at the Vuelta a Navarra the year after, which was where he came to the attention of Federico Bahamontes, who told him he had the talent to win the Tour de France. 'When I got home I had all the directeurs sportifs ringing me up because the papers had picked up on what Bahamontes had said about me,' he recalled.

Bahamontes took matters into own hands. He contacted an old racing friend, Frenchman Jean Stablinski, who was the director of the Sonolor team and had already been tracking the young Belgian's progress. A deal was quickly worked out. Stablinski spoke to Van Impe's father the weekend before the 1969 Tour began, to the rider himself on the Monday, then sorted him out with a pro licence on the Tuesday. Van Impe made his pro debut in a race at Valenciennes on the Wednesday, where he was a non-finisher, and started the Tour on the Saturday in Roubaix.

That Tour would prove a pivotal moment in the way Grand Tours were raced and for the climbers' place within them. Up to that point, almost every dominant stage racer of the past, even multiple champions such as Fausto Coppi and Jacques Anquetil, had focused on three or four stages in a race where they could make a difference on their rivals – mountain stages in the Italian's case, time trials in the Frenchman's – and otherwise ridden defensively to protect those gains. Merckx, though, adopted a far more unremitting strategy, known as *la course en tête*, racing at the front or at the head of the race, whereby attacking becomes the best form of defence. Tour debutant Van Impe said he tried to watch and learn from Merckx as much as he could, but that can't have been easy because 'The Cannibal' spent many of the critical parts of that Tour off the front on his own giving what remains arguably the greatest demonstration of power and versatility in Grand Tour history.

The first significant mountain stage illustrated it perfectly. Six decades on from René Pottier's show of power and brio on the Ballon d'Alsace, the ascent in the Vosges was the setting for another show of climbing force. Yellow jersey on the second day thanks to his Faema team's victory in his home suburb of Woluwe-Saint-Pierre in Brussels, Merckx was lying second to Frenchman Désiré Letort as the race set out for its first-ever finish on the historic pass. Wearing the white jersey as best young rider that day, the Belgian was in the five-strong lead group alongside his compatriot Roger De Vlaeminck, Germany's Rudi Altig, Dutchman Rini Wagtmans and Spain's Joaquim Galera. As the road began to rise, Merckx went to the front of the group, where, according to L'Équipe's report, 'He didn't attack, he just rode powerfully, at his own rhythm, as effective on the ramps of the Ballon d'Alsace as on the flat, and, one by one, the other racers had to submit to the steady and unrelenting increase in pace.' At the finish line, Galera was almost a minute back, Altig close to two, De Vlaeminck more than four. The gaps on the general classification were even more remarkable: Altig was two minutes back in second, defending champion Jan Janssen more than four and a half in arrears in third place.

Speaking after that Ballon d'Alsace stage, Merckx said of his success, 'I didn't set out with the idea of carrying out a major coup, but simply wanted to make the race hard and get the measure of my rivals.' He'd done that by harrying them from the start, keeping the pace high in the yellow jersey group but not making what would be defined as an attack. He'd just kept the pressure on, riding hard on the flat, 'to prevent a large peloton reaching the foot of the col because then racing becomes more difficult; you have to deal with numerous accelerations, while personally I prefer to climb at my own rhythm, and that's why I like to attack a climb at the front'.

In his biography *Merckx: Half Man, Half Bike*, William Fotheringham makes the point that the Belgian employed this strategy 'based on what he felt he could do rather than what he needed to do', because he had foreseen the eclipse of specialist climbers by strong all-rounders like himself and Ocaña, riders who could make their physical strength the critical factor in deciding races rather than stamina, as had hitherto been the case. 'We are in a time when average speeds have risen and bigger gears are used, which would exclude from the first rank riders who do not have certain physical size and athletic ability,' Merckx said in an interview with Swiss journalist Serge Lang in 1970.

> We've already seen the last of the great climbers. Riders who possess the same basic qualities as Bahamontes or [Julio] Jiménez still exist in the peloton, but with one essential difference: when they get to the mountains they have lost part of their potential because of having to use big gears in the flat part of the race: they may not be defeated in the mountains in the strictest sense but they are no longer able to create huge gaps.

During his stage-racing pomp, Merckx and his team became so adept at controlling stage races that their rivals essentially submitted to them, with just a few obvious exceptions, Luis Ocaña and Fuente the most evident, which underlines the special talent they both had. For the most part, though, they were cowed. Even when Bernard Thévenet did finally end the Belgian's Tour reign at Pra Loup in the final week of the 1975 Tour, the Frenchman's success came when the *la course en tête* strategy broke down on the race's third weekend in controversial circumstances after Merckx had been punched by a fan in the lower back on the upper slopes of the Puy de Dôme when he was, inevitably, in the yellow jersey.

The Tour doctor stated that, 'a rider with a less robust constitution might have abandoned', but Merckx not only continued but reasserted himself on the following stage, and appeared to have it won as he started up the short 6.5-kilometre ascent to Pra Loup with his main rival Thévenet more than a minute behind. He stomped up the initial ramps in his familiar manner, upper body bobbing, the metronomic side-to-side motion like a pile-driver adding extra force to his legs as they drove through the pedals, the repetitive action consistent and relentless. Gradually, though, he began to stall, the style the same but his speed dwindling, like a car running out of fuel. First Felice Gimondi caught him, then Thévenet, who didn't even glance across as he passed the race leader. The gap between the pair at the finish was almost two minutes. Thévenet was in yellow, a reward for his doggedness and belief going into the race that he could win if Merckx fell below his best.

Why had this happened? The punch and the medication that Merckx subsequently took to relieve the pain were certainly a factor. Ultimately, though, the success of *la course en tête* depended on him being the strongest and that status couldn't be sustained indefinitely, especially given the way the Belgian drove himself so furiously in almost every race that he participated in. The cracks were already showing, and Thévenet prised them apart.

Buoyed by his time trial victory at Châtel in the final days of that Tour, Van Impe's prospects were further boosted by the appointment of Cyrille Guimard as team director of his Gitane-sponsored team to replace Jean Stablinski. Forced into an early retirement because of persistent knee injuries, Guimard had a reputation as a renowned tactician and hard-nosed racer, as one of the few who had attempted to slug it out with Merckx. In Van Impe, he perceived a quality that he himself had lacked: the ability to win the Tour. But he was equally aware that the climber raced conservatively, happy in his niche, unconcerned about upsetting the established hierarchy. It was here that Guimard's influence would be most apparent, making the pair an ideal match, in the short term at least.

In the absence of Merckx, who was recovering from a saddle sore that had dogged him at the Giro, the 1976 Tour was dominated initially by Belgian sprinter Freddy Maertens, who would end up equalling the Tour record for stage wins, gathering eight bouquets. He reached the foot of Alpe d'Huez, the finale of the first big day in the mountains, but instantly lost touch with the specialist climbers, with Van Impe in their vanguard. Urged on by Guimard, the little Belgian rode everyone off his wheel apart from the dogged Zoetemelk, who, having been towed up through most of the 21 hairpins leading to the resort, told Van Impe he wasn't going to sprint, then cantered away in the final straight to claim the stage victory. 'That was typical of him,' Van Impe told me. Although he still regrets missing out on victory at what has become to climbers what the Champs-Élysées finish in Paris is to sprinters, he did clinch the bigger prize by relieving Maertens of the yellow jersey.

The Tour, one of those interregnum contests that occurs between the reigns of Grand Tour greats and often throws up a one-time winner, became a duel between Van Impe and Zoetemelk, the Belgian striking the decisive blow in the Pyrenees with an eighty-kilometre break that ended with him riding solo to victory at Pla d'Adet and opening up a race-winning lead on the Dutchman. The success appeared to highlight his supremacy, but also stoked the debate that had already been brewing about the role Guimard had played in guiding Van Impe towards the title. During the race and on many occasions subsequently, the Frenchman has depicted himself as a Machiavellian puppet-master, pulling Van Impe's strings, pushing his team leader into riding more aggressively, while manipulating his rivals. Years later, he titled the chapter in his autobiography on the Belgian's 1976 win: 'How to win the Tour de France with a rider who doesn't want to'.

Van Impe, though, suggested that Guimard is guilty of self-aggrandizement, telling me that his tactics were good, but that it was the rider himself who needed the legs to implement them. 'As a director, he was very good, but as a man he wasn't,' Van Impe said of his former DS, who went on to oversee another six Tour victories, four with Bernard Hinault, who replaced Van Impe as Gitane's leader in 1977, and a further two with Laurent Fignon.

The arguments Guimard and Van Impe have regularly propounded in their own favour were given more weight during the Belgian's defence of the title. The Belgian climber was strong enough to win, perhaps the strongest, but lost essentially because he had Lejeune-BP team director Henry Anglade in the team car behind him rather than the Frenchman. As the peloton headed towards Alpe d'Huez, Van Impe, decked out in the polka-dot jersey and just 33 seconds down on race leader Thévenet, attempted to dynamite the race just as he had done at Pla d'Adet the year before, launching an audacious attack in the toughest section of the Col du Glandon, with 60 kilometres to the finish. By the foot of Alpe d'Huez, his lead had reached almost three minutes. He had committed a basic error, though, by failing to eat during his attack. 'When I was on Alpe d'Huez I could tell that I was running out of juice. I ate on the climb but it was too late by then,' he acknowledged.

As Dutchman Hennie Kuiper closed in, with Thévenet not far

behind, the cars following Van Impe were ordered to pass the Belgian. One of them clipped him and he went sprawling into the roadside ditch. He tried to restart, but needed a new bike. While he waited for Anglade to arrive in the Lejeune team car with the new bike, which was still strapped to the roof-rack when the DS arrived, Kuiper and Thévenet passed him. Halfway up the climb, he appeared to have the Tour won; by the summit he was two minutes back in third place. 'I should have won that year. I was a lot stronger than I had been the year before,' he affirmed.

That proved to be Van Impe's last opportunity to win a second Tour title. Guimard had been nurturing France's new hope, the young Breton Hinault, who made a winning Grand Tour debut at the 1978 Vuelta and went on to establish a Merckx-like dynasty of his own, his style of *la course en tête*, though not as unceasingly relentless as the Belgian's, being buttressed by his intimidatory personality.

Although Van Impe may have never liked racing, it was very clear talking to him that he loved leading the world's best cyclists a merry dance in the mountains and is just as proud of his six King of the Mountains victories as he is of winning the yellow jersey. Those climbers' titles tied him for the record then held by his idol Federico Bahamontes, though the pair are united by more than this. Like so many of the climbing greats, including Charly Gaul, they were mavericks, too individualistic in their approach to racing to command the commitment and loyalty of a team. Eddy Merckx was right about how riders like these were becoming marginalized, eclipsed by power, higher racing speeds and team strength.

When Van Impe won the Tour in 1976 the average speed (34.518kph) was almost exactly the same as it had been when Jacques Anquetil took the first of his five titles in 1957 (34.520kph). Scroll forwards a similar distance to 1992 when Miguel Induráin won his second crown and the mean had risen to 39.504kph. Van Impe's attacks, in an era when racing speeds were generally lower on the climbs, looked more impressive and appeared to have more flair because the riders behind him weren't moving as quickly. However, having come right to centre stage on more mountainous Grand Tour courses of the 1970s and 1980s that had more summit finishes, climbers were about to get squeezed to the periphery again, as teams that had more strength in depth and were better organized tactically began to encroach into the territory to such an extent that mountain goats would become an endangered breed.

Chapter 11

What is a climber?

What is a climber? This is a question that should perhaps have been tackled earlier, but has been circumvented until this point because, I believe, the 1980s provides the ideal opportunity to observe and highlight the clear divergence in method between riders in the mould of Eddy Merckx, whose racing style was based on strength, and those who, like José Manuel Fuente or Lucien Van Impe, felt naturally at home on the long passes at the Grand Tours. In the former category were the likes of Bernard Hinault, Greg LeMond, Laurent Fignon and Francesco Moser; in the latter Robert Millar, Thierry Claveyrolat, Andy Hampsten and the first wave of Colombian climbers that broke through in Europe, notably Luis 'Lucho' Herrera and Fabio Parra.

There's a tendency, and particularly within the sport's traditional stage-racing strongholds of France and Italy, to look back on this period as a golden age of racing, the top stars battling each other from one end of the season to the other over short, steep bergs, cobbles, high mountains and through autumn's falling leaves. Although there was a dominant personality and racer in Hinault – the incarnation of bristling panache, the winner of a blizzard-hit Liège–Bastogne–Liège, a man who sorted out protests with his fists, and who called Roubaix 'bullshit' only to then go out and win it – there was also LeMond, Fignon, Moser, Sean Kelly, Moreno Argentin and Beppe Saronni. Racing was often unpredictable and even anarchic because the leading teams weren't yet completely wedded to imposing control. The homogenization that would come as a result of technological and scientific advances, in materials and design, in training methods and diet, but also, in the first place, with the widespread acceptance and employment of blood doping and use of associated products, was still some seasons ahead. As a consequence, climbers weren't yet peripheral performers in the major stage races. A good number were central actors, with strong teams built around them.

Like Van Impe, whose career had passed its zenith when they arrived on the scene, Robert Millar, who transitioned to Philippa York following her racing career, and Hampsten, were two of those mountain goats who typified the fact that genetics is at least as important as geography when it comes to defining the distinctive talent of a pure climber. Neither raced nor even trained at high altitudes until they were in their teenage years. Yet, when each of them broke through into the professional ranks, they quickly demonstrated their affinity for this terrain, which pitched them together both as opponents and friends, and as rivals to the peloton's strongmen.

Millar was the rider who cemented my fixation for the mountains, first by winning the Tour's polka-dot jersey in 1984, then by going close to winning the Vuelta a España during my stint abroad studying for my language degree, and, ultimately, due to the 1986 documentary *The High Life* that focused on him and featured what was then almost unprecedented and jaw-dropping footage of him going up and, especially, down mountains in training. Born in Glasgow, Millar became a member of the local Glenmarnock Wheelers club, where he quickly gained a reputation for being hugely talented on the bike and for being 'different' off it. Writing in the February 1997 issue of *Cycle Sport*, for which Millar was the guest editor, fellow Glaswegian Kenny Pryde described him as having 'a degree in non-verbal communication, specialising in aggression, but this couldn't hide his talent'. Willie Gibb, a friend at both primary and secondary school who would also go on to have an impressive racing career on the British domestic scene, said that even as a youngster Millar 'had a total disregard for what people thought of him and he was very obstinate'. He was, Gibb added, completely single-minded, his focus entirely on taking the steps that would lead to a professional career in Europe. 'I remember when he got his apprenticeship with Weir Pumps he said all he did was go to the toilet, lock the door and try to sleep so that he could be well rested for his training later on.'

Scottish junior champion in 1976, Scotland's national hill-climb champion a year later, Millar followed what was effectively the only path towards the pro ranks for a British rider by joining a French amateur team in 1979 – in his case the best in the country: the Athlétic Club Boulogne–Billancourt. Based in the suburbs of Paris, the ACBB already had a reputation for picking up and advancing the best English-speaking talent. Englishman Graham Jones, American Jonathan Boyer and Australian Phil Anderson had already graduated from its ranks, while the likes of Stephen Roche, Sean Yates and Allan Peiper would take the same route upwards in the seasons that followed.

Winner of the award for the best French amateur in 1979 thanks to a string of victories that season including the Route de France stage race, Millar joined the Peugeot team led by Hennie Kuiper and Michel Laurent the following season. Millar, now retired and known as York, says of those initial months at the French team:

> It was a bit of a shock at first because it's not like nowadays where you can measure where you fit into the hierarchy. You just got chucked in, starting at the bottom, going back for jerseys, taking *bidons* and other stuff, getting people's gloves and arm warmers, taking them back to the car. So a lot of the time you spent going back and forward doing domestique jobs and riding in the wind. It was only on the first couple of hill-top finishes where I realized that I could be quite near the front.

Third place on the hilly morning of the two-day Critérium International was one of those promising signals. Another came a few weeks later at the Tour de Romandie in Switzerland, where Millar was Peugeot's leading rider and raced with the whole team's backing, eventually finishing eighth. She says:

> It was quite strange. They were doing for me what I'd have been doing as a domestique, but they'd be telling me stuff. Positioning in the bunch wasn't always something I was good at, so they'd say, 'OK, we've got to move up now', or 'We'll start the hill from this position', or they'd come back and get me once I kind of fell asleep and was too far back in the bunch. It was also quite strange to be at the front with all of the best climbers who'd be at the Tour. OK, they rode away from me, but only four or five managed it.

Two-time Tour champion Hinault, who won that edition of Romandie, was one of those few, while Joop Zoetemelk, who would claim the yellow jersey that summer, was another.

Despite the handicap of being a foreign rider on what was very much a French team, Millar worked his way up the Peugeot hierarchy. He made his Tour debut in 1983, winning the stage into Luchon. The following season, he won another Pyrenean stage, this time at Guzet-Neige, finished fourth overall and took the King of the Mountains title, making him the first British rider to win a jersey classification at the Tour. Jerky footage of that Guzet stage win taken with motorbike- and helicopter-mounted cameras that weren't then equipped with in-device stabilization gimbals illustrates the freedom and flair of the climbers during that period, Millar first providing most of the impetus to ensure the little breakaway group stayed clear of the peloton, then dancing away from it, performing a cha-cha-cha on the pedals that's so rapid-fire it's easy to underestimate the size of the gear he was pushing. It was one of those moments, York reflects, when

> you look down at the other riders and they're not two inches from your back wheel – a bike length behind at the most – and you can see them chewing the handlebars, trying to stay with you. And in those conditions, seeing that just makes you go even harder. In those conditions, it's still painful but becomes quite enjoyable, if only because you're going so fast that it's unbelievable.

As he rides flat out towards victory at one of the most attractive of the Pyrenean ski stations, first Pedro Delgado, then Lucho Herrera sashay away from the peloton, the decisiveness of their accelerations quite startling when watched with eyes that have become used to seeing pure climbers given so little leeway, allowed just enough time to hang themselves out to dry before the peloton motors past them. The Spaniard looks super-charged until the Colombian, in the distinctive blue and red plumage with its yellow V-neck of team sponsor Varta, soars by, an exotic bird who has suddenly found his wings in terrain that is instinctively his own. On Alpe d'Huez, Herrera produced an even more eye-catching performance, first chasing across to lone leader Hinault, then testing his defences with two short accelerations, before unleashing a third, his legs suddenly spinning much faster as he prepares the attack and then glides away from the labouring Frenchman. Like Millar's stage-winning sally, they are moments of exquisite sporting drama and beauty, imbued with panache.

Although it's fair to say that the pure climbers could be afforded such leeway to roam because, like many Grand Tours during that era, the 1984 Grande Boucle comprised very close to 200 kilometres of time trialling, the counter to this is that all of the GC contenders raced in this same unbridled, unshepherded style at the critical points in the mountains, sometimes depending on a teammate to guide them, but usually only resorting to this when they were struggling to hold the pace of their rivals. Climbers truly were the kings of the mountains, as Andy Hampsten would discover when he turned professional in 1985.

Born in the Midwest state of Ohio, the American was brought up in North Dakota countryside set within a glacial lakebed. 'It is dead flat for 100 kilometres by 500 kilometres, and I lived in the middle of it. So riding a bike, I'd have to ride for an hour and a half to get to a little rise that was anything other than an overpass over a road,' he says.

'Radiator-thin' by his own description, Hampsten wasn't, on the face of it, well suited from a physiological perspective to the open, often windy and almost completely flat terrain where he began to ride with his elder brother Steve in order to dodge chores in the family garden. He came to the attention of the national team, who invited him to attend a training camp in Colorado Springs with 50 or so other kids when he was 15, providing him with his first opportunity to ride in the mountains. He recalls:

> I remember loving it from the start. Later on, I started spending a lot of time there and as there weren't so many young riders I'd join the elite amateurs on training rides with the coach watching up Cheyenne Canyon. It wasn't a pass, it was a short, nasty climb – probably 12 per cent or so for maybe a mile – but low enough that even in the winter we could go ride it. I had a great time on it. A lot of older riders were upset that I was even there. I just felt completely at home on a nice steep slope.

He admits that he wasn't sure to begin with whether he was simply captivated by the novelty of the mountains or because they revealed an innate talent that hadn't previously been apparent. 'I was thinking, "Maybe I'm just so excited because I'm from North Dakota and now I'm in the far west and there's mountains,"' he says, but he quickly realized the affinity went much further than initial infatuation.

> Gravity feels like a North Dakota headwind, but you don't have to tuck, you can sit up, you can stand on the pedals. It's hard, but I could actually measure my progress going up the road rather than just trying to tuck into a more aerodynamic position against the wind. It was great.

Just as Lucien Van Impe stresses the significance of the unusual training regime that his father laid out for him in the lowlands of Flanders in his development as a climber, Hampsten pays tribute to the adults from whom he first received advice in North Dakota.

I was a tiny kid and didn't have a lot of power, but they taught me to pedal very efficiently, to use my toe straps, pulling up, pushing down, spinning a lot. As a result, I was pretty efficient at pedalling and that translated well to the effort I was doing uphill, I could really focus on what my legs were doing.

Inspired by the 'big boys and girls' who were racing in the Colorado-based Coors Classic, or Red Zinger as it then was, he began to spend more and more time in that mountain state.

Even now, four decades on, I can remember my first mountain ride, climbing up a long pass that was steep in the middle to reach a hilly part on top. I didn't really know the roads, but I understood that we'd done two parts of a square and also that it was gonna be dark pretty soon, even though it was summer. Then we reached the top of the descent back into Boulder and we just flew. It only took half an hour to descend it, and I just thought that was the greatest time that I'd ever had on a bike. I can still remember the exhilaration of it.

In June 1982, he made his debut in the Coors, finishing fifth in the twelve-day, thirteen-stage race, ten minutes behind Colombian winner Patricinio Jiménez with another racer from the Andean country, Martín Ramírez, in second. Taking on the Colombians and the Mexicans, as well as competing in Central America and Colombia at junior and then amateur level, broadened Hampsten's growing knowledge of climbing as part of his racing toolkit.

I would mimic their riding style in training, by repeatedly attacking at high altitude. It was probably a terrible way to train when I read about recovery now, but doing those efforts certainly helped me. My only means of winning was by making those short, sharp attacks to get rid of stronger riders, to exhaust them, get a gap and then let them do the math, to think about chasing me down on flats later on if there were any.

Two years later, Hampsten was runner-up at the Coors Classic to fellow American Doug Shapiro, in a race that had been shifted back a month in the calendar and finished on the same day as the Tour, where Greg LeMond took third place and the white jersey as best young rider on his debut, the yellow jersey going to his Renault teammate and defending champion Laurent Fignon. By then 22, Hampsten was beginning to wonder how far he might be able to take his racing career, and acknowledges that the encouragement he received from LeMond, who had become a good friend, led to him seeking the opportunity to test himself in Europe. The following season he got his chance when the American 7-Eleven team offered him a one-month contract to ride the Giro d'Italia after they'd received an invitation to make their Grand Tour debut in the race. 'It was my first pro race. I'd been riding amateur races in Europe like the Tour de l'Avenir and the Grand Prix William Tell, doing well in the mountains, but this was a huge step up. Yet I really wanted to turn professional, so I leapt at the opportunity,' he says.

As with Van Impe's professional stage-racing debut at the 1969 Tour, Hampsten stepping into the top level at one of the biggest races on the calendar seems almost ridiculous now, when new pros tend to be nurtured for a season or two before being pitched into a Grand Tour, and he confesses that there were times when it felt exactly like that to him. In the opening few days, having tried but failed to take the mountains jersey on a third-category climb, he found himself sweeping back down into a Lombard valley close to the front of the lined-out peloton. 'Four of the people ahead of me,' he says, 'had the rainbow bands on their sleeves – it was Greg LeMond, Bernard Hinault, Beppe Saronni and Francesco Moser. And I'm thinking, "What am I doing? If the helicopters zoom in on us, they're going to name all these riders and then *Hampsten*. This is crazy."'

Halfway through that first week, as 7-Eleven's principal climbing specialist, he had his first opportunity to test himself in the high mountains on a 237-kilometre stage to Val Gardena in the Dolomites.

> It was a really hard, long climb, it was raining and it came at the end of a really long day. I started with the front group of sixty riders or so and just didn't have any energy. I lost a tragic amount of time and I was like, 'I thought I'd be a climber and here we are on the first day . . . I'm not really cut out for this.' I had a pretty bad experience. But as the race went along, we did more hilly stages and I started being in that first group of favourites, and pretty comfortably.

Eighth on the Gran Sasso, alongside race leader Hinault, the Frenchman's recently signed teammate LeMond and the other favourites for the *maglia rosa*, seventh the next day on a hilly stage to Perugia where Ron Kiefel gave 7-Eleven their first stage success, Hampsten served up a second victory in the final week on the short stage to the Aosta valley resort of Valnontey di Cogne. Having already been tipped off by LeMond about his countryman's talent, Hampsten subsequently received a contract offer from La Vie Claire for the 1986 season.

Victory at the Tour of Switzerland in the June of what was his first full season as a pro guaranteed him a place on the French team's line-up for the Tour de France. The shenanigans- and controversy-spiced story of that epic edition has been well told, the central characters being La Vie Claire co-leaders LeMond and Hinault, who would finish first and second, with their teammate Hampsten among the leading supporting actors in fourth place and the white jersey winner as the best-placed Tour debutant. It was epic in other ways too, featuring the biggest field in the race's history, 21 ten-man teams at the start at Boulogne–Billancourt, the peloton 50 per cent bigger than it had been just three years earlier. Among those 210 riders was arguably the deepest line-up of climbing talent in Grand Tour history, including Millar, Peter Winnen, Laurent Fignon, Pedro Delgado, Steven Rooks, the young Miguel Induráin, Joop Zoetemelk, Thierry Claveyrolat and the two outstanding Colombian teams of the era, Café de Colombia and Postobón, the former featuring Herrera, Parra and Patricinio Jiménez. In all, there were more than two dozen possible contenders for the polka-dot King of the Mountains jersey.

Reflecting on those names, let's return to that fundamental question: what is a climber? The American offers a good basis for examination of this question with a concise dissection of the qualities that made his two leaders at La Vie Claire such formidable racers. 'I don't think LeMond was a climber,' Hampsten asserts.

> He was the strongest rider I ever rode with, because, physically, he didn't hurt. When he was fit, he could go fast up, very fast down, he could sprint, he could certainly time trial, he just went fast. As for Hinault, he was famous for not liking the climbs. He'd only have one bad day in the Tour – he'd usually suffer on the first mountain day. But he'd always be attacking on that day to put climbers like

me on the back foot. I think they were just extraordinarily powerful riders who could use that power going uphill. They also knew how to suffer, and they knew how to demoralize climbers by just being there.

York explains how this strength would be manifested. 'They would ride in a much more controlled manner, setting a pace which has you on your limit, and there's only so long you can last like that,' says the Scot.

To try to upset them, you'd put in a couple of accelerations to try to break their rhythm, but if they were really strong, they'd just continue as they were and come back to you. Gradually, that wears you down because you'd be right on your limit, and eventually you'd let go, because you couldn't sustain that power output.

York adds that this pressing wouldn't just be confined to the final climb of a mountain stage, or even just these critical stages.

They might not even drop you on a mountain by riding a really hard tempo, but on the next mountain you'd be so tired that you'd never recover. You'd get dropped near the bottom and then it was a case of getting to the top as well as you could.

According to Hampsten, Hinault essentially followed the example of Eddy Merckx, who, it should be remembered, had foreseen at the start of the 1970s that strength on the climbs was going to subdue natural flair. 'Merckx wanted to keep everyone worried about him and Hinault wanted to keep everyone terrified about him,' he insists.

They were both so strong that, even on their worst day, they were going to climb out of their skin. They also had climbers figured out, they knew how to organize, they had the politics to organize other climbers to chase them down if they were dropped, they were master racers.

The same could be said of Miguel Induráin, Chris Froome and, more recently, of Tadej Pogačar. Each of them could climb phenomenally well, but each of them also preferred to race at a set, but very fast, tempo. 'Induráin, as I learned when I was on his team in 1995, could not recuperate if he went over his anaerobic threshold,' says Hampsten to back up his point. Forcing him past that point was the key to breaking him, but in five consecutive Tours no one managed to achieve that, although Italian climber Claudio Chiappucci came close on a number of occasions.

While the climbers were always likely to be strong-armed by the power and versatility of the pre-eminent stage racers, as Merckx had anticipated, the outcome of their contests in the mountains wasn't as easy to predict. For a start, it benefited climbers like York and Hampsten that Grand Tours were raced at a markedly slower pace than they are nowadays: in 1986, for instance, Greg LeMond's average speed as he claimed the Tour title for the first time was 36.2kph, while Tadej Pogačar's in 2021 was 41.2kph. Averages for individual stages in the mountains during those respective races also suggest a five-kilometre per hour differential. The extent of this margin goes some way to explaining why Delgado and Herrera's accelerations on the Guzet-Neige stage now appear so remarkable. They probably weren't even travelling as quickly as a contemporary racer would be when making a similar attack, but the group behind them was moving considerably slower than it would be in the 2020s, so gaps could be opened with extraordinary speed.

Says York, who was tutored in this style of climbing by Peugeot leaders Kuiper and Laurent:

> Those natural accelerations, that kind of dancing on the pedals stuff, comes naturally to most climbers. What doesn't come naturally is the ability to ride the whole mountain at a steady pace without hurting whoever you're riding for. That's something you have to practise and get used to, that you learn how to do through trial and error. If I had to ride for them, they would shout at me to stick to a steady pace instead of riding in the little spurts that you would do as a climber in order to hurt people. They'd be shouting at me when to speed up and when to slow down, and gradually I got the idea of riding at a tempo in order to look after your GC guy. It's a different way of climbing to when you're riding for the win, to be competitive and to hurt the other guys, than if you're riding to take the team leader to the top of the mountain.

Having risen through the racing hierarchy to become a leader, York was able to put this knowledge to use when going up against riders who wanted to climb in that same steady fashion as Kuiper and Laurent.

> You'd have to break their rhythm. It's very rare that the mountains are always a steady gradient, there's always little bits where it's harder or easier. So on the little harder bits, that's when you would tend to stand up, so that coming into them, you wouldn't slow down, you'd keep the same

speed on a slightly harder part. And that's really annoying. When you're on your limit, you come to a kind of slightly harder bit, and it doesn't slow down, that's rude. It really hurts.

Hampsten concurs. 'I loved playing with the curves, trying to take the gentler path around them and changing my rhythm,' says the American.

A lot of French climbers, Thierry Claveyrolat for instance, would always take the inside path, using a huge gear and try to accelerate by taking the steeper route. But I would always take the longer way and actually try to change my speed as I did that because I knew the fact that I used my gears to accelerate in the flatter bit of a curve bugged Induráin and lots of other riders on the climbs.

According to York, these *rouleurs-grimpeurs*, the French term depicting accurately their tendency to climb at a steady pace, like the Spaniard or, in more recent years, Bradley Wiggins, can usually sustain one or two often lengthy accelerations, but can be undone by constant niggly accelerations.

Natural climbers tend to climb at a certain speed, then put in an acceleration, then slow down. Often when they do this, the other guy will be thinking, 'Oh, yeah, that's the end of it.' But if, after slowing down for a little bit, they accelerate again that's likely to mean a whole heap of trouble for the other guy because the acceleration part of climbing is the hardest part. I'm not saying that keeping to a sustained power output is easy to do on the climbs, but it's the more common way of racing. So if you slow the group down and then you put in another big acceleration, the people who are kind of hanging there will get dropped because they've got used to riding at that slower speed and won't want to speed up again. They'll be thinking, 'OK, I've had enough of that change in pace.'

There were, York reveals, other ways to disrupt the smooth running of the *rouleurs-grimpeurs*. 'Sticking it in the big ring intimidates everybody who's climbing on the little ring,' she says.

You might be using much the same gear on the big ring as you were on the little ring and going at exactly the same speed, but it looks so much more impressive, and it's that mental aspect that counts. So, when the other guys saw you change into the big ring, sometimes their head would fall off. They'd be thinking, 'Oh, Jesus! What's this?'

Like York, Hampsten says that his main weapon as a pure climber was the accelerations he could deliver – 'I would practise them and Hinault and LeMond did not like them,' he confirms – but his unconventional route into the sport also led to him getting advice on ways that he could improve as a racer that would then have seemed quirky but have since become more mainstream.

None of us had coaches when we were juniors, so Eddie Borysewicz, who coached the national team, told us to learn whatever we could from whomever we could. When I was at the Olympic Training Center in Colorado Springs, I had a completely random encounter with a kinesiologist, who taught me something I used the rest of my career. He didn't know anything about cycling, rowing was his sport, but he knew that some aspects were fundamental to good performance, feeling relaxed being one of them.

My bike was set up indoors on a trainer and he got me to get on, click in and then reach for the bars. 'OK, your back's a little bit curved,' he told me. 'I've been looking at other riders and it's not as curved as some others, but curving your chest and your back really constricts your diaphragm and you want to open it up, as this will boost your overall strength and improve breathing. So instead of reaching for the bars, why don't you just bend at the waist, put your arms where they're going to be and fall onto the bike.' I tried this and it was completely different. I had an open chest, I was relaxed and my neck wouldn't be as taut. And I'd often go through this routine when I was trying to relax on really long climbs, purposely trying to isolate my legs as I didn't want a lot of upper body movement. I'd be telling myself, 'Relax, relax, relax.'

While this kind of exercise, which effectively engaged Hampsten's core muscles, has become a standard part of racers' training programmes, the kinesiologist also offered a more esoteric suggestion about the process of climbing by attempting to get the American to think he was being pulled up a climb rather than simply pushing his way towards the summit.

He asked me, 'What do you feel when you're climbing?' I said, 'I like going up because instead of tucking and trying to push air out of my way, I can sit up, I can be unaerodynamic. I can sit up, I can breathe, I can just think about pushing up against gravity. I love seeing the road go by.' He said, 'I hear you saying that you're trying to push yourself, and that's kind of hard. But why don't you try to feel like you're being pulled up the climb?' I said that was pretty nuts and asked him what he meant. 'Why don't you imagine that you feel a thread, not a rope, but a thread attached to you, and let it pull you up the climb?' I wasn't totally convinced, but I have to confess that it did work sometimes.

In the time trial that I won in the 88 Giro that finished on a big uphill, I was going as hard as I could to keep the pink jersey and Erik Breukink was way too close. I was going as hard as I could as I went onto the climb, but I was quite relaxed, and then it just hit me – the golden thread. Once I was into the climb, I thought, 'I'm going to see if it's there. I'm going to see if I can relax into feeling like I'm being pulled up the climb instead of psychologically stressing myself by telling myself to pedal harder and making my legs hurt more.' The golden thread doesn't work all of the time, but that day it did and I won that Giro.

York and Hampsten both stress the different strategies that they would employ in races where they were going for stage wins and those where they were focused on the overall. What's interesting about hearing their perspective on this is how both, as pure climbers, felt like they were often riding against their nature when set on a GC goal and how liberating it would often be to put aside this self-nullifying quest for consistency that the Grand Tours demand from their contenders and just let rip. Hampsten recalls, for instance, a conversation with Motorola team coach Dr Max Testa in which the Italian revealed he could see how frustrating three-week races were for climbers and suggested that the American climber should drop the Giro from his pre-Tour programme each season and focus on week-long stage races instead. Says the American, his face beaming:

When I'd do a three-week race, he said, 'You have to hold back so many days, it's a negative for you because you're a climber, you just want to tear it up, you want to see people fall over on their bike and then you get all excited and fly up the road. That's what a climber does.' And he was absolutely right. I really did like seeing my rivals' eyes roll back in their skull.

Testa reasoned that because there was less at stake at races like the Dauphiné Libéré and the Tour of Switzerland, Hampsten could sit up if he wasn't doing well and then try to win a stage. Significantly, he also pointed out that by riding these shorter races, the American would accumulate the same number of mountain days as he would have done at the Giro and that there'd be more days when he'd be allowed to tear it up.

Says Hampsten:

Max told me, 'If you win the Dauphiné it's awesome, if you win a stage then it's great. But this way it's better training to race aggressively, rather than negatively trying to just conserve energy like you would in a Grand Tour.' That was a big help to try to prepare me once I was a marked rider, to go into the Tour de France and really be ready for battle against these other top riders.

York reached a similar conclusion in 1988, when she exchanged the constant pressure and demands for consistency as the leader at Panasonic for what should have been – until Tour champion Stephen Roche got injured – a freer role at Fagor. A subsequent move in 1989 to Z, now the backers of what had been Peugeot, confirmed this switch of emphasis. 'There's pleasure in both, there's value in both,' she says when asked if she had a preference for one approach over the other, but then she adds:

> It got to the point where I didn't really want to be the GC rider any more, because I found more personal satisfaction in being one of the best climbers in the world than being in the top ten GC riders. I'd rather just be the best climber and be happy with that because riding the GC race was always slightly frustrating. The way I looked at it, if I was in the front as best climber, I'd be in the front of the race anyway, but I could allow myself to ride in a way that I wanted to.

Hampsten admits to sharing this exasperation as a climbing-focused GC leader who was always going to be eclipsed by the *rouleurs-grimpeurs* on such time-trial-heavy courses.

> Year after year, we were doing well in excess of 100 kilometres of time trials, almost 200 with the team time trial thrown in, with just two or three big mountain stages. It was clear that they didn't want a climber like Claudio Chiappucci to win, but I'm not sure why they were so amazingly generous to Induráin by having those 60-kilometre time trials. I always hoped that a Tour would come around with more mountains, but it never happened. In 92, I did absolutely the best I could and ended up fourth again, but I was able to win a stage on Alpe d'Huez by riding away at a hard part with other climbers, so at least the formula did finally work out in my favour.

The Grand Tour routes might have been formulaic during that period, but the approach to them was changing. Although the strong naturally still prevailed, out went anarchy and in came organization.

Remarkably, given the reputation Spanish squads had long had for internal disorder, Spain's ONCE team was in the vanguard of this competitive shift. Established in 1989 by Manolo Saiz, who had a mercurial touch when it came to developing and coaching riders – as well as for more illicit practices, it later turned out – and substantially backed for the next 15 seasons by Spain's lottery for the blind, ONCE's distinctive yellow jerseys (substituted for an equally conspicuous pink version at the Tour to avoid a clash with the leader's jersey) would cluster at the front of the peloton at key points in races, mimicking the lead-out 'train' tactic that was becoming more widely employed by sprint teams in the late 1980s but with the intention of keeping their own leaders well protected while applying pressure to their rivals.

'ONCE introduced that high tempo with a train of riders, which would hurt you quite a lot, and then Banesto took it up with Induráin,' explains. 'The gearing got bigger because those guys were stronger and they had support riders of a higher level.' In that 1992 Tour when Hampsten won at Alpe d'Huez, Induráin's eight-strong support crew comprised a former champion in Pedro Delgado, a podium finisher in Jean-François Bernard, one of France's most promising GC riders in Armand de Las Cuevas and a clutch of other strong domestiques. The strength in ONCE's line-up led by Laurent Jalabert and Alex Zülle went equally deep, while other teams were following the example of these two.

Some long-standing professionals were also becoming aware of a more sinister development. Doping had always been an issue for cycling, but in the early 1990s the use of a new generation of blood-boosting products, notably erythropoietin (EPO), radically altered the physiological limits of the riders who took them. Says Hampsten:

> You did see good riders becoming superstars, all-rounders starting to climb extraordinarily well. I guess in a way it was levelling out the differences between riders. I had the same trainer, Doctor Testa, and he'd say to me, 'I've tested you every year for your entire career. You're just the same. You're the litmus test for what's going on.' I remember that by the mid-90s it was over for someone like Robert Millar or me – it was just over.

Chapter 12

The Queens of the Mountains

'If it's not on Strava, it didn't happen' is one of the tropes of modern cycling. Looking back through the history of women's road racing to discover the great climbing feats that might be bracketed alongside Luis Ocaña's decimation of Eddy Merckx and the rest of the Tour pack at Orcières-Merlette in the 1971 Tour de France or Andy Hampsten's epic ride over the blizzard-swept Passo di Gavia that went so far in enabling him to win the 1988 Giro d'Italia, you quickly reach a similar conclusion. While newspaper archives present countless pages on the exploits of the sport's pre-eminent male climbers and YouTube channels serve up footage of most of these mountain specialists in the post-Second World War period, there's comparatively nothing on their female peers. It's almost as if they didn't exist.

In the introduction to *Queens of Pain*, in which she highlights the careers and achievements of two dozen of cycling's legendary female riders, Isabel Best comes to the same conclusion. 'Women's racing gets such scant mention in cycling literature you'd be forgiven for thinking it had no history,' she says, adding: 'Where is the folklore about the epic rivalry played between two riders who *should* be up there in the Pantheon of the greats: Maria Canins and Jeannie Longo?'

Best's book does a good deal to fill that gaping hole in cycling's histories, bringing to life pioneering racers from the late nineteenth century through to the end of the twentieth. Yet the exploits of most of those mentioned took place either on the track, in time trials or in place-to-place long-distance tests. There is little mention of mountains until the last quarter, and specifically the chapter that evokes the achievement of Marianne Martin in winning the first Tour de France Féminin in 1984. While there had been a Tour de France before then, the one-off, five-day event won by Britain's Millie Robinson in 1955 had started in Paris and travelled north through the rolling pastures and hills of bucolic Normandy. It wasn't until two decades later and the first edition of the Red Zinger Classic that the mountains appeared as a significant feature in a major women's stage race, American Hannah North winning that inaugural edition in 1975.

When Colorado-based brewing giant Coors took over as the primary sponsor of the Red Zinger in 1980, the prize purse doubled, close to half of it awarded in the women's race, which became the first well-established, -funded and -supported multi-stage event that featured the high mountains. The winner was Beth Heiden, a speed skating bronze medallist at the Lake Placid Winter Olympics at the start of that year who went on to triumph in the World Road Race Championship on the very hilly Sallanches course in the French Alps towards the end of the season. However, triggered to a significant extent by Red Zinger (later the Coors Classic) and also by the introduction of women's events to the Olympic programme at the Los Angeles Games, the real lift-off for stage racing took place in 1984, which saw the launch of the Ore-Ida Women's Challenge in Idaho and the Tour de France Féminin.

Félix Lévitan was the driving force behind the latter. Prompted by the success of the Coors Classic and his belief that the United States

In one of the Tour's all-time great mountain duels, Luis Ocaña leads fellow Spaniard José Manuel Fuente towards Les Orres in 1973. Fuente attacked Ocaña as many as 20 times climbing the Télégraphe and Galibier.

Having been encouraged to attack by Gitane directeur sportif Cyrille Guimard, Lucien Van Impe heads for victory and the Tour's yellow jersey at Pla d'Adet in 1976.

Luis 'Lucho' Herrera on his way to victory at Alpe d'Huez in the 1984 Tour, the first stage success by a Colombian rider.

The first British racer to win a classification jersey at the Tour, Robert Millar, now known as Philippa York, is decked out in polka dots as he leads Laurent Fignon (right) and Greg LeMond (left) up the Col de Joux Plane in 1984.

Arguably the greatest climber in the history of women's racing, Maria Canins will soon swap the polka dot jersey for the race leader's yellow at the 1985 Tour de France Féminin.

In the midst of one of the most memorable mountain stages in racing history, Andy Hampsten climbs towards the summit of the Gavia pass during the 1988 Giro d'Italia. Second place at the finish put him in the leader's pink jersey, which he held to the finish.

Jeannie Longo in yellow leads Maria Canins in the polka dot jersey at the 1989 Tour de France Féminin, which the Frenchwoman would win for the third year in succession.

Marco Pantani nears the summit of the Col du Galibier during his stage-winning attack in icy conditions on the road to Les Deux Alpes in 1998.

Following Pantani's death in 2004, a number of memorials have been erected in his memory. This one stands atop the Colle Fauniera, setting for one of the Italian's attacks during the 1999 Giro.

2011: Andy Schleck races past fans from his home country of Luxembourg as he climbs towards the summit of the Galibier pass, the Tour's highest-ever finish, during his legendary solo raid in the edition.

Already in the yellow jersey, Chris Froome all but wrapped up victory in the 2013 Tour de France with a stage win at the iconic summit of Mont Ventoux.

Julian Alaphilippe resplendent in polka dots during the 2018 Tour stage to La Rosière.

Ashleigh Moolman Pasio is tracked by Giro Rosa leader Annemiek van Vleuten on Monte Zoncolan in the 2018 edition of the race in which the South African climber finished second overall to her Dutch rival.

Winner of mountain stages in all three Grand Tours, Dan Martin on the climb of Jebel Hafeet at the 2019 UAE Tour.

Urged on by compatriot and Ineos teammate Dani Martínez, Egan Bernal strives to maintain his hold on the pink jersey on the climb to Sega di Ala in the 2021 Giro d'Italia.

The new King of the Mountains, Slovenia's Tadej Pogačar, celebrates victory after dropping rival Jonas Vingegaard on the final steep ramp up to the Col du Portet in the 2021 Tour.

would be fundamental to the future of bike racing, the co-director of the men's Tour put together a 1,066-kilometre, eighteen-stage race featuring half a dozen six-rider teams. It ran ahead of the men most days and included a sortie through the Vercors massif into Grenoble, a summit finish at the Alpine resort of La Plagne and a stage over the Col de Joux Plane into Morzine.

Before it got under way, there was a good deal of scepticism about the new event, some of it ridiculously narrow-minded. 'I have absolutely nothing against women's sport, but cycling is much too difficult for a woman. They are not made for the sport,' opined five-time Tour winner Jacques Anquetil. 'I'm sorry to see women suffer. On a bicycle, there's always a lot of suffering.' Yet, just one rider failed to complete the route starting and ending in Paris. The Dutch dominated the race until the Alps, winning all bar one of the eleven stages as their leader Heleen Hage held the yellow jersey. The USA's Marianne Martin trimmed that lead back with a solo raid over the Rousset and Chalimont passes in the Vercors to Grenoble, then took it for herself when she once again finished clear of her rivals at La Plagne, Hage yielding five minutes to the American on the 32-kilometre stage. 'I'd never actually ridden up a real mountain before. I didn't know what it was like to ride uphill for twenty kilometres,' Hage told a Dutch newspaper in 2019. 'I think I should have ridden at my own pace a bit more. I let the others push me too much. The rest day beforehand also affected me. I didn't like that in any stage race. My legs always felt bad afterwards.'

Colorado-based Martin, though, had no problems coping with climbs of that magnitude. Set back by anaemia early in that season, she explains that she wasn't in her best shape going into the Tour.

I rode into my fitness so that by the time we were in the Alps I was at my peak. My feeling at that time about American cyclists, both the men and the women, was that they all overtrained, apart from Andy Hampsten. I used to rest a lot, and I'd been very smart with my training up to the Tour because I had been out of shape. When I felt my fitness coming around, which was probably in May, I was very focused on everything that I did. Everything had a purpose, every breath, every workout. There were no junk miles. It was all very deliberate. I remember climbing towards La Plagne and I didn't even know where the road was until the people parted just in front of me. That is so cool – slightly stressful but so cool. You feed off that excitement, that thrill.

Her biggest test came on the next stage from Scionzier to Morzine over the Joux Plane, where Hage and her Dutch teammates took turns in attacking the yellow jersey.

I can remember looking up the mountain ahead and seeing people for miles, which was really amazing. But at the same time I was thinking, 'I can't ride this fast over that kind of distance.' But then you do. You're racing up and the fans on either side of you are just a blur. My name was written on the road on a couple of occasions and I loved the fact that in the mountains there were no barriers or anything. I liked the rawness, the realness of it.

Although Hage won in Morzine, Martin limited her losses to a mere twenty-two seconds, then safely negotiated the final three stages into Paris, where she finished more than three minutes clear of her Dutch rival on the Champs-Élysées.

Unfortunately, she was unable to defend her title after falling ill while in France during the early part of the 1985 season and retired from competition the year after due to a persistent problem with allergies. Martin says, though, that winning that one race in the yellow jersey changed her significantly.

> The whole champion thing was definitely wasted on me because I'm a behind-the-scenes person, but it's in my heart. It's not like I'm not incredibly proud of it. It's just that that's not who I am, it's just something that I did. But it definitely did have an impact on me. It taught me that we can do way more than we think we can. I think that applies to absolutely anybody. It didn't affect me in a way that I went around waving it and saying, 'Look at who I am.' It was an internal thing, something that made me say to myself, 'Look what I can do.' It helped me set my sights very high. Unless you do that, you'll never get there.

That inaugural 1984 edition of the Tour had clashed with the cycling events at the Olympics, preventing many of the biggest names in women's racing from competing in France. A year later, though, most of the riders who had focused on the LA Games were in the Breton town of Lanester for the second edition, a dozen teams lining up in a race of two parts. Due to a UCI regulation restricting women's events to a maximum of twelve days, Lévitan and his organizing team ran it as two separate but contiguous races, the first comprising a prologue and a dozen stages, the second the final five, the yellow jersey decided on points that were carried across from the former to the latter rather than on time.

Heleen Hage was one of the early leaders, but the race quickly developed into a battle between the two foremost stage racers of that era, France's Jeannie Longo and Italy's Maria Canins. Both riders had a long competitive history in the mountains, the Frenchwoman as a downhill skier and the Italian as multiple national cross-country skiing champion – Canins also won the Italian mountain running title and, later, the world veterans' mountain bike championship.

The younger of the pair by nine years, Longo, a waif-like 47kg at her competitive best, had been encouraged to shift her focus from skis to wheels in 1979 by her coach and later husband Patrice Ciprelli. She won the French road title that season – and retained it for the following decade! – but didn't make a full-time switch to cycling until 1983, tempted by the prospect of winning gold in Los Angeles. Although she was overpowered by US riders in the medal-deciding sprint, Connie Carpenter taking gold and Rebecca Twigg the silver as Longo finished sixth, she was by then almost peerless in stage races and began the Tour as favourite for the title.

Just a touch more powerfully built, but still an elfin figure on the bike, Canins initially used the bike as a training tool for skiing until 1982, when she won the Italian road title. Also coached by her husband, international cross-country skier and mountaineer Bruno Bonaldi, she had bright blue eyes that almost matched the navy of her *azzurri* jersey, was soft-spoken and a rather reluctant star, the archetypal rider who let their legs do their talking for them. Fifth in Los Angeles, she'd claimed her first major stage race success just prior to the Games, beating Longo into second place at the Coors Classic.

The pair finished within a second of each other in a time trial at Reims on day five, Canins edging it as Longo took the yellow jersey. Two wins approaching the Alps appeared to give the Frenchwoman the upper hand, but the mountains then delivered a true reckoning. Canins, fittingly wearing the Café de Colombia-sponsored Queen of the Mountains red polka dots, won by almost three minutes at Avoriaz, taking the lead from Longo. She followed up with what, in terms of the time gaps it yielded, was an Ocaña-like demonstration on Longo's home roads at Lans-en-Vercors close to Grenoble, finishing more than eight minutes clear of the second rider, France's Dominique Damiani, with Longo way back in fourteenth. 'Jeannie fought desperately to keep the flying Italian mama in sight,' wrote Owen Mulholland, using the nickname given by the Italian press to Canins. 'On the last climb, Jeannie blew up spectacularly, dismounting three times,' he added, describing how the soundly beaten Frenchwoman had 'crawled in' to the finish.

When the second part of the race reached the Pyrenees, the Italian was just as untouchable, dropping all of her rivals almost from the start in Sainte-Marie-de-Campan on the eastern flank of the Col du Tourmalet. She crossed the pass minutes clear and pushed her advantage out all the way up to the summit finish at Luz Ardiden, Longo coming in nine minutes later in second. She was 'Coppi in a skirt' said Lévitan, the comparison with Il Campionissimo indelicately made, but a fitting one. There was a gulf between Canins and the rest, Longo twenty-two minutes behind overall, third-placed Cécile Odin almost thirty-five.

The Canins–Longo rivalry was reprised at the 1986 Tour, when the presence of 22-year-old Inga Thompson added extra spark to the battle between the two veterans, the trio winning three-quarters of the sixteen stages between them. They were evenly matched in time trials and the flatter road stages, and it was the mountains that once again proved the difference. On the stage over the Aspin and

Peyresourde passes into Luchon, the Italian, described by Longo in her race diary in *Miroir du Cyclisme* as 'the queen of the mountains', went clear on the first climb, but for once she was not alone. Thompson, a former California college runner who started training on a bike when recuperating from an ankle injury and discovered she had a talent for it, to the extent that she ended up racing the Olympic road event in LA during her first competitive season, stayed with her. Although the American, with her distinctive long blonde plait, lost some ground on the Peyresourde, she limited her losses to two minutes, which enabled her to leapfrog the Frenchwoman into second place.

'It's magical when your form comes together like that. When everything clicks, you've got so much awareness of your body, you're in touch with it all but above it all. You're listening to your breath and heartbeat, and you're focused on the pedal stroke,' says Thompson. 'It's a lot like meditation, like an active meditation when you're really in tune with it all.'

Although she was in her third year at the top level, the Tour was only the third stage race that the American had started. Part of the US Olympic squad in 1984, then affected by a brain abscess and, subsequently, overtraining as she came back from that illness, Thompson affirms that the 1986 season was her first full one, but she did have experience from the 1984 Coors Classic of racing against Canins.

> She was such a good rider, but not a beautiful rider. She wasn't a dancing-on-the-pedals type of climber, but she had a set of lungs on her. She was all ribcage. She had another gear, the ability to ride five pedal strokes faster than you, so you'd

just have to watch her ride off and accept there was nothing you could do about it. You just had to smile and think, 'I'm OK getting second to Maria Canins. I'm good with this.' At the same time, though, it made me mad and I didn't want to accept it, but I had to.

Thompson continues:

If it was a shorter climb, I could hang with her. When we'd go to, say, like Leadville, Colorado, on the Coors, even though we got really high up in the mountains and had perhaps 5,000 feet of climbing, I could stay with her. I was a really good climber. But once we got into the Alps, where there are ten-mile climbs, I could stick with her for half to two-thirds, but in that last couple of miles . . .

It was in the Alps that the contest between the three riders was decided, on a 69-kilometre stage from Guillestre that took the race over the towering Izoard pass and then to the even loftier Col du Granon for a summit finish. 'As in the Pyrenees, I decided to ride at my own rhythm. There's no point in trying to follow the wheel of Maria Canins when she shoots away,' Longo recorded in her diary. 'For five kilometres, the Italian was with Inga Thompson as I stuck to my tempo behind. On the pass's hairpins, I suddenly noticed the American had blown by trying to follow the infernal Canins.' The Frenchwoman rode away from the struggling Thompson, only to suffer with hunger 'knock' and lose six minutes to the incomparable Italian, who had produced another magnificent climbing recital.

'We didn't have the proper gearing, because the race bibles we had were so bad,' Thompson recalls.

I blew up big time. I was doing what I call 'the paperboy', going back and forth across the road because I wasn't going to get off and walk. And I never quite recovered from that stage. I just blew chunks. It was an ugly day. I'd got really confident and on the Col du Granon I was thinking, 'I'm going to stay with her. I don't have the right gears, but she has those same gears.' But I just went 'Poof!' When Longo passed me, it was the ultimate low for me because I knew that I was stronger than her on the climbs. I learned a good lesson, though. That was the only day that I can ever remember in my ten-year career that I blew up.

Thompson's admiration for Canins's ability and achievements is palpable.

When you look at her overall speed compared to Greg LeMond's that year in the Tour, it was only one kilometre per hour slower. Sure, the women's race was shorter. Well, yes, it was. But I used to joke that the men got the flats to warm up on, whereas they just started us at the bottom of the mountains and said, 'There you go . . .' The men's peloton also had more than two hundred riders in it, while we had half that number and only thirty or so of us were really strong. We didn't have the depth. So really it was a good comparison of how well Canins was climbing, because she was off the front all the time, to how well LeMond was climbing. I finished twenty-two minutes behind her. Longo was fifteen on her. It shows you what a stunning athlete Maria Canins was.

As well as making a commitment to come back even stronger the following year, Longo's race diary also highlighted the difficulties already affecting this marquee race in the women's calendar. First, she noted that there was very little press coverage of the Tour Féminin stage based in Villard-de-Lans despite it coinciding with a rest day for the men. 'As Hinault and the rest weren't racing, everything stopped for the press. L'Équipe and the local paper, Le Dauphiné Libéré, didn't even cover our stage,' she noted. Reflecting on the race as a whole, she picked out Thompson as emblematic of the emerging talent in the women's peloton, but lamented the event's likely future. 'We've finished what is perhaps the last Tour Féminin worthy of the name. Félix Lévitan has announced that next year we will race in September in conjunction with the Tour de l'Avenir. What a retrograde step that would be.' As it turned out, that prediction proved a little hasty. The race continued in its July slot for another three editions before being pushed back to a September date in 1990, when it was also rebranded as the Women's Tour of the EEC. This ran for four editions before the Société du Tour de France closed it down for good.

In the first of those final three editions of the Tour Féminin in 1987, the balance of racing power began to shift. Although Canins got the better of Longo at the Tour de l'Aude in the French Pyrenees that spring, the Frenchwoman won the Coors and the tours of Colombia, the Drôme and Norway. Finally, she also won the Tour, beating the now 38-year-old Italian at Luz Ardiden, La Plagne and Morzine to claim the title by almost three minutes in Paris. Longo retained the title in 1988 and 1989, when she won every mountain stage and reached the French capital almost nine minutes up on her perennial rival, Thompson once again third on her first appearance since her 1986 podium.

Like her compatriot Andy Hampsten in the men's peloton, the American was by then becoming aware that the competitive playing field was changing, that doping was becoming much more sophisticated. She declares:

> Those years in the mid-1980s were the best because racing was still clean at that point. But you could see a change taking place in certain riders, and Longo was one of them. When we saw her at the Tour of Texas in 1987, she looked like she always did – a fit, healthy athlete with the appropriate amount of body fat for a woman. Six weeks later, she looked like a mini Arnold Schwarzenegger. In Texas, I'd been beating her in the time trials and out-climbing her, it was just like 1986. Six weeks later, when we went over to France to race, I couldn't touch her. She was putting two minutes on me in a time trial and she was gone in the mountains. I couldn't even see her. You don't make changes like that after you've been an elite athlete for ten years.

Her allegation is supported by the fact that Longo did test positive at the end of the 1987 season, a control done following a three-kilometre world record attempt in Colorado Springs that revealed use of the stimulant ephedrine. While this was the only positive test during a career that lasted until 2011, when she bowed out after capturing the French time trial title at the age of 52, in 2018, her husband and coach Patrice Ciprelli received a year's suspended sentence for the illegal import of EPO on 8 separate occasions between 2007 and 2011. Ciprelli maintained the blood-boosting product was for his 'own, personal use', but the two judges who conducted the investigation into the offence said of him that he had 'excuses that aren't credible and that are in certain aspects complete fantasy in the face of overwhelming evidence'. Their report also stated that they had 'suspicions of doping' with regard to Longo due to 'exceptional sporting performances and longevity', but added that they had been 'unable to provide irrefutable proof of this doping'.

As the Tour withered, other races flourished from the late 1980s, notably the Giro d'Italia, its inaugural 1988 edition won by Canins, and the Ore-Ida Women's Challenge. This was established by former Green Beret and Vietnam veteran Jim Rabdau, who had first seen road racing during a stay in Italy in the early 1960s and had instantly been captivated. In 1984, while working in the human resources department at the Ore-Ida potato snack company based in Idaho, he was tasked with promoting the brand among women and came up with the idea for a six-day race. 'It has the colour, the speed, the thrill,' he said of the sport. The first edition that year was dominated by members of the US national team, Rebecca Twigg taking the title ahead of Cindy Olivarri and Inga Thompson.

In 1990, Rabdau decided to mark the centenary of Idaho's foundation with a race that matched and perhaps even surpassed the scale of those early editions of the Tour Féminin, piecing together a route that covered 17 stages over 16 days, extending to 1,067 kilometres with 6,705 metres of climbing. As it didn't fit within the parameters set for stage racing, the UCI refused to sanction it, declaiming in a letter the 'excessive number of stages . . . excessive individual stage distances . . . excessive climbing . . . excessive duration'. Rather than back down or find a fudge to get around the rules as Lévitan had done in 1985, Rabdau used the ruling body's naysaying as fuel to publicize Ore-Ida under the tag line 'Let's get excessive in Idaho'.

Winner of five stages, Thompson, who describes Rabdau as 'a visionary and such a huge supporter of women's racing', took the title for the second time, beating compatriot Ruthie Matthes and Britain's defending champion Lisa Brambani. The contest between the three riders had echoes of the 1986 Tour Féminin, Thompson being the early leader, until Brambani – 'this tiny little thing that could go up hills like crazy' Matthes said in a 2021 feature in *Rouleur* – claimed top spot in the mountains on day five. The Yorkshirewoman's advantage was fleeting, though, Thompson leading the way up the final 13 kilometres and 64 bends of the Spiral Highway climb the next day to regain top spot, one rival saying she'd ridden like she had 'three lungs'. The battle continued to rage on a stage over the 2,192-metre Banner Summit and another that crossed the 2,652-metre Galena Summit, where Brambani and her teammates constantly harried Thompson, who refused to crack.

In that *Rouleur* feature, written by Isabel Best, Brambani described the Ore-Ida as being 'ahead of the game'. It supported Lévitan's belief that cycling's future lay in the US, for women racers at least. 'Only the Giro Rosa comes close with length but really, it bears no comparison with the slick Ore-Ida event. I honestly cannot say enough good things about this race. It simply was *the* best,' said the Briton. The race's upward trajectory was maintained even when Ore-Ida ended their sponsorship after the 1992 edition. Rabdau brought in other heavyweights to back it, first the energy food company PowerBar and then Idaho-based computer giant Hewlett-Packard, who pushed the prize fund up to $125,000 in 1998, making it the biggest race of any kind in the US and one of the largest anywhere in the sport. That edition was also broadcast for the first time on network television by CBS and attracted most of the world's leading racers.

Sadly, the 12-day edition of 2002 won by Germany's Judith Arndt was the last. The sponsor that had been lined up for the following year pulled out and Rabdau opted to retire. Although the Giro Donne, the Grande Boucle Féminine, which was the successor to the Tour Féminin, and the Tour de l'Aude continued as flagship events, their profile was undermined by their organizers' meagre resources and, fundamentally, by TV and press indifference, with coverage mostly limited to local stations and papers.

In a *Rouleur* feature tracing the history of the Giro Donne, which became the biggest stage race on the calendar in the first decade of this century, Collyn Ahart described it as being 'enigmatic', as an event that essentially existed within its own space rather than being a pillar of cycle sport. She wrote:

> It's not a story of heroes and great narratives that have been rehearsed in the same way the Tour or the Giro have. Even Fabiana Luperini, arguably one of the greatest cyclists in history with five Giro Donne titles to her name (four consecutive wins from '95–'98 and then again ten years later in 2008) goes practically unheard in the cycling press. This year, in 2012, she was on the podium of one of the stages. And yet, if I saw her in a cafe I wouldn't know who she was.

Luperini's lack of public profile, and that of other climbers such as Spain's Joane Somarriba, Switzerland's Nicole Brändli, and Lithuanian duo Edita Pučinskaitė and Diana Žiliūtė, illustrated the poverty of the women's racing scene compared to the men's. The latter's win in the 1999 Grande Boucle Féminine, which at 1,581 kilometres was and remains the longest event in women's racing history, appears to have taken place in a journalistic vacuum. Despite featuring several renowned Pyrenean passes, a stage over Mont Ventoux and a summit finish at the Alpine resort of Vaujany, barely any details of the action remain. Here was a race that ran counter to the argument put forward in the post-war years by Albert Baker d'Isy, a doyen of French cycling writers, who declared: 'Before the mountains appeared, the Tour was seldom spoken about.' Despite those famous climbs, this one, the successor to the event won by Martin, Canins and Longo, appeared to pass with barely a mention.

Coverage of women's racing has improved hugely in recent years, coinciding with the emergence of a new generation of stars led by Dutch riders Marianne Vos, Anna van der Breggen and Annemiek van Vleuten, and Britain's Lizzie Deignan. Yet their notoriety has not been forged in the mountains, as is the case with so much of men's racing history, but primarily in the calendar's one-day Classics and at the World Championships and Olympic Games. Although infamous ascents such as the Stelvio and Zoncolan have occasionally appeared in what has become the Giro d'Italia Donne, these have been one-offs, appearing so rarely on race routes that most racers don't even do specific training for them.

Confirms Ashleigh Moolman Pasio, runner-up to van Vleuten in the 2018 Giro and also on that edition's ascent of the fearsome Monte Zoncolan:

> This is the interesting thing with women's cycling. Tour riding for men is very specialized, whereas tour riding for women isn't. The long climbs that the men do, the ones that all fans know, have actually sometimes been a bit of a challenge for the women's peloton, and even for a climber like myself because we don't race on them that often. The way you ride a very long mountain pass is very different to the way you'd ride a five- or an eight-kilometre climb, so it's more difficult for us

to prepare for the longer ones when they come up just once a year. Whereas the men have very specific preparation for the Tour de France, which is the pinnacle for them, and the high mountains are almost their sole focus.

The establishment of the Tour de France Femmes in 2022 looks likely to change the dynamic of women's racing in a similar way to its forerunners on both sides of the Atlantic did in the mid-1980s. Run, like the men's race, by ASO, the inaugural eight-day event is set to feature some notable climbs on its final weekend, including the Tour's first ascent, the Ballon d'Alsace, where René Pottier laid down the first marker for climbers in 1905, and one of the modern race's favourite summit finales at La Planche des Belles Filles, or more precisley at La Super Planche des Belles Filles, a kilometre or so higher than the resort and accessed by a gravel road, a finish first used by the men in 2019. Starting in Paris on the day that the men's race finishes, it will be covered on live television and by a large press corps. Sponsored by Zwift, a hugely popular online bike training programme, the race will, says ASO, be self-sustaining in terms of its revenue and, if that does indeed turn out to be the case, it will also help to provide a clear narrative to the season based around obvious milestones. What's more, the step into the high mountains, to Alpe d'Huez, the Ventoux and the Tourmalet, won't be too far away. By the time they are included, a new generation of climbers will be emerging, belatedly following in the wheeltracks of Marianne Martin, Maria Canins and Inga Thompson, while at the same time highlighting the exploits of those and so many other racers.

Thompson can't wait to see it, to find out who these queens of the mountains will be.

> Initially, I was against having it at a different time to the men's race because, if they're run concurrently, the fans are already there, the route's already in place. That's how it was before and it was beautifully run. But I've changed my stance, because this way they can showcase the women. Instead of the women being the support race, they are *the* race and that really will be beautiful.

Chapter 13

Every climber in one

'Are climbers a dying breed?' This pessimistic question was one of the cover-lines on the August 1994 issue of *Cycle Sport*, which appeared on the shelves just before the Tour de France was due to arrive in Britain for only the second time in its history. Inside, a feature entitled 'Mountain Men: In Memoriam' declared that more than five years had passed since a thoroughbred climber had last won any of the three Grand Tours, that success being Pedro Delgado's 1989 victory in the Vuelta a España, which came a season after the Spaniard had won the Tour de France and Andy Hampsten had won the Giro d'Italia. 'Riders like this, the ones who provide what many feel are the most spectacular moments of cycling, keep getting harder and harder to find,' said the story by William and Alasdair Fotheringham, adding that these moments might 'represent the last gasp of a type of rider whose likes may prove difficult to see again'.

The article canvassed a handful of riders with a distinguished reputation in the mountains. Colombia's Oliverio Rincón, winner of a famous Tour victory through the Pyrenees the previous season, asserted that the odds of pure climbers like him contending in the Grand Tours and other big stage races were lengthening because riders were better prepared than ever before, not only riding faster on the flat but also able to stay with the pace of the best in the mountains for longer, while at the same time having the security blanket of frequent long time trials to provide them with an insurmountable time buffer. Three-time Vuelta winner and the 1993 Tour's King of the Mountains, Tony Rominger, concurred. 'It's partly the training: riders are better prepared for the mountains,' stated the Swiss. 'I don't think we will see the days of the great climbers again – the other guys are so much stronger, and they'll stay that way.'

Halfway through what would prove to be his last full season as a professional, Robert Millar, now known as Philippa York, also emphasized the fact that pure strength was prevailing over innate climbing talent, highlighting how

> races are getting faster and the use of a 12 sprocket on the freewheel is becoming a requirement for almost every race for everybody, climbers included. The problem is that if you train to handle a big gear more easily, you lose part of the natural suppleness a climber uses to accelerate when climbing.

He concluded: 'One thing is for sure, 53×12 and pure climbers are not compatible.'

Spanish climbing legends Federico Bahamontes and José Manuel Fuente, meanwhile, bemoaned the lack of initiative and daring on the part of climbers, the tendency to wait until the final ascent on a mountain stage rather moving earlier in the day. 'They just can't or won't,' Bahamontes observed of the reluctance to attack early, adding, 'They've got no blood in them' – a comment that, with hindsight, can't fail to produce a wry smile bearing in mind the red-blood-cell-boosting practices of many in the peloton at that time.

In a final section under the headline 'RIP: The Grimpeur', the article declared: 'The inescapable conclusion seems to be that the great days of the specialist climber are over', and suggested that exploits to compare with Lucien Van Impe's Tour win at Pla d'Adet in 1976 or Luis Ocaña's incredible break to Orcières-Merlette three years earlier might not be seen again. The story summed up: 'The mountain men are dead: long live the mountains.'

As the sub-editor on *Cycle Sport* at that time, I must have read, checked and corrected William and Alasdair's rather bleak assessment of the future for the sport's climbers. I can also say with some certainty that I would most likely have done so in late May or early June for an August-dated issue that probably went on sale on the first Wednesday of July, to coincide with the Tour's two stages in southern England. In other words, the story would have been written at least a week and maybe two before Marco Pantani completely torched the idea that the mountain men were dead with back-to-back victories in the Dolomites at Merano and Aprica in the Giro d'Italia, the former the first of a professional career that had started the year before.

This was an era when the use of computers and email was only just becoming widespread, the internet was almost unheard of, and British television companies weren't interested in any bike race apart from the Tour, so details of events in Italy would probably have reached the office via a day-old copy of *L'Équipe* or of *La Gazzetta dello Sport*. Yet Pantani's achievement must have had a significant impact on us in our London South Bank offices, because, following a September issue that focused on Miguel Induráin's fourth consecutive Tour victory, Pantani, runner-up at the Giro and then third and best young rider at the Tour, was the cover star of the October issue, proclaimed the 'New king of the mountains'. So much for them being a dying breed . . .

In the side-on cover photo taken in a deluge during his Tour debut for the Carrera team led by Claudio Chiappucci, the most striking aspect is that it doesn't look like Pantani at all. He has hair for a start – a tonsure, already receded to the crown of his head, but still fairly abundant at the sides. There's no trademark bandanna or earring, no sign yet of 'Il Pirata', the persona he would later adopt. With his gaze fixed just ahead of his front wheel, there's no trace of star status at all. He looks like an old pro who's done his job for the day and been dropped, rather than the new climbing sensation of Italian cycling.

Inside the magazine, there's no hint either of the esoteric and sometimes poetic statements for which he's best remembered. Instead, there's something more substantial from the climbing perspective: an awareness rapidly acquired that, like so many before, the odds are stacked against him. He admits to being frustrated, saying, 'The climbers have disappeared because the climbs now, the ones they do at a steady pace, they do at 20 kilometres per hour . . . They go so quickly now that strength is what really matters and you see that with riders like Induráin and Rominger.' He agrees with Robert Millar's comment from the issue before last that climbers are being killed off by the need to spend so much time racing in the 12 sprocket. 'In the Tour, you have 10 days without a proper climb, and I think that climbers are knocked out at the start,' he asserts, adding that the Tour organizers need to change their approach to route-planning if riders like him are to have a realistic chance of challenging for the yellow jersey.

The moment that offers the most enlightening insight into his approach comes right at the end of the interview when he says, '*Fare il vuoto*, getting a gap, is the most beautiful thing, and people value it. It's hard, but when it's good, it's the most beautiful thing there is.' This is the essence of Pantani – and perhaps even the best explanation why climbing as an art bewitches us: the reason why, despite the scandals, suspicion and controversy that ultimately beset his career, the Italian was and still is so revered, the leading climber of all time according to most polls. Pantani's anointment as the sport's, and above all Italy's, new superstar was captured at the end of that Tour in *La Gazzetta dello Sport*, which reported millions of Italians sat down for each stage, captivated by the prospect of what Pantani would serve up. He was, the paper said, 'invariably there, ahead of everyone on the climbs, whirling his bony legs at a rhythm no one else could keep up, with King Induráin at the top of the list.'

In between a training ride crash that led to him missing the 1995 Giro d'Italia and a life-endangering, head-on collision with a car that was driving up a descent at Milan–Turin that October, Pantani served up a triptych of climbing brilliance that furthered his standing as the most captivating racer in the sport. This began on the penultimate stage of the Tour of Switzerland that finished on the Flumserberg, a nine-kilometre autobahn of a climb – wide, immaculately surfaced, the gradient steady until the very final section up to the finish. Coming onto it, the Italian's Carrera teammate Leonardo Sierra is just ahead of the group of favourites that includes race leader Pavel Tonkov, second-placed Alex Zülle, as well as Pantani, looking more familiar now with his head completely shaved.

When, with seven kilometres remaining, Zülle attacks, Tonkov is quick to respond. Moments later, Pantani bridges up to them, tracks them around the next hairpin, then makes his move. He doesn't so much jump as glide away, with a perfect illustration of the grace and control evoked by the term 'dancing on the pedals'. Toes pointed downwards in classic, almost balletic, climbing fashion, in very much the same style as Charly Gaul but pushing a much bigger gear than those preferred by the Luxembourger, Pantani's rhythmic tempo has hypnotic elegance that compares with ice dancers Jayne Torvill and Christopher Dean performing their Olympic-winning routine to Ravel's *Boléro*.

In an article in the *Cycling Anthology*, Daniel Friebe says that performances like this one in Switzerland were evidence of Pantani possessing 'what Italians in the Renaissance called "*sprezzatura*"'. The term first appeared in Baldassare Castiglione's *The Book of the Courtier*, written in the 1520s, and was defined as 'a certain nonchalance, so as to conceal all art and make whatever one does or says appear to be without effort and almost without any thought about it'. According to Castiglione, *sprezzatura* was a vital quality for the ideal courtier, denoting their skill in a variety of areas, including combat, music and dancing, and their studied carelessness in performing them. Compared to the other riders on the Flumserberg, who are surging, slowing, grimacing, fighting with their bikes as much as each other, Pantani makes climbing look painless and uncomplicated. It's easy to imagine amateur riders witnessing his poise and trying to replicate it on their next outing on a climb, standing on the pedals for a few seconds until the burn of lactic acid in the thighs forces them back into the saddle again. He might have made it seem effortless, but it certainly wasn't.

The Italian was even more imperious at the Tour. He won his first stage at Alpe d'Huez, where his victory highlighted the contrast in style with race leader Miguel Induráin, already well on the way to his fifth consecutive title. Coming onto the famous ascent with its 21 hairpins up to the ski station, Pantani was tucked into the yellow jersey group where the pace was being set by a line of Induráin's

Banesto teammates. The TV cameras cut away just before this group reaches the first switchback on the steepest part of the climb, focusing briefly on the gaggle of escapees a few hundred metres ahead. When the focus returns to the favourites, Pantani has just breezed away from them, French champion Laurent Madouas hanging gamely on his wheel until he realizes he can't possibly match the Italian's pace.

As he presses on, gobbling up each of the breakaways in trademark fashion that earned him the nickname 'Pac-Man', Induráin sits in behind teammate Gérard Rué, monitoring his closest GC rivals. Pantani, 14 minutes down, is not on his radar. The Italian might have an edge on the big Spaniard in the mountains, but the truth is that, as had been the case with so many previous match-ups between climber and GC hitter, we'll never know because they're in different races. Unlike Induráin, Pantani has nothing to lose. His final victim, ten kilometres from the summit, is long-time rival Ivan Gotti, a sudden quickening of Pantani's cadence splintering the urgent rhythm of his compatriot, who's insouciantly swatted aside, a hammer-like blow delivered with a velvet glove that leaves Gotti visibly reeling.

The third victory in the set was quite different to the first two. For a start, in a sign that he was growing into the role of high-altitude provocateur, he predicted it the night before in an interview with Italian broadcaster RAI. Yet, while everyone was expecting it, few could have imagined that Carrera's blistering pace into the first steep ramps of the Port de Lers, with 40 kilometres and another 3 climbs remaining, was not a softening-up process that would be maintained over most of that distance but a brief prelude before Pantani's offensive commenced. 'Ah, *bene*! Pantani's attacked and the stage is starting to liven up,' says RAI TV commentator Adriano De Zan as the elfin climber closes in on Tony Rominger and Ramón González

Arrieta, a couple of hundred metres ahead of the peloton, neither able to raise their pace as the Italian eases by on their left. Moments later, escapees Maarten den Bakker and Jean-Cyril Robin suffer the same fate, and, as he enters the thick woods through which the narrow strip of road rises towards the Port de Lers, De Zan declares, '*Un uomo solo al comando . . . Marco Pantani*' – the reference to Fausto Coppi unmissable, especially to the millions watching the coverage in Italy for whom the fragile climber had already become a sporting hero.

Pantani's aggressive approach to mountain stages – he was the winner by two and a half minutes after leading over the Lers, Agnes and Latrape passes – contrasts not only with that of Induráin and other GC leaders, but also with other riders who made their careers on the climbs, notably Richard Virenque, then on the way to the second of what would be seven King of the Mountains titles, one more than the previous record held by Federico Bahamontes and Lucien Van Impe. There's no doubt the Frenchman was a strong climber, but he was one who very rarely managed to *fare il vuoto* and get a gap on the very best in this terrain. Unlike Pantani, who was beset by vulnerability and strove to allay this with hugely dramatic athletic gestures, always attacking from the group of favourites, Virenque was a cycling Fagin who played the angles, often attacking on stages where the GC leaders were likely to sit tight, and, very obviously, he took advantage of the work other teams and riders did on the climbs before nipping around them at the last, pickpocketing the King of the Mountains points.

After that high, another low followed three months later, when a Jeep found its way onto the course at the season-ending Milan–Turin semi-Classic, and Pantani was hit by it when descending at

80kph, the impact shattering his left leg so seriously that there were fears about whether he would be able to race again. The accident also revealed what in hindsight would prove to be a more critical concern. Doctors who treated him at Turin's Centro Traumatologico Ortopedico were bewildered by his blood levels. His haematocrit (red blood cell count) was 60.1 per cent, considerably higher than the normal range between 40 and 50 per cent and well above what was then the permitted safe level for competition of 50 per cent that had been set by the UCI. This value plummeted to a quarter of that within a week, requiring a blood transfusion, then returned to normal levels. The abnormality highlighted that Pantani had been receiving injections of genetically engineered EPO to boost his red blood cell count, these taking place sufficiently frequently that his own body had stopped producing the hormone. What's more, the head physician at the hospital, Professor Massimo Cartasegna, told an Italian court in 2000 that he believed Pantani had been receiving EPO injections during his hospitalization without the knowledge of the medical staff attending to him.

He was, we now know, far from alone in this practice. Virenque would eventually confess to using the product during his time with the Festina team. Bjarne Riis, winner of the 1996 Tour that Pantani missed, also admitted he had used EPO to win the yellow jersey, while Lance Armstrong would, much later, acknowledge that he had taken the same banned product during the seven Tour victories that he was later stripped of for sporting fraud. Yet, when Pantani eventually returned to racing in 1997 at the head of a Mercatone Uno team that was built almost entirely around him in the classic Italian mould, the lack of an EPO test and the consequent dependence by the sport's ruling body on the 50 per cent haematocrit limit – which had been introduced 'for health reasons' but only forced riders found to have a higher percentage to sit out from racing for a fortnight before being able to compete again – he continued almost unchecked.

After a stuttering start to the season, partly as a result of a crash at the Giro when a black cat crossed his path, 'Il Pirata' re-emerged at the Tour, initially at Alpe d'Huez once again. He reprised 1995's winning method, but introduced a new touch, removing his peaked *casquette* and casting it away, a ritual that would signal his readiness to attack and would become part of a longer striptease. Then came the acceleration. Within a couple of hundred metres, Pantani had just three riders on his wheel: King of the Mountains Virenque, yellow jersey Jan Ullrich and the young German's teammate Bjarne Riis. As the Italian sprinted up through the lower hairpins, hands on the drops as he danced on the pedals, his characteristic style allowing the TV camera to pick out the pirate motif on his saddle, the 1996 champion yielded first. Next, Virenque gave a little shake of the head and slipped back. Ullrich lasted just a little longer before he too conceded. This was an archetypal instance of a cycling David taking out *les grandes carcasses*, the peloton's Goliaths, with a precisely aimed and majestically delivered blow, an irresistible triumph for the sporting underdog, achieved, it should be noted, with the fastest-ever ascent of Alpe d'Huez at a touch under 37 minutes.

As with Charly Gaul in 1958, Federico Bahamontes in 1959, Lucien Van Impe in 1976, Pedro Delgado in 1988 and Andy Schleck in 2010, Pantani's Tour victory in 1998 required a very particular set of circumstances to unfold and offer the opportunity to a pure climber to upset the established order, which favours riders with much greater all-round capability. This doesn't lessen their achievement so much as once again highlight to what extent the odds are always stacked against racers who are completely dependent on the mountains offering them a competitive edge. Pantani acknowledged this when, following the October presentation in Paris of the following 1998 season's Tour route, he criticized a *parcours* that featured just two summit finishes: at the tiny Pyrenean cross-country station of Plateau de Beille and at Les Deux Alpes, the neighbouring resort to Alpe d'Huez. He focused instead on his own national tour, where the organizers RCS held resolutely to their by then well-established trend of going heavy on the mountains and limiting the time trials to less than a hundred kilometres in total.

The battle for the *maglia rosa* became a duel between Pantani, who took the lead halfway through the race's final week on a fearsome stage over four Dolomite passes into Val Gardena that was won by Giuseppe Guerini, and Pavel Tonkov, a doughty and stony-faced Russian who edged 'Il Pirata' on Alpe di Pampeago the next day. The showdown came a day later on the *corsa rosa*'s fourth and final summit finish at Plan di Montecampione, in the Alps north of Brescia. Reaching it, Pantani cast off his cap, then let Mercatone Uno teammates Dmitri Konyshev and Massimo Podenzana set the tempo for the opening few kilometres of the climb. When he sensed the Italian was slowing, Pantani quickened by, with Tonkov the only rider able to match his pace. Over the next dozen or so kilometres, the stoic Russian matched the Italian's regular bursts, until, with less than three kilometres to go, Pantani finally sprang clear, first sensing the gap was opening, then taking flight as it widened, the *tifosi* jumping with glee at the roadside as he swept past them, millions more equally jubilant in front of their television screens. The Giro was his.

Thanks to France's hosting of the World Cup, there were four weeks instead of the usual three between the Giro and Tour, but Pantani didn't initially consider doubling up. His change of heart came with the death of his mentor Luciano Pezzi in late June. At his funeral ten days before the Tour was due to start in Dublin, Pantani told DS Giuseppe Martinelli of his decision, made as a tribute to Pezzi, who had played an instrumental role in putting the Mercatone Uno team together.

As the teams and the rest of the Tour entourage gathered for the start in Dublin, the traditional pre-race conjecture and predictions were sidelined by the news that a Festina soigneur, Willy Voet, the masseur of French darling Virenque, had been stopped at the France–Belgium border with a vast supply of doping products, including EPO. From that point, twin narratives developed, revelations about 'the Festina affair' competing for headlines with the action on the road. By the time the race had reached Luchon for the stage to Plateau de Beille, Festina manager Bruno Roussel had confessed to systematic doping within the team, Tour boss Jean-Marie Leblanc had expelled Festina from the race, while defending champion Jan Ullrich had taken the yellow jersey, lost it, then regained it. Pantani, now sporting a moustache and goatee together with what had become his de rigueur pirate bandanna, was on the threshold of the top ten, almost five minutes down on Ullrich, but boosted by a gain of 23 seconds with an attack over the Peyresourde pass the day before and, a 2013 French Senate report into doping revealed, an injection of EPO.

Pantani's plan was to attack right at the foot of Plateau de Beille and the bandanna was tossed away as the preliminary to this. But he held off when told that Ullrich had punctured approaching the climb and was still being led back up to the group containing his rivals – one of the inconsistencies of this period was a strict adherence to the unwritten rule of not attacking the yellow jersey when he'd punctured or crashed, while at the same time methodically taking banned products and repeatedly insisting that you weren't. Once the German had returned to the front, dropping his teammates in his panic to achieve this, Pantani waited briefly, then went. The yellow jersey chased for 200 metres, but had to relent. Like Coppi at his best, once Pantani had got the gap, it was only going to get bigger. Victory promoted him to fourth place, three minutes behind Ullrich.

In the immediate aftermath of that success, *La Repubblica*'s Gianni Mura asked the stage-winner why he climbed so fast, a question that almost any other rider would respond to with a pat explanation of better focus on training, the input of a new coach, or perhaps experience providing better management of physical resources. Pantani, however, replied gnomically, saying, 'To abbreviate my agony.' It's a brilliant summation of the climber's art. Four words that say everything about racing at your limit up a mountain. Yet his response also fitted with the mythology and mystique that was building around Pantani: his portrayal as a rider apart, and even as the Tour's and cycling's saviour while the race continued its descent towards drug-induced meltdown. This sense of hidden depths, of mystique, was fed also by the Italian's old-school approach to the sport, going out training with slices of watermelon and a handful of nuts in his jersey pockets, drinking from roadside fountains, eschewing the use of technology such as a heart rate monitor. Mura had himself said, 'the fascination of Pantani was that of an undiscovered island or continent'.

Daniel Friebe suggests that this tendency to lionize Pantani, perhaps even to see depths that were actually only shallows, stems partly from the characteristics that have always been attached to climbers, elevating them because we feel that they have some kind of mystical relationship with the mountains themselves.

> You can talk about that feeling of racers being pushed into a different dimension by the physical effort they're making in all forms of cycling, but I think only when you're talking about mountains does it really bring in that almost epic dimension of conquering nature. Particularly in the case of Pantani, Charly Gaul and some others, there's also a sense of a relationship with and almost a mirroring of the mountains, in the sense that mountains are silent, they're stormy, they're enigmatic. I think we often project the same qualities onto certain of those who we define as pure climbers. They are kind of mirror images of the natural obstacles that they're conquering in a certain way.

Pantani, a slight and fragile figure who looked like the archetypal underdog, became a lightning rod for this acclamation because he was the incarnation of almost all of the qualities that we revere in climbers. He had the perfect style of Gaul, the grace of Bahamontes, the ballsiness of Fuente and Bartali, the class and killer instinct of Coppi, the tendency for theatre of Vietto, the diminutive stature and vulnerability of Trueba and Jiménez. He was the epitome of *sprezzatura* and fired by *duende*, which drew thrilling performances from him, but also led him into the abyss and, ultimately, to a tragically premature and lonely death.

All these attributes were displayed on what would be the defining victory of his career at Les Deux Alpes. Run in driving rain and in chilling temperatures, the stage from Grenoble crossed the Croix de Fer and Télégraphe passes to reach the critical ascent of the Col du Galibier. Climbing from the ski station of Valloire, the road runs due south to Plan Lachat, where it switches back over the Valloirette river and starts to rise more steeply towards the 2,642-metre summit, still 8 kilometres away. With almost two of these completed, Luc Leblanc attacks, Adriano De Zan, who had just been highlighting the presence of fans from all over Italy on the climb, declaring on RAI's coverage, 'Attention, this is a very important moment . . .' His co-commentator, ex-pro Davide Cassani, concurs, describing how, 'Pantani has his hands on the drops, Ullrich keeps turning to look at him, this could be a good place to attack . . .' As if prompted by Cassani's words, Pantani accelerates away, instantly forging a gap. Ten seconds into his offensive, he pauses in mid-pedal stroke and glances back over his right shoulder to see if the German is chasing. There is a figure coming out of the murk towards him, but it's Leblanc, not the yellow jersey. Then he goes again. '*Pantani ha fatto il vuoto,*' De Zan declares a few moments later.

At the summit, where Mercatone Uno directeur sportif Orlando Maini is waiting in the road to hand Pantani a rain-jacket, the Italian's advantage is just over three minutes, making him the Tour's virtual leader. He's lucid enough to stop a kilometre or so down the mountain to pull his flapping jacket on securely, a manoeuvre that enables Christophe Rinero and José María Jiménez, breakaways dropped just before the crest of the Galibier, to regain contact and, crucially, share the pace-making with him down to the Lautaret pass and on the long, steady drop into a headwind from there to the foot of Les Deux Alpes, during which they're joined by three more riders. Ullrich, on the other hand, doesn't get a jacket and, following a puncture approaching the final climb, repeats the mistake he made at Plateau de Beille by chasing back with too much gusto. When he starts to climb again, now four minutes behind Pantani, he looks like he's pedalling through treacle.

'Pantani, with his way of racing that's instinctive and creative, based on a talent that's beautiful but can also be defined as a bit naïve because he doesn't calculate but instead makes big attacks on any climb, is returning the sport to its most beautiful dimension,' says Cassani when the Italian is halfway up the climb. He's right, or at least at that moment he was, because even as that Tour sank into the mire of doping and deceit, Pantani rose above it and was lauded for saving the race and the sport with a performance that was a throwback to the glory days of Coppi and Bartali, turning a three-minute deficit on Ullrich into a six-minute lead. The last time the Tour had seen anything that compared to this was Luis Ocaña's dismantling of Eddy Merckx in 1971.

The next day, the front page of *L'Équipe* featured a picture of Pantani attacking on the Galibier with the headline '*C'est un Géant*'. 'When he crossed the line, he closed his eyes and spread his arms, like Christ on the cross. This man was forged in suffering,' wrote Jean-Michel Rouet inside the sports daily, before listing the Italian rider's many injuries and setbacks, then suggesting he'd given 'an extraordinary lesson in perseverance, in courage, in grandeur . . . his charisma and genius returning to us the legend of the solitary rider in the storm, the legend of Fausto Coppi and of Charly Gaul'. Gianni Mura, too, highlighted this Christ-like moment, suggesting that it was almost like Pantani was saying, 'I could have done less, but I carried my cross and did it for you.'

Once again, though, the reality was more prosaic. As he crossed the line, Pantani did throw his arms to the side, but then quickly brought them together with a self-congratulatory clap above his head, just as he had done at Plateau de Beille, at Piancavallo and at Montecampione. As with some of his curious comments, which, says Daniel Friebe, 'if you thought that you were in the presence of some kind of shaman, then all of a sudden it took on this pseudo-religious significance', it was a case of seeing something that wasn't there, but overlooking the evidence of what was there.

This changed on the pre-penultimate day of the 1999 Giro, when, after claiming his fourth summit victory at Madonna di Campiglio, Pantani took a blood test that recorded his haematocrit at 52 per cent, two above the permitted limit. Forced to leave the race, he didn't compete again that season. Now hounded rather than lionized by the press, he also became caught up in a series of legal investigations that would drag on for the next few years. Humiliated by his very public downfall, he railed against the injustice of his expulsion from the Giro, declared himself to be a clean rider, asserted that he would never touch a bike again and that he was the victim of plots and conspiracies.

'If I know Marco, he will never recover from this disgrace,' said Giuseppe Martinelli. Sadly, the Mercatone Uno directeur's comment would prove prescient. The paranoia, self-doubt and vulnerability that had been cloaked by his success on the road overwhelmed Pantani. Cocaine became his lifeboat.

He did make comebacks, notably in 2000 when he returned to the Tour. He won the stage to Mont Ventoux after a duel up the final kilometres of the famous peak with the Tour's new champion, Lance Armstrong. 'I could have accelerated again, but what point would there have been?' the American said at the finish, acknowledging that he'd gifted the win as a mark of respect to the Italian. Pantani, though, saw the act as a slight. Angered by Armstrong's gesture and words, he offered a riposte on the road, first by winning the stage over the mighty Galibier and Madeleine passes into Courchevel, then, as the feud over events on the Ventoux raged again on the rest day that followed this, by attacking 130 kilometres out on the next stage to Morzine with the express idea of torpedoing the American's progress to a second Tour title. Although this was in vain, the pressure that Pantani had applied led to Armstrong suffering one of the few bad moments during his seven-year Tour reign on the stage's final ascent of the Joux Plane.

This short flurry of contests between a rider at the peak of his form and one for whom the success in Courchevel was the last of his career marked the changeover between the old world order of climbing and the new. Pantani was the link to the past, almost born in the wrong era, who said of himself, 'I like to listen to what my body and the mountains are telling me, nothing else.' You watched him because, as with Diego Maradona, another brilliant but flawed athlete, there was always the possibility that he would produce something exceptional, a feeling beautifully encapsulated by Italian writer Marco Pastonesi. 'Pantani's every acceleration is a little treasure, which no one needs to keep secret; it's money in the bank, in the bank of our senses and memory, free money', he wrote.

Armstrong, on the other hand, was clinical, ruthless and, ultimately, predictable. You knew he was going to win. As he did so, there was no sense of him trying to capture or resonate with the mythology of the mountains. There was no romance. The Tour route was just a race track. It often looked impressive, but it wasn't stirring. Speaking to *Cyclingnews* on the tenth anniversary of Pantani's death in 2014, the American professed: 'If I was the carpenter, then he was the artist. He had all the panache in the world, all the panache you could fit into a small climber, and I, if I'm honest, didn't have that.' What's more, as the victories stacked up, so did the doubts and questions about his probity, and these became more captivating than his performances on the road as evidence gradually piled up indicating that the renewal that was heralded for the sport in 1999 had never taken place.

After news emerged of Pantani's death in a hotel room in Rimini due to a drug overdose on 14 February 2004, Gianni Mura wrote that 'Il Pirata' 'would probably become a myth, like they always do when they die young'. The many monuments that have appeared in his memory or marking the locations of his exploits, as well as his undimmed popularity, confirm that Mura was right. The Giro organizers were quick to contribute to this, paying homage every year since his death with a *Montagna Pantani*', a climb on the race route that had particular significance during the Italian's career. In 2020, it was Piancavallo, the setting for the first of his three stage wins in 1998 – that edition also visited Rimini, his home town of Cesenatico and Madonna di Campiglio. When, in 2021, the race held a knock-out poll to select the fans' favourite rider in the Giro's history, Pantani came out on top, beating Fausto Coppi in the final match-up after more than a million votes had been received.

His ongoing popularity can be explained partly by the depth of Italy's cycling culture and the awareness that so many of the sport's heroes have been tainted by questions and scandals relating to doping, including Coppi, Merckx and Moser, and a long-standing acceptance of this. Pantani is also viewed as a victim of a corrupt system, the fall guy for so many others who got away with the same transgressions, including Armstrong, who we now know was shielded by the UCI's leadership despite strong evidence that he was doping. Equally, the polls and Giro tributes feed the mythology that has always made Pantani such a compelling athlete and personality, leading to the disconnect where he's portrayed as a martyr for a sport that was mired in deception and venality.

Ultimately, though, the idolization of Pantani stems from his unforgettable exploits when racing in the mountains. Writing in French magazine *Pédale!*, Lucas Duvernet-Coppola and Stéphane Régy described how:

> We didn't love him because he used to win . . . We loved him because he upset the odds and brought the strong men down, the favourites and title-holders, Induráin, Tonkov and Ullrich. We loved him because life didn't offer him any presents . . . We loved him because he appeared fallible, and he actually was. We loved him, above all, because we felt that when he accelerated again and again that there was something more than a simple victory at stake, but what?

And so the myth continues . . .

Chapter 14

All aboard the Sky Train

In view of Andy Hampsten's comment about his competitive career being 'over' once blood-boosting practices began to flow through the peloton in the mid-1990s, the downfall of Marco Pantani at Madonna di Campiglio, and the subsequent confessions of EPO use by Tour de France winners Bjarne Riis, Jan Ullrich and, most famously of all, Lance Armstrong, it's reasonable to wonder when, if at all, performances in the mountains and indeed every other kind of terrain became credible again. Bearing in mind subsequent scandals that saw Floyd Landis stripped of the 2006 Tour crown after a positive test, Michael Rasmussen's removal by his Rabobank team from the 2007 Tour when he was on the verge of winning it after it was revealed that he had lied about his whereabouts in order to avoid out-of-competition anti-doping controls, and Alberto Contador's disqualification as the 2010 Tour winner following a positive test for the bronchodilator clenbuterol, you might wonder if they ever have done. I'll admit that the absolute cynicism that filled me between the late 1990s and the early years of the twenty-first century's second decade took many years to dissipate and still bubbles up after performances that strike me as unusual.

In March 2015, the Cycling Independent Reform Commission (CIRC), which had been established by the UCI, the sports ruling body, produced a comprehensive, if not completely convincing, answer to questions about cycling's credibility in the shape of a 228-page report detailing the year-long investigation by its 3-member panel into doping within professional road racing, and with a particular focus on the role the UCI had played over the previous 25 years. The report underlined that, historically, 'the culture of doping grew from an approach to the sport where taking performance enhancement substances was not illegal and indeed was perhaps seen as "the done thing"'. Up to the late 1980s, the products used were principally stimulants such as alcohol, cocaine and amphetamines. From that point, there was a change towards the use of EPO, which was described as a 'game changer' due to a reported 10 to 15 per cent increase in performance, and, from 2001, blood transfusions and microdosing – the administration of small amounts of EPO – which persisted to 2007.

Focusing on the ruling body, the report stated 'that decisions taken by the UCI leadership in the past have undermined anti-doping efforts', and highlighted numerous violations of the federation's own anti-doping rules and good governance, as well as collusion with certain riders, most notably Armstrong, the tone of this relationship having been set by an incident during the 1999 Tour when the American's doctors provided a backdated prescription for cortisone after he tested positive for the drug. 'The UCI failed to apply its own rules', the report stated bluntly. Armstrong should have been kicked off the race before he took his first victory that year.

According to the report, anti-doping initiatives, and particularly the 2008 introduction of the Athlete Biological Passport (ABP) – designed to monitor selected biological variables over time that indirectly reveal the effects of doping rather than attempting to detect the doping substance or method itself – signalled an end to what had been 'endemic' doping within cycling. In the three years following its introduction, twenty riders tested positive for EPO as a result of targeted controls carried out after blood abnormalities were flagged up. Yet, the CIRC also underlined that it was hard to establish the extent of doping, some of its interviewees suggesting it had almost been eradicated, others that use of banned products was still widespread, although it was generally recognized that the performance increase provided by drugs had dropped substantially and to the point where clean riders could once again hold their own in races. In short, the situation still wasn't perfect, but was far improved on what it had been prior to 2008.

The shift back from scepticism towards belief has been slow and halting. By the second decade of this century, though, spectacle finally began to replace scandal as the main dish at the Grand Tours. If there was one race that encapsulated this, it was the 2011 Tour de France, which was by general agreement the best since the eight-second race of 1989 when Greg LeMond edged out Laurent Fignon by a mere eight seconds following the final day time trial that finished on the Champs-Élysées. There were initially two drivers in this: first, the route, which exemplified race director Christian Prudhomme's determination to draw the yellow jersey favourites front and centre in the opening week. The second trigger was Thomas Voeckler taking the lead just before the first rest day. The Frenchman's terrier-like defence of the jersey from that point meant that there was still a possibility of a first home winner since 1986 with the race just four days from Paris.

Voeckler's lead was little more than a minute over Cadel Evans and Fränk Schleck, with Andy Schleck two and a half minutes behind in fourth place, but he'd only lost a couple of dozen seconds to these riders, all much stronger climbers, at two summit finishes in the Pyrenees. Could he limit his losses to similar minimal amounts in the Alps? Fired up by the yellow fever that can raise the performance of a Tour leader, Voeckler and French fans were starting to believe he could as the riders prepared for a fearsome mountain stage that commemorated the centenary of the Tour's first passage through the high Alps and culminated for the first time in history on the top of the Col du Galibier. The Frenchman only needed to defend his position, as did Evans, the strongest time triallist of the quartet, who would have an advantage in the 42.5-kilometre Grenoble TT on the penultimate day. The Schlecks, though, needed to gain time on both of their rivals. If either of them were to win, they needed to have a cushion of at least two minutes going into that time trial.

Younger brother Andy had been mulling over a plan for this stage since the Pyrenees, where the pair had failed to make any useful gains. Rather than wait for the final ascent of the Galibier to attack, he was pondering an offensive on the previous climb of the Col d'Izoard, with 60 kilometres or more to the finish. He'd mentioned it to Leopard Trek teammate Stuart O'Grady, who'd told him, 'Andy, you can do this. I believe in you.' During the pre-stage team briefing on their bus in Pinerolo, Andy laid out his plan. Some of his teammates were sceptical, Maxime Monfort describing it as 'PlayStation cycling', and adding that it was unlikely to work. 'It was nice to hear that the team was ambitious, but this, I thought, was too much. Modern cycling does not work like this', said the Belgian in Richard Moore's *Étape*. Leopard DS Kim Andersen wasn't convinced either, pointing out that there was likely to be a strong headwind on the long drag up to the Col du Lautaret, where the riders would turn onto the 8.5-kilometre ascent of the Galibier. 'Let me do it, I want to try,' said Schleck.

The stage unfolded as the Luxembourger had hoped it would. Teammate Joost Posthuma got into the seven-man break and was soon joined by Monfort as the escape swelled to sixteen. Approaching and then climbing the southern flank of the Izoard, Posthuma did the bulk of the pace-making to ensure the break stayed five minutes or so ahead, then, with five kilometres to the summit, he pulled aside and dropped back. At almost the same instant, Schleck, who had been sitting on O'Grady's right at the front of the peloton, accelerated away. After a glance back to check that no one was following what seemed like a kamikaze attack from so far out, the Leopard leader powered on, joining Posthuma coming into the dramatic scree and rock formations of the Casse Déserte towards the top of the Izoard, where the Dutch domestique upped his pace for a few hundred metres, allowing Schleck a chance to recuperate before he surged past in pursuit of Montfort in the lead group.

Reflecting on the stage in an interview with Luxembourg paper *Le Quotidien*, the Leopard Trek climber confessed that he'd made a mistake at this point by leaving Posthuma. 'If I'd stayed with him it would have made a two-minute difference. But I was nervy, I'll admit. Instead of one guy, I could have had two guys with me. That's where I made a mistake,' he said, alluding to the time that he might well have gained in the valley between the Izoard and Galibier with two teammates pacing him.

Two minutes clear of the yellow jersey group cresting the Izoard, Schleck joined forces with Monfort. The pair flew down into

Briançon and onto the long and headwindy haul up to the Lautaret, on the southern 'shoulder' of the Galibier. With occasional help from other breakaway riders they had picked up, but with Monfort setting the tempo for the most part, they extended their advantage over Voeckler and the other yellow jersey contenders to almost four minutes. When Monfort yielded, Schleck took up the tempo himself, Nicolas Roche and Maxim Iglinskiy either unwilling or unable to do no more than sit on his wheel – the latter it soon transpired, as first the Irishman fell back.

Nearing the Lautaret, Schleck's lead was close to four and a half minutes, giving him an advantage of two on Voeckler and three on Evans, who had decided to take responsibility for what had hitherto been a faltering pursuit. Schleck told *Le Quotidien*:

> If I'd stayed in the wheels, the leaders' teammates would have kept on doing their usual work and the leaders wouldn't have had to work. My idea was to force them to work. I kept riding at 420 to 430 watts, all the time. Who could ride at those power levels? Cadel, Alberto Contador, only the leaders. My plan worked even though most of my teammates thought that it wouldn't.

After Iglinskiy dropped away on the early slopes of the Galibier, Schleck was all but guaranteed the stage win. But could he take the lead? That all depended on how he matched up against Evans in what was effectively a mountain time trial to the summit of the Galibier. The Luxembourger, tall and extremely lean, composed and graceful as he pedalled, hands on the top of his bars, an occasional and fluid dance on the pedals helping to maintain his momentum, won the contest on style. His smoothness gave the impression he was making faster progress. Evans, teeth gritted and eyes hidden behind dark lenses, the epitome of the Aussie battler, like cricketer Allan Border on a bike, his style punchier and cadence a touch slower, didn't look as comfortable, particularly with the rest of the favourites sitting on his wheel apparently waiting to attack. He was, though, pushing a bigger gear than the lone leader. He chiselled steadily away at Schleck's lead. In the final kilometre, the steepest on this flank, the Leopard Trek climber lost the thick end of a minute. At the line, the yellow jersey eluded him by 15 seconds, as Voeckler retained the lead. Although he'd slipped from second to fourth, Evans was just 57 seconds behind the Luxembourger. As expected, the Australian gained more than twice that amount in Grenoble, and the title was his, Andy Schleck finishing second in Paris and Fränk third.

'I didn't want to finish fourth in Paris. I wanted to risk everything. It either worked or it didn't,' said Schleck after that Galibier stage, adding that he had no fears about inflicting the pain on himself that his break had demanded. 'He has something inside of him that is really special, like a killer instinct. He can push himself to the point where he forgets everything around him,' said Karsten Kroon, who was Schleck's teammate at CSC for four seasons. 'He could hurt himself so bad you cannot imagine.'

This ability of racers, especially climbers, to self-hurt will be examined later, so let's pick up on two aspects of that Galibier stage that would have particular significance in the mountains over the next few seasons, starting with Schleck's comment about obliging the other team leaders to respond to his 'Hail Mary' attack. His bet that his tactic had a good chance of producing a dividend was based on sound logic, primarily the fact that the team defending the yellow jersey, Voeckler's Europcar, was in the sport's second division. Like the rider himself, they were solid performers who made the very best of the opportunity they had, but they were not well equipped for the task of nursing a rider through the biggest race of the season. Moreover, although the Tour wasn't in an interregnum period because Contador, the winner of three of the previous four Tours did start and was backed by a very strong team, the Spaniard's resources had been sapped by riding and winning the Giro a few weeks earlier and also by the ongoing uncertainty over a possible ban for his clenbuterol positive at the 2010 Tour – in February 2012, his ban was confirmed, one result of which was Schleck being declared the victor of that Tour.

Schleck's raid was also well timed for a reason few could have foreseen. A new order was coming, imposed by a team whose top finisher had been way back in twenty-fourth place in that Tour. In what was their second year in the peloton, Team Sky had gone into that race with extremely high expectations of contending for the title after Bradley Wiggins had won the Critérium du Dauphiné, where Evans had been the distant runner-up. Unfortunately for the Londoner, having worked his way up to sixth place on GC heading into stage seven, he got caught up in a crash that left him on the deck with a broken collarbone. Out of the Tour, Wiggins opted in to the Vuelta, which would prove a pivotal race for him, his team and one of his teammates.

The sixty-sixth edition of Spain's national tour showcased the race's recent resurgence. Overshadowed for many years by the Giro as well as the Tour, it attracted a strong field, produced the third closest finish in Vuelta history, had nine different leaders and – although it took another eight years to be confirmed – two different winners. It started disastrously for Sky, who finished twentieth in the Benidorm team time trial, a discipline that was usually one of their strengths. Asked where it had gone wrong, Swedish rider Thomas Löfkvist answered, 'The uphills, the downhills and the corners', adding, 'there were misunderstandings'. Yet, 24 hours later, they were celebrating sprinter Chris Sutton winning in Orihuela. After Peter Sagan had grabbed his first Grand Tour win in Córdoba and Dan Martin had emulated him atop La Covatilla, Chris Froome became the seventh leader in ten days when he finished second to Tony Martin in the mid-race time trial at Salamanca, where his leader Wiggins was third. Would this change Sky's game plan?

The following stage to the Manzaneda ski station provided the answer. After their teammates had set the pace into the climb, Xabier Zandio, Löfkvist and then Morris Possoni kept the tempo high on the front. When the latter ran out of gas, there was a flurry of attacks, little climbers with dynamite in their pedals like Joaquim Rodríguez and Dani Moreno prominent, while Wiggins was suddenly isolated and looking around for support. Then the cavalry arrived. Having been enveloped by the pack when those rapid-fire attacks had kicked off, Froome had found his groove and was up to cruising speed. With Wiggins tucked in on his wheel, the Briton set a consistently fast rhythm. Attacks still came from behind, but on each occasion, the red jersey of Froome quickly led the peloton back up to the escapees.

Finally, with three kilometres remaining, an attack by Dan Martin ended Froome's show of force, only to trigger a similar demonstration of power and consistency from Wiggins. It wasn't spectacular, but it was very impressive and equally effective, the group behind the Englishman thinning out as he time-trialled to the line and into the leader's jersey.

Ultimately, Wiggins and Sky's hopes splintered on the horribly steep tarmac-coated goat track leading to the Alto de l'Angliru, where surprise package Juan José Cobo – himself undone by abnormal biological passport readings eight years later – took victory and the lead. But what became the Sky Grand Tour method had been successfully road tested. Better still, the Vuelta had revealed a hidden Grand Tour talent in Froome. Not selected for the Tour that year, he was on the verge of being released by the team until that Vuelta performance.

By the time the 2012 Tour came around, he was an integral part of the Sky 'train' that set the pace for Wiggins in the mountains, Australians Michael Rogers and Richie Porte being the other two key engines in upland terrain. Befitting a team from Britain, where time trials have traditionally been central in the racing scene, Sky set the 2012 Tour up as what was effectively a series of team time trial tests, each rider assigned a position and a task on key days, pulling over when they'd fulfilled it, as their next teammate came through. The strategy stripped the romance from mountain stages, in the same way that Banesto and US Postal's approach had, but proved just as effective for Sky as it did for those teams. Wiggins took the title in Paris, with Froome the runner-up in a race that British fans will remember fondly but that was much less captivating than the previous year's show-stopper.

Sky's method would prove to be the best version ever of cycling *catenaccio*, the tactical system in football that has a strong emphasis on defence and nullifying the opposition, and that proved so effective for Italian teams during the 1960s and 1970s. 'It was negative, it was all about protecting a lead, everything that, say, the 1986 Tour wasn't,' says Andy Hampsten.

My friend Sean Yates was the Sky directeur sportif and I heard him say the worst words when he was asked what the team would do during that Tour, whether he would send Froome up the road because he was in second place. And he was like, 'No, we're not Bernard Hinault. We're not going to go swashbuckling up the road with our second-placed GC man.' I just wanted to throw the TV at him. You should go swashbuckling, but his team just wasn't going to. They followed US Postal tactically, protecting the lead with strong riders at the front, buying up climbers to do tempo at the front, which Miguel Induráin did particularly well on the Tour.

As Hampsten indicates, the British team made good use of the biggest budget in the sport, above all when it came to bringing in riders to support Wiggins and Froome. Michael Rogers and Christian Knees arrived in 2011, Richie Porte in 2012, Vasil Kiryienka in 2013, Mikel Nieve in 2014, Wout Poels in 2015, Michał Kwiatkowski in 2016, Jonathan Castroviejo and Dylan van Baarle in 2018, each of them becoming critical links in the chain. The team also focused on their core of homegrown talent that's included stalwarts such as Ian Stannard, Luke Rowe and Geraint Thomas, the domestique who became so super that he ended up winning the yellow jersey for himself in 2018. Over those years, the only occasions they missed out on the Tour title were in 2011 and 2014 due to race-ending crashes for Wiggins and Froome, their respective leaders in those editions.

The best tribute to Sky's approach has been the way that other teams have mimicked it. When I spoke during the 2018 Tour to Richard Plugge, manager of what was then LottoNL-Jumbo and has subsequently became Jumbo-Visma, he told me the Dutch outfit were watching Sky closely, employing some of the British outfit's 'marginal gains' while endeavouring to find some of their own. As Primož Roglič began to emerge as a veritable Grand Tour contender and, in 2019, Jumbo took over a lead sponsor, providing a big budgetary boost at the same time, the Dutch team began to beef up both its Grand Tour attack and its support crew, Tony Martin, Wout van Aert and Mike Teunissen arriving that season, Tom Dumoulin the next. The result was what many rival riders described as the most powerful train ever put together. During the 2020 Tour, Jumbo reached the foot of the final climb on mountain stages with as many as six riders working for Roglič, more akin to the lead-out for a bunch sprint than a mountain-top finish.

It was hugely impressive, but the strategy was undermined by one fundamental flaw. Jumbo's leader wasn't the race's strong man. As the Dutch team led the Slovenian around France, his young compatriot Tadej Pogačar was tucked in on his wheel. When it came to the final time trial on the penultimate day to the Vosges ski station of La Planche des Belles Filles, the precocious UAE Team Emirates leader blitzed his countryman in unforgettable fashion to seize the yellow jersey at the very last.

Yet even before that astonishing success, Pogačar's team were already going down the same path as Sky and Jumbo by recruiting a string of experienced and highly talented three-week performers to support their precocious leader, such as Davide Formolo, Rafał Majka, Marc Hirschi and, for 2022, George Bennett, João Almeida and Marc Soler.

The finessing of this strategy has occurred as a consequence of better understanding of physiological preparation, underpinned by the knowledge and instant feedback that power meters supply in training and, most crucially, when racing. 'Everyone is focusing on their numbers,' says Nicolas Roche, who raced as a GC leader in his early years before becoming a mountain domestique and road captain for Alberto Contador and then for Froome at Sky. Said the Irishman during the 2021 season, his final one after seventeen years in the peloton:

> The playing of games that we used to see in the mountains, riders looking at each other, attacking each other to break their rhythm and trying to make sure your opponent isn't going to come back, that was the approach when Alberto and Andy Schleck were at their peak in 2010. No one was really looking at watts or whatever, it was more on feeling.
>
> When you're climbing, it's now more a case of knowing yourself by having those numbers, and not racing on feeling as much. It's more scientific. It's a little bit less about what the others can do and more about what you can do. When riders are climbing now, they drop the wheel before they crack, going at their own pace that they can sustain rather than pushing over the limit. When you see a guy disappear from the TV pictures, another five minutes will pass and, although he's not back on the wheel, he's still only ten seconds behind. Before, when you exploded that was it. It was a matter of survival to the top. Now, no one really explodes any more, everyone paces themselves, it's a completely different feeling.

Roche elucidates how this might play out on an individual basis.

> Apart from the very strongest one or two guys, most riders are thinking, 'OK, today the climb is about twenty-two minutes, my average power for that should be around 6.1 watts per kilo, so I'm going to try to hold six, and if I can hold it and push on a bit in the last kilometre, then, etc., etc . . .' That's

the way the climbs are coached now. It's completely different even to how it was three years ago. Riders don't look at the profiles of the climbs and think, 'I'm gonna have to hang until kilometre six, then it flattens out' . . . They don't really look at the terrain. If they feel the pace is too high after three kilometres of climbing, they'll just swing off and make their own pace, losing maybe thirty seconds less than they would have lost ten years ago.

It would be reasonable to assume, given the continuing domination of the *rouleurs-grimpeurs* at the Tour since Sky's first success in 2012 and the constant refinement of their 'steamroller' strategy, that the peloton's climbers have been relegated to bit-part roles. However, this hasn't been the case. Thanks to the Athlete Biological Passport and other anti-doping initiatives, as well as a shift in focus from the science of doping towards other scientific specialities, whereby watt output and power-to-weight ratios have trumped haematocrit as the key indicators of likely competitive success in a more monitored racing world, pure climbers have rediscovered their natural advantage in the mountains, re-emerging not only as contenders for the major stage-racing titles but, regularly, as the victors.

In 2017, for instance, as Froome ground out what was the least impressive of his four Tour de France victories, the final top ten featured another *rouleur-grimpeur* as runner-up in the form of Rigoberto Urán, followed by eight riders who were essentially pure climbers – Romain Bardet, Mikel Landa, Fabio Aru, Dan Martin, Simon Yates, Louis Meintjes, Alberto Contador and Warren Barguil. Of these, Aru, Bardet and Barguil all claimed mountain-summit victories with attacks from the yellow jersey group. What's more, climbers Nairo Quintana, Contador, Richard Carapaz, Tao

Geoghegan Hart and Egan Bernal all savoured victory at the Giro, while Contador, Aru, Quintana and Simon Yates triumphed at the Vuelta.

Dan Martin, Roche's cousin who also retired at the end of the 2021 season having won stages in all three Grand Tours over the course of a fourteen-year career, suggests the steady rise in the amount and difficulty of climbing in the Grand Tours – the Tour de France following the two other three-week events in this trend – has enabled climbers to hold their own. 'The Tour is tougher,' Martin affirms.

> There are a lot more mountains, it didn't used to have 50,000 metres of vertical gain like it does now. Teams can also pack a lot of climbers in because there aren't as many sprints as there once were in the Tour. It's got to the point where there are so few that some teams don't bring a sprinter, so not only are there more mountains, there are more climbers too, more strength in depth.

Yet, says Martin, while the emphasis on the mountains has increased, playing in the favour of the sport's mountain goats, climbers have still had to adapt because their natural performance advantage has been squeezed simultaneously by other factors. He explains:

> We are racing faster than ever, the speeds and the powers involved are so much higher than they were even five years ago. The training and the technology have made a real difference, while aerodynamics have too. There's less standing on the pedals because teams and riders have become increasingly aware that you can generate more power if you stay in the saddle, and you're more aerodynamic at the same time. There's real strength in depth as well, because

with all this knowledge everybody knows the training that needs to be done and the numbers that you need to do to be competitive. Guys at a very young age are training towards that. Whereas, obviously, when I was a junior, I didn't even know what a power meter was, I didn't even use one until I was pro effectively. As the level of professionalism and the climbing speeds have shot up, so has the difficulty of winning, unfortunately.

Denmark's Jakob Fuglsang agrees. 'When I was seventh in the Tour de France in 2013, if I had the numbers I have now back then, I would have won the Tour,' he told *VeloNews* at the end of the 2021 season. According to the Dane, he and other racing veterans all agreed that they were recording their 'best numbers ever', but, of course, everyone else had advanced too. 'Today the whole level is so much higher. Everything counts so much more now. You need the newest, the lightest, the best TT bike, the most aero wheels if you want to win. It's because the competition is so close, much closer than it used to be,' Fuglsang explained.

This is borne out by the margins between the riders at the Tour. In 2016, Froome beat Bardet by four minutes to win the title, but second to tenth were covered by just three minutes. The three editions that followed were similarly tight. Indeed, for the most part the Tours that followed the 2011 edition and the race in 2019 that was equally enthralling were largely devoid of panache. There was tension, moments of brilliance, but often not right until the very final kilometres of a mountain stage. To gauge how tough it was to compete, the TV cameras would have been better advised to focus on the back of the peloton, where riders were drifting out of contention, rather than at the front, where the picture was largely unchanging.

Boosting the amount of climbing and climbers, coupled with better training methods, the growing prevalence of high-altitude training camps, better aerodynamics, and the widespread use of power meters to gauge and set performance, packed everyone together, says Martin.

> It changed the way of racing. Every race got harder, which I wasn't complaining about because it suited me. It meant there was more fatigue and that guys were waiting further and further into the stage before making an attack. It made it more negative, though. It was more a wearing-down process.
>
> There used to be a dozen places on the Tour where you could make a difference by attacking your rivals, and if you missed one opportunity you didn't have to wait too long for the next one to appear. Now, though, there are just five or so opportunities where you can make that difference. It's harder, which I wasn't unhappy about, but it doesn't leave much room for flair. Although it's still the same scenario, with the main GC guys ending up fighting it out with each other at the end, there aren't the long-range attacks that we used to see. There was a lot more risk involved in making attacks like that.

Roche shares his cousin's perspective on the trend for risk-free racing in the mountains, pointing out that the sheer difficulty of getting a gap because the overall level is so high means that

> Attacks come very, very late. If you look at Roglič, he attacks in the last 500–600 metres of races, gets ten seconds or fifteen seconds, and often that's all you need. There's no more attacking with 10k to go, or at least if there is it's from guys who are in eighth or ninth position and trying to recover places. If you're going for the win or the podium, it's all about the last kilometre and having that explosion in the last kilometre.

He adds, though, that this strategy carries its own risk, pointing to Roglič's 2020 defeat by Pogačar as what can happen if a rider is making small gains regularly but without completely seeing off his rivals.

Yet, says Roche, there are also clear indications of a fundamental change taking place, or at the very least a significant reaction to the softly-softly strategy, a sense that panache and *duende* can prevail over watching your numbers. The most evident example was Julian Alaphilippe's joyride through the plans of the GC favourites at the 2019 Tour de France, which began in the hills of Champagne, continued in the high rolls of the Massif Central into Saint-Étienne, and was then maintained in the Pyrenees despite the tactical spike strip Team Ineos (formerly Sky) and Jumbo-Visma tried to throw in front of him by rolling out their trains.

With his wonderfully punchy style, an attitude buoyed up by panache, his handsome musketeer looks and family background in dance bands, rhythm and music, the goateed Frenchman took the yellow jersey and, like Voeckler in 2011, squeezed every atom of inspiration out of it. It was *duende à la française*, gloriously committed and totally enrapturing, that also swept up compatriot Thibaut Pinot, who, as Alaphilippe inevitably began to fade, emerged as the likely and long-awaited home champion, only to be cut down at his swashbuckling zenith by a mystery thigh injury.

As the French duo wilted, Colombia's Egan Bernal extended the display of sporting fireworks, attacking on the towering Iseran pass with 42 kilometres remaining to the finish in Tignes and gaining enough time on Alaphilippe by its 2,770-metre summit to move into yellow before a freak mountain squall produced landslides that closed the road into the finish. Although the victory continued the long Sky/Ineos sequence of success, it will be interesting to assess whether Bernal's win falls into the interregnum category, coming between Froome's reign and the start of what looks set to be the Pogačar dynasty, or whether the Colombian climber can add to it.

It will also, says Roche, be intriguing to see how this shift in the stage-racing dynamic will affect the Grand Tours in the years ahead. Referring to Richard Carapaz's gung-ho performance to win the 2019 *corsa rosa*, Tao Geoghegan Hart and Jai Hindley's gripping battle in the mountains during the final days of the following edition that the Englishman just edged, and Bernal's 2021 victory in the same race, he observes:

> Although everyone's kind of pacing themselves, it's not just about doing a time trial on your own and getting to the top as quick as possible. There still is that thing about dropping the guy on your wheel. I think the Tour, the Giro and the Vuelta have given us some pretty cool battles.

Those final two races took place, of course, in the midst of the coronavirus pandemic that affected almost every part of our lives, including cycling, resulting initially in a swathe of race cancellations and, in the second half of 2020 and all through 2021, in events taking place with the possibility of sudden postponement always evident. As a consequence, when riders did get the opportunity to compete, they all tended to give it everything. 'COVID-19 added a new hunger to it all and changed the style of racing. We were initially racing every race as if it was the last. Now we know that's not the case but the aggressive style has held,' Michael Woods told *Cyclingnews* in late 2021. The Canadian added: 'If I'd ridden like I'm doing now just three years ago, I think I'd have won 10 races. Performances in the peloton have gone to another level.'

The sense that attitudes are changing, that racing for the pure fun of it is central to the competitive philosophy of the peloton's biggest names, is underpinned by the performances of Tadej Pogačar, who has shown that he's got a quite different approach to stage racing than the Grand Tour kings who immediately preceded him. Andrej Hauptman, a former Slovenian road champion who took the bronze medal in the 2001 World Road Race Championship and became Pogačar's team director at UAE, has been the young Slovenian's mentor since his early teenage years. He was, Hauptman confirms, always very promising, even as a late-developing fifteen-year-old:

> Back then he was really small compared to the others, but he was really competitive with those bigger guys. I thought he could be good, but you never know with kids how they will turn out. You could see, though, that he was always really clever, always in the right place at the right moment, tactically very smart, maybe because he was so small and he needed to be smart to be competitive. When he became a second-year junior, he grew and put on some kilos and I thought, 'OK, now let's see how you climb with these extra kilos,' and he was even stronger. I said to myself, 'This kid could really go far,' but you never know. Someone who's eighteen years old can be really good but then the improvement doesn't come. But I had a really good feeling because he wasn't training a lot and had a significant margin for improvement. And once that training started, well . . .

The dominating winner of the 2018 Tour de l'Avenir, the sport's premier under-23 event and often an accurate indicator of emerging stage-race talent, Pogačar turned professional with UAE at the end of that season. Winner of his second stage race, the Tour of the Algarve, in February 2019, he romped through the year, collecting another prestigious victory at the Tour of California in May, before lining up at the Vuelta a España that September. Each of his three stage wins in the mountains on his debut appearance in a three-week event were the result of aggressive racing, the last of them on the penultimate day forged with a 39-kilometre solo break from the group of favourites that included race winner Roglič. There were three more wins when he made his race-winning debut at the Tour in 2020, two in the mountains, the first of them in Laruns coming after a gripping attack-and-counterattack contest with his compatriot on the fearsomely steep western flank of the Col de Marie-Blanque, that remains etched into my own memory from my painful encounter with it in 1990, the pair each looking for the haymaker punch that would knock the other down but eventually being split by just a narrow margin in a small group sprint at the line.

Pogačar was even more impressive in his defence of the yellow jersey. There were three more stage wins, two at Pyrenean summits in the final days after riveting contests with Jonas Vingegaard and Richard Carapaz. Best of all, though, was his performance on the opening Alpine stage into Le Grand-Bornand, where, after being ruffled and, he admitted, riled by his rivals on the long stage the previous day to Le Creusot, he slammed them all down with a searing attack on the penultimate ascent of the Col de Romme that was sustained over the Col de la Colombière and into the finish, where he took yellow and effectively had the race won. It was one of the best demonstrations of *la course en tête* since Eddy Merckx was in his pomp, the Belgian saying as much when he declared, 'In Tadej, I think we've really got the new Merckx.'

Riding on teammate Formolo's wheel, Pogačar seemed to sense the pace was dropping and was instantly on his pedals, sprinting by on the Italian's left with a relaxed urgency. He has the acceleration of a *puncheur*, not quite as rapid as Julian Alaphilippe or Mathieu van der Poel, but enough that day to drop everyone in the yellow jersey group bar Carapaz. What sets him apart is that when he's back in the saddle, he maintains that speed, which a pure climber like the Ecuadorean can't. Soon, he too had to yield. 'Without a doubt it was the most beautiful solo of my career,' he later said of that performance. 'It was chaos from the start that day, but I had extraordinary legs. On the penultimate ascent I could see all of my rivals were suffering: I asked the guys to ride very hard at the front, then I attacked and no one could follow me.'

Watching him at these moments, Pogačar actually looks like he's enjoying himself, and he confessed in the race winner's final press conference at the 2021 Tour that there's a strong element of fun in his racing.

> For me, it's similar to when I was playing games or sport with my brother or my friends when I was a kid. I always try to win, have fun and enjoy the sport, the battle between each other. Even if I lose sometimes, I accept it. I always try to enjoy the bike and be happy on my bike because it's a beautiful sport. I think that's the point of sport, to have fun and to enjoy it. My coaches, my sport director, all tell me, 'Just keep having fun, it's just a game, one time you win, one time you lose, just keep having fun.' Even if I have bad days, I still see fun in it.

Speaking to *L'Équipe* following the 2021 season, he expanded on this a little more, explaining that he felt like he was obliged as a professional athlete to try to entertain by making long-range attacks, by shaking up the established schema.

> When you sit on your settee and turn on the TV, that's what you want to see: guys attacking 100km from the finish, not cautious racers waiting for the last ten kilometres to enter into the action. I feel like professional cycling hasn't ever been as entertaining as this and we should all be pleased about that.

The dilemma for his rivals is how to compete with and beat Pogačar. At his best, he appears to be a level above anyone else in the peloton and very capable of adding more substance to those comparisons with Eddy Merckx. But can the likes of Ineos and Jumbo perhaps take a lesson from the riders and teams that unsettled and in some rare cases got the better of 'The Cannibal' – from Luis Ocaña and José Manuel Fuente, superlative climbers who relished a long-range attack? I suggest this not on the basis of any great understanding of the tactical niceties of racing at Grand Tour level, but simply as a fan who'd love to see a twenty-first-century version of a team like Kas that was stacked with pure climbers.

It appeared that Ineos were starting down this path in 2021, when they selected Geraint Thomas, Tao Geoghegan Hart, Richie Porte and Richard Carapaz for the Tour, only to see the chances of the first three hit by crashes in the opening week, leaving the Ecuadorean as their only GC option. But what a prospect it would be if, rather than rowing back from this strategy and getting behind one leader, they kept going in the other direction and added Egan Bernal, Dani

Martínez and Adam Yates to the mix, countering Pogačar's potent brand of *la course en tête* with a modern revamp of Bernard Hinault's version of this strategy with the La Vie Claire team, which was packed with opportunistic racers, always looking to get riders in the breakaways, forcing their rivals to chase, gradually chipping away at their resources. After Sky perfected the mountain train, could this be the way for their successors to send it off track?

Chapter 15

The realm of the mountain kings

If climbers were fashioned by elevation alone, not only would the sport not have witnessed the mountain exploits of Lucien Van Impe and all the riders who turned Alpe d'Huez into 'the Dutch mountain' in the 1970s and 80s, but Colombia's place as the realm of the mountain kings would also have been severely diminished. With an average altitude of 593 metres, it's dwarfed by Switzerland (1,350m), looked down on by Austria (910m) and even overlooked by Spain (660m). Yet those statistics hide salient facts when starting down the path towards understanding why this Latin American country has become as unequivocally associated with climbers as the Flemish half of Belgium is with Classics riders who can conjure a race-winning opportunity out of a cross-wind and stomp up a cobbled wall in the big ring.

When it comes to Colombia and climbers, geography matters hugely. The country is split between five regions: almost 60 per cent of the land mass rests to the east of the Andes in the Llanos, low-lying gently rolling plains where a Belgian *rouleur* would be in their element, and, to the south of that, the Amazon Rainforest area, its rivers flowing into the vast water system that empties into the sea thousands of kilometres to the east on Brazil's Atlantic coast. There are coastal regions on the Caribbean and Pacific, to the west of the Andes, its peaks and huge valleys filling the remaining 35 per cent or so of the country. These highlands are, though, home to almost 80 per cent of Colombia's 51 million inhabitants.

In a similar way to the sport's traditional strongholds of France, Belgium, Italy and Spain, the popularity of cycling grew organically in Colombia, although in a quite different way to those European countries because of its Latin American location and Andean topography. In his book *Kings of the Mountains*, in which he traces the links between cycling and Colombia's social, economic and political development, Matt Rendell offers evidence that racing was taking place at the very end of the nineteenth century and of riders travelling from neighbouring countries to compete in Colombia during the 1920s. Yet it was the establishment of the Vuelta a Colombia in 1951 that proved the pivotal moment.

It was the idea of road and track racer Efraín Forero Triviño, known as 'The Indomitable Zipa' after his hometown of Zipaquirá, just north of Bogotá, which later produced Egan Bernal. Inspired by tales of the Tour de France, he planned out a ten-stage, 1,154-kilometre route that was primarily in the Andean massif and included what has become the country's most famous climb, the 3,230-metre La Línea pass. 'If we may be permitted the comparison, the roads of France and Colombia are as different as a billiard table and a big dipper. Its difficulty and demands will make the Tour of Colombia singular, if not unique, among the great trials of world cycling', declared *El Tiempo*, the newspaper that backed the event.

The terrain may have been completely unlike that used for the Tour, but, like the first edition of that race in 1903, the Vuelta a Colombia was an instant popular success, drawing large and enthusiastic crowds to the roadside and huge audiences for radio broadcasts. Having been the driving force behind the event,

Forero won it, his victory prompting an official day of celebration in Zipaquirá. 'At the midpoint of the twentieth century Forero had tapped a nation's resources of hope. Through cycling, perhaps, Colombia might achieve some unexpected absolution,' says Rendell, although another three decades would pass before this became clearly evident.

There were moments when it appeared Colombia might join the cycling mainstream centred on Western Europe. In 1958, Fausto Coppi, Hugo Koblet, Luigi Casola and Ettore Milano, the latter pair two of the Italian's *gregari* as domestiques are known in Italian, participated in the 160-kilometre Clásico El Colombiano based in Medellín. Koblet won the first sector of the race, but the quartet all succumbed to the effects of the heat and altitude on the 42-kilometre ascent of the Alto de Minas and failed to finish, victory going to five-time Vuelta a Colombia winner Ramón Hoyos – known as 'El Escarabajo' after a type of flying beetle, due to the smoothness and grittiness of his climbing style, his nickname would eventually encompass all Colombian climbers. In 1974, Bianchi star Felice Gimondi travelled to the Andean nation with his Colombian teammate Martín 'Cochise' Rodríguez and Spaniards José Manuel Fuente and Txomin Perurena to participate in the Clásico POC.

Although these occasional encounters with the European racing elite didn't change Colombia's position as a remote outpost of international cycling, racing was flourishing domestically. Cycling writer Klaus Bellon Gaitán asserts that the impact of the first editions of the national tour can still be felt in Colombia in the current era. 'Regardless of what age you are, it's very, very likely that your parents and even grandparents were active fans,' he says. In an article for *The Cycling Anthology*, Bellon explained that the impact of this popularity was such that cycling became, 'part of Colombian life. It's not a sport, a hobby or a pastime. It's part of Colombia itself . . . it taught its citizens about themselves and what they were capable of. But, perhaps more importantly, it taught them about their own country and its geography.'

Religion played a fundamental part in this symbiosis, Rendell describing how 'Cycling, Colombia and Catholicism are an ineffable, indivisible trinity.' Not only are Colombians among the most devout of Latin American Catholics, but their variant of Catholicism is one of the most conservative and traditional on the continent, and it has traditionally had a strong emphasis on martyrdom. Cycling, particularly in the mountains, has obvious resonance with this. 'Suffering alone offers a beautiful idea of the martyr,' Bellon affirms. 'Because of the terrain, but also because there's this aspect of the suffering of lone cyclists, cycling really touches on something inherent in Colombians, especially in its religious background.'

As had been the case in Europe during the eighteenth century, altitude was also venerated. In what Rendell describes as 'a nation of mountain-top Madonnas', shrines, churches and crosses tend to stand in high places, with the bicycle offering the opportunity for pilgrimage as well as the competitive challenge. 'In a landscape like this, any belief system intending to take root has to make a virtue of the uphill struggle,' says Rendell. 'Christ's agonies on the way to Calvary provide a model for Colombia's athletes.'

In 1980, these athletes, hardened by the Andes and its thin mountain air, finally began to travel to Europe in numbers, following in the footsteps of lone raiders like Cochise who had already made a success of professional careers on the old continent. That year, thanks to the prompting of ex-racer-turned-journalist Héctor

Urrego, whose ebullient radio broadcasts from the Tour and other leading races would make him something of a celebrity in Europe, a Colombian amateur team received a last-minute invitation to the Tour de l'Avenir, a race that has always highlighted the best upcoming talent. Despite losing five minutes to the strongest nations in the team time trial, Alfonso Flórez took the lead in the Jura mountains at the mid-point and held it to the finish, beating the Soviet Union's defending champion Sergei Sukhoruchenkov, renowned as one of the greatest amateur racers in history, into second place by more than three minutes. On their return to Bogotá, the Colombian riders were feted like heroes by hundreds of thousands lining the capital's streets. This, it should be noted, for an amateur race that would barely have made any waves in Europe.

Says Bellon:

> The thought that one of ours could go to Europe and 'beat them at their game' was and still is hugely important. Any sport or event where a Colombian can and then does do well means a whole lot. You can see the same thing with the Colombian football team and also with Formula 1 when Juan Pablo Montoya was driving.

Expanding on this point, he stresses how cycling captures the nation's imagination in a very specific way:

> Colombians don't see ourselves as being highly patriotic, or at least that quality plays out in a very different way to American patriotism, for example. The reality is, we are underdogs in every single way in terms of geopolitical standings. As a result, the possibility of a lone rider, not even a team, but

a lone rider winning in this way has particular resonance. I don't think it's outlandish to say that we feel like he's doing it for us. While that's actually sort of unfair because, of course, this person has trained and he is doing it for himself. But it almost feels always like he's doing it for us, for the nation, not just him and his team.

Three years on from that Tour de l'Avenir success and thanks to a relaxation on the rule that prevented amateurs from participating in the Tour de France, a Colombia team backed by the Varta battery company lined up in Fontenay-sous-Bois on the outskirts of Paris for the start of the seventieth edition of the world's greatest race. 'We didn't understand anything that was happening, and we were scared to death,' admitted Patricinio Jiménez, a stage-winner at the Avenir. Set back by the loss of their leader Flórez before the race had even reached the Pyrenees, the Colombians struggled until the race reached Pau for a stage through 'the circle of death' to Luchon. After battling with cross-winds, long days on the flat and in team time trials, here, finally, they were in terrain that could draw the best out of them.

Jiménez was in the vanguard. After Lucien Van Impe led over the Aubisque, the most experienced of the Colombians went clear with another Tour debutant, Philippa York. Jiménez led over the iconic pass and the Aspin that followed. However, 500 metres from the top of the Peyresourde, as Pedro Delgado, another Tour first-timer, began to close on them, the Scot accelerated, went clear over the top and held that advantage into the finish, where Jiménez was fourth, a place ahead of his 20-year-old teammate Edgar Corredor, and, more importantly, became the new leader of the mountains competition. He held the polka-dot jersey for a week until Van Impe lifted it off his shoulders at Alpe d'Huez. In the end, there was no fairy-tale victory, although there were highly commendable third-place finishes for Jiménez in the Puy de Dôme time trial and on consecutive stages for Corredor at Alpe d'Huez and Morzine, the youngster just edging out his teammate in the GC standings by reaching Paris one place ahead of him in sixteenth.

The victories weren't long in coming, though. Martín Ramírez won the Critérium du Dauphiné Libéré title the following year despite insults, elbows and runner-up Bernard Hinault's attempts to make him fall as the Colombian tracked the Frenchman on the final road stage. A month later at the Tour, Lucho Herrera, of whom it was said by one of his Colombian contemporaries that fame couldn't have happened to a more unwilling participant, earned himself a place as a sporting immortal in his country by riding away from Hinault at Alpe d'Huez.

Reflecting on the Colombians who emerged during that period, York believes they didn't change the nature of racing very much, but adapted quickly, especially when climbing. As she explains:

> Guys like Fabio Parra and Herrera would climb more in the style of Bernard Hinault and Greg LeMond, riding a really steady tempo. The reason for that is in Colombia the mountains tend to be twenty to thirty kilometres long, so you can't ride in a series of little accelerations. They tended to push a fairly large gear as well, a bigger gear than the Europeans would because they were used to less air resistance at altitude. As a consequence of this, they would tend to be good in the Alps where the road surfaces were slightly better and the climbs were slightly longer, and they could pull that bigger gear more efficiently.

But they did tend to wear themselves out by climbing like that because they'd maybe do it for two days and then on the third they'd be knackered. When they had to use the 21 or the 23 sprocket you knew that they were struggling. The rest of the time, they'd use 17 and 19 on the mountains and often stand up a lot, and you'd be thinking, 'That's a giant gear. What are you doing?' They didn't really change the overall speed that we climbed at, just the manner in which they wanted to climb was slightly different to what had come before.

Back home in Colombia, though, the performances of Herrera, Ramírez, Parra and their peers had a very significant impact, firing their compatriots' sense of national pride, in a similar way to Flemish riders in the early decades of the twentieth century, when their performances in one-day Classics like Paris–Roubaix and the Tour of Flanders gave the people of Flanders a cultural reference point that helped to forge their identity and to an extent encouraged use of their native Dutch language rather than French, which had hitherto predominated throughout Belgium. In his *Cycling Anthology* article, Bellon picked up on this in a discussion with Corey Shouse Tourino, a professor in Hispanic studies in the United States, who described Colombia as being

a nation of nations until radio broadcasts united Colombians with a shared invisible sense of belonging to a shared space and culture. Given that cycling was both the most important sport and national spectacle (at least of a positive and popular nature), first the Vuelta and the Clásico RCN, and later the Tour, the Giro and the Vuelta a España were essential to convincing Colombians that Colombia existed as a singular concept that was worth defending and celebrating at home on the world stage.

Thanks to his experience of racing against Colombians and also in Colombia both before and after he turned professional, Andy Hampsten says that he often felt much more of a bond with the *escarabajos* than he did with European riders. 'We definitely had an affinity for each other, we were in a brotherhood of Americans putting up with grouchy old Europeans resenting our presence there. We would mysteriously not chase each other as hard as we could have in the European peloton,' he says. Thanks to a Colombian friend who acted as his coach and manager when he raced in the country, Hampsten also got a particular insight into cycling's importance, and specifically the significance of climbing's distinct part within that.

'I raced there enough to know that you're crazy to go down a mountain fast because the roads are covered in oil and you can't possibly trust the road surface, so it's a different version of racing, but they love going uphill,' says the American.

> We'd go hard right away and there would be kids with no toe clips who were so young that I'd feel kind of sorry for them. We'd be down to twenty riders and they'd still be hanging in there. Then, with their last breath before they got dropped, they'd attack on these terrible bikes and wearing clothes that didn't fit.

It struck the American that these kids were following their dream in the same way American youngsters were when they play Little League baseball, soccer or American football.

> Some kids want to, say, be the goalie when they play soccer, and that's how it is for kids when it comes to climbing and riding a bike down there. That's what makes them happy.

They want to attack. If you only manage to make the first attack, then that's enough. You don't have to win the race, you just have to play the game.

Hampsten asserts that that delight in climbing and attacking remains as Colombian racers rise through the ranks. They were all ready to attack and be attacked.

There were never any hard feelings. They didn't play the politics. They were a little jealous of each other, I'm sure, but there was a really nice camaraderie, there was sportsmanship between the riders, and I think at a much higher level than there was between most of my European and North American colleagues. I think that sense of togetherness enabled them to relax and do their pesky attacking that used to drive the more powerful riders crazy. They didn't need to win the Tour de France at that point, they were heroes just for their way of racing.

In pointing out this relish for aggressive racing, for making attacks just at the moment when there's nothing left in the legs at all, the American touches on a Colombian trait that Bellon believes has a key role in their approach to racing: *malicia indígena*. He describes it as a shrewdness or astuteness, a kind of street-smartness that keeps you a step ahead. 'It's not a matter of, "I'm going to cut in front of you and take something from you." It's more like, "My eyes and ears are always open. Although you're stronger, faster or richer, I'm smarter,"' Bellon explains.

What's most telling, I think, is that the word *indígena* is there, indigenous, native or Indian, as people might call it.

> We as Colombians are aware that this doesn't come from our European blood, but from the indigenous part of our heritage. In the US, they say, 'You can't get one over on me,' and that's absolutely *malicia indígena*. There's that sense of, 'You can't pull a swift move on me and try to attack. I know it's coming. I have eyes in the back of my head.'

Bellon sees this quality not only in the way that Colombians at all levels race, in the commitment to attacking before you get attacked, but also in the way that riders are determined to claw their way out of poverty.

> I think there's a real fighting spirit in the Colombian psyche, and that this comes from our upbringing and being very aware of our place in the world. If you're a category one racer in the United States, for instance, and your career falls apart, you can get an education either because your parents will pay for it or because you can take out a loan and go to college. But for a lot of riders in Colombia that possibility doesn't exist. And I think that that only makes them work harder, and what's interesting is that they're not just doing it for themselves. I talked to some of the riders on the Colombia-Coldeportes team, guys who weren't making huge amounts of money. Yet, they were earning more than their entire immediate family combined and were putting their siblings through college.

There are obvious echoes with the background of so many European pros from the early days of the sport through to the 1960s, and markedly with Spanish climbers such as Vicente Trueba, Federico Bahamontes, Luis Ocaña and José Manuel Fuente, each of whom saw cycling as their opportunity to escape from the privations that marked their childhood years. Speaking to Bellon, Patricinio Jiménez said of the generation he raced with, 'We were all peasants. We had an insatiable hunger for winning, in part perhaps because it meant more to us. We needed to win. We were an amazing group, and we were willing to sacrifice everything.'

Where Colombia stands apart from the traditional cycling nations is in the way cycling is retaining its central importance to sporting life as the country's economy expands and poverty levels, though still comparatively high, are coming down. While in France, Italy and Spain, cycling has lost its attraction and status because it's seen as lacking glamour, being too hard – as an old man's sport that's been tainted by doping scandals – in Colombia it remains woven into the cultural fabric, in a similar way again to how it is in Flanders. The scene is vibrant. There are countless cycling academies, clubs, teams and races; bike touring companies are flourishing. The sport's roots are so deeply set that it will continue to thrive, constantly replenishing the production of talent that has established Colombia as one of the great powers of road racing in the twenty-first century.

Loitering outside team buses is one of the staples of life as a cycling journalist. But this was a first for me. You quickly get accustomed to being asked to wait, for team briefings to finish or for another media commitment to be fulfilled. But on this occasion, the brief hiatus before my intended interviewee emerged from the little camper van he and his teammates were crammed into was due to their pre-race prayer.

I'd travelled to the Vuelta a Castilla y León because I'd been offered the opportunity to interview Alberto Contador. It was April

2011. The Spaniard and the rest of the cycling world were waiting for the Court of Arbitration for Sport to announce its verdict on his positive test for clenbuterol from the previous year's Tour de France. In the meantime, Contador was still the winner of that title and was still competing.

On the lookout for other stories, I'd noticed that the 4-72–Colombia es Pasión team were also participating in the five-day stage race taking place to the west of Madrid and that their line-up featured Nairo Quintana, the winner of the previous year's edition of the Tour de l'Avenir. Also there was Víctor Hugo Peña, then in the penultimate year of a long professional career that had included a three-day spell in the Tour de France's yellow jersey when he was with US Postal. Always friendly and approachable, Peña would, I hoped, be able to provide an insight into a team whose primary objective was to nurture the pick of Colombia's young road talents and into whether a new wave of climbers was about to emerge from the Andean nation.

After a few moments, the riders spilled out of the bus and into the dusty backstreet of the small Castilian town of Medina de Rioseco where their bikes were lined up ready for the start of the race's opening stage. I had no idea which of them was Quintana until he was pointed towards me by the team's manager, Luisa Fernanda Ríos. I was, like most people are on seeing him for the first time, surprised by how small and slight he is. He looked young and fragile, inscrutable and rather worn at the same time. We chatted for a couple of minutes, him smiling a little guardedly, me vainly trying with my faltering Spanish to get something more than the pat answers that most riders serve up when their focus is, naturally, on the race they're about to start.

Then I spoke to the easy-going Peña, the road captain and mentor for the much younger riders around him. He told me:

> The one thing I would say about them is that they're big talents. They know how to ride on the climbs and that's where their talent stands out, but they also know how to suffer. But on the climbs, they really have my respect. They are the sons of the mountains. But these guys are not like the Colombian riders we all used to see before. They can ride on the flat no problem. They can hold their place in the bunch no problem. The only thing they have to learn is to be cold, to stop themselves being swayed too much by their Latin blood. They have to learn what it takes to race. The other aspects of the sport are no problem for them. They are really professional.

With those few sentences, Peña broadly summed up the past, present and future of Colombian road cycling. Quintana and Colombia es Pasión teammate Esteban Chaves, together with the likes of Rigoberto Urán, Egan Bernal and Miguel Ángel López, would go on to emulate and exceed the exploits of their country's first wave of riders who challenged and beat the European elite, climbing stars of the 1980s including Lucho Herrera, Fabio Parra, Pacho Rodríguez and Patricinio Jiménez.

There were obvious as well as less transparent reasons for the decline in Colombia's racing fortunes from the early 1990s and the second decade of the twenty-first century. The loss of its three professional teams from the European scene was fundamental. The emblematic Café de Colombia team was the first to go, folding at the end of 1990 after the deregulation of the International Coffee Agreement led to the wholesale price of beans dropping by

75 per cent. Twelve months later, Pony Malta pulled the plug on their team after five seasons. A year on from that, in the wake of a catastrophic 1992 Tour when only two of its riders reached Paris, Postobón cut back substantially on its investment and focused on a domestic team. Although the best of the Colombian riders found places elsewhere, Álvaro Mejía joining Andy Hampsten at Motorola and Hernán Buenahora moving to Kelme, for the majority of their compatriots the most straightforward route into the European peloton had been closed off. A steady trickle did manage to make the jump, Nelson Rodríguez, Chepe González, Santiago Botero and Víctor Hugo Peña among them.

'Only the really talented ones would last,' says Philippa York. 'Most of the teams tried to take two or three Colombian climbers, but they'd find that they'd last half a season before they were worn out. It was probably quite difficult coming from South America to Europe and having to deal with all of the cultural changes.'

Doping, too, had an effect. Just like Hampsten, who steadily became aware that his best level wasn't good enough to give him an edge in the mountains, some Colombian riders struggled to excel in the terrain where they had hitherto stood out. Henry Cárdenas, Herrera's loyal domestique who was with him when he won the Vuelta in 1987 and finished second himself in the Dauphiné that year, admitted to Bellon that he realized that the EPO had triggered a fundamental shift in the racing environment.

> There was an obvious change in the early 90s. When you train, you have ways of measuring your performance: best times and records on climbs. So you know how you're doing. I was training, doing well, but I would go to Europe

and everyone would be so much faster all of a sudden. They were using something strong, something serious. It started with just a few riders, but then it seemed like everyone, just everyone, could beat us. They could all climb faster.

While Colombia wasn't immune from the industrialization of doping within cycling, economic recession, political instability and escalating violence related to drug cartels and guerrilla and paramilitary groups had a more significant impact on the sport. By 1999, the country didn't have a single professional team registered with the UCI. The sense of breakdown was underlined by the kidnapping in early 2000 of 1993 Tour stage-winner Oliverio Rincón. He was released quickly, but abducted again two months later. Days later, Lucho Herrera suffered the same fate. Once more, both were soon freed.

As the economy picked up and Colombia began to emerge from decades of civil war and the worst of the cartel-related violence, the nation's trade body began to promote investment, business and tourism under the slogan 'Colombia es Pasión', which led to the investment in the eponymous bike team in 2005. The emphasis was put on developing young riders and clean sport, although the team's adherence to the latter was undermined by a positive test at the 2008 Vuelta a Colombia. Luisa Fernanda Ríos, a former adventure sports athlete who represented Colombia three times at the world championships in that discipline and then became an event organizer, was headhunted from the government's department of external relations to help change the internal culture, which included the introduction of UCI biological passport protocols. Rather than focusing on the riders' almost pre-ordained strength as climbers, team coach Luis Fernando Saldarriaga worked with the riders on aspects of racing that didn't come naturally, such as time trialling and riding in cross-winds. They worked with a psychologist in order to make them more confident on the road and off it, got advice on diet and training, tailoring them all the while to be more rounded as racers.

Thirty years on from Alfonso Flórez's victory in the 1980 Tour de l'Avenir, which heralded the advent of the first wave of Colombian stars into Europe, Quintana's success in the same race proved similarly providential. Esteban Chaves won it the following season. In 2012, Quintana moved to Spanish squad Movistar, winning a mountain stage into Morzine at the Critérium du Dauphiné in that first season. A year on from that, he was runner-up, King of the Mountains and best young rider at the Tour de France. He could, if his team had shown more gumption and courage with their tactics in the Pyrenees when Chris Froome was isolated from all of his teammates, even have won the title.

He returned to a hero's reception in Colombia. 'The footage of his arrival into Bogotá was just astonishing. The roads were six deep as he made his way to go and see the president,' says Bellon. 'It was absolutely insane. And thereafter after every great success, his win at the Giro in 2014 for instance, he's been greeted the same way in Tunja, where he lives and where the central plaza holds 80,000 people.' When he outwitted Froome to win the Vuelta in 2016, his local Boyacá radio station's crowing headline was: 'Boyacá's malicia indígena has beaten British science'.

By the time Egan Bernal clinched what had been an elusive first Tour de France victory for Colombia in 2019, the twenty-first-century *escarabajos* had accumulated no fewer than 13 podium finishes,

Chaves, Rigoberto Urán and Miguel Ángel López contributing to that collection. As Víctor Hugo Peña suggested, these riders can do everything. There is no sign of this well of talent drying up either. Harold Tejada, Dani Martínez, Iván Sosa, Einer Rubio, Sergio Higuita and Andrés Ardila have all proved themselves to be thrilling climbers. Lower down the ranks, the leading junior race, the Vuelta del Porvenir, is hugely oversubscribed and is watched closely by scouts from the peloton's biggest teams. Thanks to a thriving track programme, there are sprinters too, Fernando Gaviria the pick of them.

This latest generation is feted and recognized in a wholly different way too. Bellon explains:

> Nairo Quintana is a David Beckham-style star. He was just in a TV show, *The Masked Singer*, where a person comes out and sings and dances, and you don't know who it is until they reveal themselves. Rigoberto Urán is doing Pepsi commercials and impersonating Mick Jagger. Chaves has a big profile too, as of course does Egan Bernal. They're also very socially aware in a way the riders in the 1980s weren't. Nairo has spoken out about farmers and also in support of truck drivers who were on strike, issues that are close to his heart as it used to be his job to take his family's fruit and potatoes to market.

When, in April and May 2021, Colombian police suppressed protests against corruption and the government's health and tax reforms, Bernal was among major sporting and entertainment figures who joined the demonstrations and urged the authorities to listen to what the protesters had to say.

Yet the mountains remain their true stage, an arena where their next show of verve is never far away and each one is a reminder of what sets climbers apart in our affections. Among the pick of them were Quintana's ten-kilometre solo ride to victory at the Chalet Reynard ski station on Mont Ventoux in the 2020 Tour de la Provence – 'I was pulling on the front and when he came from behind it was amazing to see the speed he was going,' French climber Kenny Elissonde told me – and 'Superman' López's flight from the 2020 Tour favourites on the Col de la Loze, one of the new generation of acutely steep ascents being sought out by Grand Tour organizers because they reduce the speed to such an extent that no advantage can be gained from sitting in the wheels and it becomes an every-man-for-himself contest.

Perhaps best of all, though, was the Sega di Ala summit finish at the 2021 Giro, where, after scattering his rivals the day before with a winning raid to Cortina d'Ampezzo, race leader Egan Bernal looked to be on the verge of crumbling until teammate Dani Martínez, who had been pacing him, interceded. 'When I turned to look for him, he wasn't there. When I saw him, he was in a very bad way, I shouted at him with practically everything I had; I pushed on him, I encouraged him, even swearing at him,' said Martínez, who accompanied this volley with fist-pumping exhortations. Bernal acknowledged that it did the trick. If Lucho Herrera, blood running down his face after crashing on the stage into Saint-Étienne in the 1985 Tour, was the image of the first generation of *escarabajos*, depicted by the Colombian press, says Bellon, as 'a Christ-like fallen figure, a deity', this was the encapsulation of their twenty-first-century successors, leaders of the sport's biggest teams, tightly fraternal, winning the biggest races, very much the sons of the mountains.

Speaking to Klaus Bellon, Corey Shouse Tourino asserted that, 'The success of the "Colombian way" on the bike is the end result of their appropriation and reinvention of cycling as a Colombian practice. In this sense, Colombians cycle the way Brazilians play soccer – we have *o jogo bonito* and *el escarabajo*.' As he suggests, we've come to appreciate Colombian racers for their style, their courage, for the fact that they are so wedded to the terrain in which they seek to thrive. Formed physiologically, geographically and spiritually by the mountains, the Colombians have come to epitomize the ideal of the climber.

Equally, although we may not know the Andean nation's great passes, they – like the cradle of Classics racing that is Flanders – provide cycling with an essential and sustaining ingredient that can't often be found elsewhere: not simply a passion for climbing mountains, but the fundamental need to climb them. The same essence can be felt during the height of the European racing season, but it is fleeting. In Colombia, it is inescapable.

Chapter 16

Hammers and nails

Bike racing may be about aesthetics, focused essentially on the drama of the landscape and the way that the riders respond to it, but the fundamental beauty and essence of the sport is also built on what sports writer Jeff Moag has suggested is 'a kind of sympathetic voyeurism'. Thanks to our own experience of the effort required to climb a slope, hill or mountain, we can empathize, admire and respect racers for pushing themselves to their physiological limits, wanting them to succeed, some no doubt a little more than others. At the same time, we're captivated by and even relish the suffering that they're enduring, spectating, often at very close quarters, on what Mark Cavendish has described with typical cutting precision as 'physiological torture, the competitive equivalent of someone pulling your fingernails out very slowly'.

I've felt these contrasting emotions many times, particularly when I've been at the roadside on a long climb in a big race. Indeed, they're what draw me to be there. I'm simultaneously awed, thrilled and fascinated by the spectacle they present, by this self-inflicted violence. I suspect that almost every time I've walked back down the mountain afterwards I've engaged in a variant of essentially the same conversation: 'How do they do it? What do you feel when you race up a climb full bore? Do you remain lucid? Does it bring any sense of enjoyment?' These are, I admit, dumb questions, but during the course of writing this book I've asked them again and again, and the answers to them draw us closer to an absolute understanding of the beauty of racing in the mountains and the pull it has on us.

The best place to start towards a better appreciation of the unique, onerous and magical path of the climber is in a relatively pain-free zone, as described by Ashleigh Moolman Pasio, twice runner-up in the Giro d'Italia Femminile, a six-time South African road champion and renowned as one of the best climbers in the peloton. She first discovered this talent in her early twenties when she joined her then boyfriend Carl Pasio on rides around his home town of Knysna on their country's southern tip. 'I was on a borrowed bike. Knysna has a lagoon and there's two big headlands called The Heads that are the gateway to the sea with a viewpoint at the top. It's pretty steep going up there and that's where he noticed my raw talent,' she explains. Encouraged by Pasio, who'd been a world-class triathlete as a junior, Moolman began to train seriously, using climbs to measure her progress.

> In the beginning, I was doing intervals up climbs, then I started competing in local league events in South Africa. In one of the first races that I did, there was a climb soon after the start and I dropped from the first group. After the race, Carl asked me, 'So what happened?' And I told him that I'd given it my best, but I just couldn't stay with them. It provoked a little bit of an argument between us because he'd say, 'For sure, you didn't give it your best.' And I'd be like, 'How do you know? I gave it my hardest and I couldn't stay with them.' But he wasn't convinced that I had given everything.
>
> Ultimately, though, he was right. It came down to the fact that I just didn't know how to push myself deep enough. I think most normal people stop just outside their comfort

zone, while professional athletes go well into the red, far out of our comfort zone. And that's what makes us professional athletes. And I had to learn how to do that. Not long after, there was a league race in Stellenbosch that went up this climb called Helshoogte that I used to use a lot for intervals. I stayed with the front group on that climb and finished the race with them. I didn't end up on the podium, but that race has always been pivotal for me because it was when I realized, 'Wow, now I know what he means. I wasn't going my hardest. I wasn't going into the red zone.' We have to learn to love the pain is what everyone says. But that is literally the case, you have to learn how to find some kind of enjoyment in that suffering, to overcome that challenge. It's the reward at the end that makes us do it over and over and over again.

In his book *Endure*, which examines the limits of human performance, Alex Hutchinson – by adapting the definition of effort proposed by Samuele Marcora, a professor investigating the psychobiology of endurance performance at the University of Bologna – offers a helpful explanation of this eureka moment shared by every top-class endurance athlete. Endurance, says Hutchinson, is 'the struggle to continue against the mounting desire to stop'. Evidently, this could also be applied to climbing. Most amateur cyclists will be familiar with the moment when the mounting desire to stop wins out. Push hard on a climb, perhaps with a short dance on the pedals, and your thighs quickly start to burn as lactate begins to build, the pain persuading you back into the saddle and to slow down. For elite racers, the key to training is to delay this moment for as long as possible and then, when it comes, to carry on anyway because success lies somewhere at the far end of it, knowing that lactate production is a strain response to metabolic stress and acts, says

Hutchinson, 'as a crucial source of emergency fuel during intense exercise. Top athletes, far from being immune to lactate, are actually able to recycle it into fuel more efficiently than lesser athletes.'

'You welcome that feeling because you know that if your legs are burning then someone else's legs are going to be burning all that much more. So it needs to burn for you to know that you're doing it right. You welcome it because it's something you become familiar with,' says Moolman Pasio.

> If we didn't train as much as we did and didn't have that sensation over and over again, it would be an uncomfortable feeling. But because every climber would train by climbing, your body becomes familiar with it and that's the way that you're able to relish it and go through it. Whereas if you weren't accustomed to it, then it would be unpleasant, just as it was the first time that I experienced it. I was like, 'No, it's too uncomfortable. I'm not going to do that.' But the really strange thing about pro cyclists is that we inflict this pain upon ourselves and that pain brings us satisfaction.

The key to adapting to this discomfort isn't simply getting fitter by 'getting in the miles', but also entails training intermittently at high intensities that induce suffering and, as a consequence, enable the brain and the body to cope with this stress and ultimately result in bigger improvements in racing performance. The focus on this kind of training has grown significantly since the early 1990s when I first started reporting on the sport. At that time, riders were still using early-season races to sharpen their condition, but that's gradually changed, to the extent that most riders often now push themselves harder in their training sessions than they will do in most races.

Dan Martin, who turned professional at the start of the 2008 season and retired at the end of 2021 having won mountain stages in all three Grand Tours, explains that this change in training methods has come about largely due to the widening use of power meters and the focus on the data that they deliver. Says the Irishman:

> Early in my career, they were very much in their infancy and with that came a lack of understanding of the data. Whereas now, we've had fifteen to twenty years when coaches have been working with power and as a consequence there's a better understanding of how to create a stimulus, of what's required.
>
> We used to just go out and do twenty minutes at threshold three times and then go home, whereas now there's a better understanding of what racing involves and how to train for that. So training sessions will involve going under and above threshold – say, twenty minutes of one minute above threshold and one minute below, or even shorter efforts than that, what are effectively sprints during the climb, really strong accelerations, because that's what you do in a race. Often training sessions are harder than racing, because you're obviously pushing the limits, while in a race when there's the prospect of winning that gives you the motivation to stay on the wheel. On the other hand, though, in a training session you can collapse on the side of the road and stop completely, but in a race you've got to keep pedalling.

Martin suggests that cycling has lost the simplicity it had when he first started racing, that science and technology have altered the competitive landscape in other significant ways, to the point where some teams are out of the running before the action has even got under way. 'Equipment plays a bigger role than it did because everybody's pushing the limits. It's like Formula 1,' he says.

> If you don't have the right equipment now, you can't win the race. Some teams get to the start line and they've already lost because of their clothing. I think that the difference made by the aerodynamics of the bikes, the wheels and tyres, and the clothing has been massively underplayed as a factor in how the sport has developed in recent seasons. If you have a slow package, you don't have a chance.

He adds that dietary knowledge and its application is another area where there have been huge advances in knowledge, pointing out that this was a realm where he was ahead of the curve, but the rest of the peloton has gradually reeled him in.

> I've always been told that I've got a very good feeling in terms of pacing when it comes to nutrition, of knowing what to eat when. My instinct has always been good and it meant that I did have a better nutrition plan during races. Whereas now my instinct is up against a team of scientists sitting in an office planning out a guy's race. Everybody is so well trained and understands nutrition so well now, to the point where you hardly ever see guys having a bad day in the mountains, or getting sick and blowing up on the last mountain stage of the Tour. Nobody makes mistakes with nutrition any more.

Martin believes the focus on the difference that power meters have had on racing has also led to the importance of dietary expertise being underestimated.

I know people often say, 'Yeah, but they're all looking at their power meter and racing according to what it tells them.' In all honesty, I don't think most people do look at their power meters when they're racing, because you can't. You just have to focus on holding the wheel in front. It's more a case of everybody knowing exactly how much to eat and what to eat when. It's drilled into you and, as a result, the human error element has been reduced. You're basically given a guidebook of exactly what to eat and when and that means you're going to be good at the finish. It's another key part of the professionalism of the sport. The sacrifice involved has increased as well. Guys are willing to go to extremes to get results – weighing their food every day for example. I think you've seen that quite obviously from the way cyclists' bodies have changed over the last twenty years.

Another interesting aspect I noticed when talking to riders about changes in racing and training over recent seasons was how many of them felt they had a more profound connection to the mountains when training out on their own. 'I can't do a training ride without doing some hills or some kind of a mountain or climb. They really stimulate me. I love that kind of scenery, those roads,' says Nicolas Roche. 'When I think about mountains, I think of good training sessions, of the enjoyment I get from the scenery while I'm working.' Moolman Pasio has a very similar perspective, explaining how 'the mountains always present a sense of freedom, of escape, the opportunity for some good mind space. There's something special about fresh mountain air, especially when you go to altitude. It's something you just can't find anywhere else.'

According to Michael Woods, being in control of your training ride rather than at the mercy of the peloton's unpredictability, dangers and whims, and especially if you're going easy, is cathartic. 'You're going at a slow enough pace that you're enjoying everything that's around you, and it's taking you to this high point where you get incredible views and from where you get to earn the fun of the descent that follows. You have a lot of time to think and process thoughts.' What's more, says the Canadian, as well as the restorative stimulus that the landscape provides, it can also foster a very particular connection with a riding partner.

> It's a great opportunity to just chat. Somebody once told me that was one of the reasons why you have such great conversations on a bike is that there's almost a bit of anonymity to it, because you're not directly facing the person. You're looking forwards and because of that you're in your head a bit as well and that enables a more comfortable conversation. I believe that, because when I'm riding with somebody up a climb we have these wonderful conversations.

Racing situations, however, leave no room for these kinds of reflections and conversations. On days that will suit climbers, other feelings predominate. Anticipation, anxiety and excitement are all part of the cocktail, says Moolman Pasio.

> Climbing is an interesting thing, it's what I absolutely love, it's what I ride my bike to do, it's why I'm a professional cyclist. But there's a contradiction, because it's not the case that every experience or every pedal stroke on a climb is enjoyable. But that challenge, that pain, being the first to the top of that mountain, makes what might seem

excruciating actually really enjoyable. You know that you're going to be hurting, but there are plenty of other people in the peloton who are going to be hurting that much more than you.

When you're racing, you can generally always see the climb looming, then coming closer and closer. As you approach it, there's this excitement, but also a nervous feeling that starts to bubble up. Based on what you've done before and the fact you're a climber entering your terrain, you have confidence, but it's mixed in with joy and nerves, because you know that it's going to be a real battle to the top.

As the critical action unfolds, anticipation soon gives way to a realistic appraisal of the situation, which essentially boils down to one basic question: do your legs feel good or not? Or, in current cycling parlance, are you the hammer or the nail? Woods says that there's so much depth within the peloton at WorldTour events that you're almost always likely to be the nail. 'You're often just getting hammered. Ninety-five per cent of the season is spent like that. You're just at the mercy of the guy who's *on* that day,' he says.

I'm there, I'm riding, I'm on the bike, but I want to be anywhere but there. I'm suffering and fighting, wishing that I had that same sensation I had on my best days.

But those moments shape you and make you stronger as a rider if you learn from them. This is such an endurance sport, such a mental sport, that I find those experiences callus your mind a bit, make it stronger. They make a subtly easier day feel that much easier. And even on a harder day, they make you realize that you've gone through something almost as bad before.

Roche puts it like this:

> On days like those you lose a little bit of focus, everything
> starts to hurt – your arse hurts, your shoes are tight, your
> hands are swollen, your jersey's too tight, you're thirsty,
> you're hungry, you've got sore legs, you feel fed up. You're
> asking yourself: 'Where's the top of the climb? Bloody hell,
> there's another 10k to go.'

The key on days like this is to 'dig into your mental toolbox', as one rider put it, and say, 'OK, this is going to be over at some point even though it might hurt like hell right now.' Rather than reflecting on it negatively, the next step is to analyse how you can improve or make things better. Sometimes that might be a change of racing focus, a decision to stop focusing on GC and look for stage wins instead, as Philippa York did towards the end of her career, and as Woods did at the end of the 2021 season, having come to realize that he wasn't at the same level as the likes of Tadej Pogačar and Primož Roglič. It might even mean a more fundamental change, riding for your teammates in the mountains instead of chasing your own ambitions, as Kenny Elissonde did when he joined Team Sky in 2017 and spent three seasons working for Chris Froome, Geraint Thomas and Egan Bernal.

On the other hand, and no matter whether it's a GC rider chasing a leader's jersey, a specialist climber with their focus on a stage win or a mountain domestique who's been assigned the task of setting the tempo for a rider in either of these categories, the sensations are quite different when you're the hammer. For Woods, these moments produce something he describes as being close to an out-of-the-body experience.

When I'm on my best form, I'm able to really separate myself from my body. I almost imagine myself watching from the helicopter above. I know when the climb is going to end, I can see. I'm imagining myself watching on TV where I can see the countdown to the finish line, the time gap to the chasers. I'm able to break the climb down into pieces. I have this incredible kind of perspective.

Those rare moments when he's the hammer produce what he says is effectively an analgesic effect within him.

When I've been successful, it's been the most painless experience from a memory perspective. I know that I suffered, although suffer is not quite right. I know that I was hurting. I know that I was experiencing pain, but I don't remember that. I just remember having the presence of mind to know that I was going to have success, and, in retrospect, that it felt easy.

The Canadian climber adds that he also gains an extraordinary degree of insight into the condition and tactics of his rivals at moments like this.

When I'm on a bad day, I assume that the other guys are feeling better than me. I'm unable to have perspective on how they are doing. Whereas when I'm on my best days, I can almost feel how they are feeling, and I know when to push. When that moment comes, I almost know how to crack another guy. I'm able to remove myself and get away, and even if the guy's chasing me, I can say to myself, 'OK, if I just push this much further, he'll break first.' That's when I have most success, when I win on a mountain top or when I break away on a mountain top, I have that perspective. In those moments, it's just beautiful. It's what I live for in cycling, those fleeting occasions that occur a couple of times a season when you understand what's going on in front of you, behind you and how you're going to react in response to that.

Woods says that his stage win in the 2021 edition of the Tour des Alpes Maritimes et du Var was a good example of him wielding the hammer on his rivals on the wall-like finish into the beautiful Provençal town of Fayence. He explains:

I was that guy. Although it was a really short climb, I knew exactly when to attack, and I knew that if I went at that point it'd be very difficult to beat me, and it was almost shocking to me coming into the final fifty metres how, in my mind, easy it felt. But, obviously, it was very difficult.

Woods isn't alone in his depiction of moments like these when form, objectives and tactics all come to intersect and produce this out-of-the-body effect. 'I kind of agree with that. Because when you're at the front, you get that drive and the adrenaline because you're going for something big or you're defending something,' says Roche.

You have that feeling of not wanting to disappoint yourself, getting as quickly as possible to the top, and you focus on your numbers, you're focused on your rhythm, on your cadence, on your breathing. There's so much happening that you're right in your zone, you're not enjoying the scenery, but you're enjoying the climbing in kind of a vicious way, because you're actually trying to get something out of this climb, rather than just getting over it to survive.

Roche's cousin, Dan Martin, describes how in moments like these the race seems to slow down while, at the same time, the control you have over what's happening around you increases. 'It's almost like a slow-motion thing. When you do have that form, when you are feeling that good, you're not gasping for breath, you have a lot more control over your breathing and a lot more clarity of mind,' he explains. 'It's something that you learn with experience as well, to slow things down, to kind of relax a lot more. Obviously, if you're more relaxed on the bike, the legs are going round smoothly, you can make better decisions.'

Moolman Pasio is in broad agreement too. Says the South African, who describes it as being a quite different sensation to the one she'd tend to have when she's training and, therefore, riding alone:

> These are situations where you do end up detaching yourself, and that's when you have your best performances because you have that ability to be completely in the moment, not really thinking about anything other than just riding your bike as hard as possible. When you're training it's more like a battle with yourself. Whereas in racing, there are other riders around you and the crowds, and that makes a big difference. The noise they create when you're in that moment does enable you to kind of detach yourself and not necessarily feel the pain.

Could this be the rider's perspective of *duende* as it presents itself in cycling, a moment of intensity, nurtured by the fierce discipline of training, that builds within the athlete, pushing them towards the extraordinary, while at the same time there's a communion with the fans forming a narrow corridor on either side of them, their proximity and noise adding even greater dynamism to the experience, transmitting energy to the racer, compelling them to give their best? However you want to depict it, this amalgamation of landscape, athletic prowess and raucous enthusiasm can be hugely intoxicating, the spark for something quite exceptional, for what Kenny Elissonde describes as 'a transcendent feeling', being right in the moment and apart from it at the same time.

The Frenchman was the last man in the Sky line before Chris Froome made his stage- and what proved to be the race-winning break on the Colle delle Finestre in the 2018 Giro d'Italia. Picking up on what Roche says, the diminutive Parisian knew that he was set to play a key part in something big, a strategy that involved not only all of the team's riders, but also every member of the staff on the race, each of them posted along the route to provide Froome with food and bottles if his all-or-nothing raid was to be successful.

> I remember we went to the front of the peloton on the Finestre and with all the switchbacks we could see that the bunch was getting smaller and smaller. Our directeur sportif, Nicolas Portal, was telling us who had been dropped, like the pink jersey Simon Yates. So we knew we were on the verge of something special.
>
> I remember my turn was coming slowly but surely, and I was like, 'OK, let's do it! Let's do it!' I started my pull just when the gravel section of the climb started, and Chris was telling me 'Squeeze! Squeeze!' because he wanted me to go faster and faster. I remember my wheel sliding a bit in a corner and at the next bend I looked behind and there were maybe just five guys in my wheel. The bunch had completely exploded and Nico, who liked to spur us on over the radio, was saying, 'Go Kenny, squeeze, squeeze!' I realized then that we

were making history, that whatever happened, even if we blew totally, it would still be an historic day, a story that would go down in the history of the sport, and I was glad to be part of it. Then I finished my turn, flicked my elbow to say, 'OK, I'm done.' At that instant, I saw Chris was on his own, and I was already thinking, 'Well that's pretty special.' It was only then that I started to think about the pain, about the fact that I'd ridden myself almost to a standstill and still had to ride 80k to the finish.

For her part, ex-professional Philippa York asserts that the out-of-the-body experience isn't something that she was familiar with, or at least initially she does.

There were times, though, when I felt like I was going that fast it was ridiculous. When you're going really, really well, you're riding so fast that you know that nobody is going to go any faster than that, no matter who they are. And the mountain just goes past like it's not there.

Then, pausing to reflect on this last comment, she continues:

Maybe you're right. In those conditions, it is actually quite enjoyable, but only because you're going so fast that it's unbelievable. You also get a lift from the fact that the other riders are struggling. You look down and they're not two inches from your back wheel, a bike length at the most, and you can see them chewing the handlebars, trying to stay with you. That just makes you go even harder.

Andy Hampsten, too, plays down the suggestion of a transfigurative effect.

I'm not going to call it an out-of-body experience, as to me it was the ability to relax mentally and physically under that huge physical stress. My daughter once said when she was reading an article about me, 'Dad, you look so stressed in all of these racing shots.' I was a bit surprised. 'I wasn't stressed,' I told her, 'racing was really fun. I was just on a climb and, as a climber, I didn't get many occasions to show the best of myself, so I had to perform well. As a result, psychologically I pushed myself to go as hard as I could physically. I was stressing myself, but I felt good. I was telling myself that I had to pedal harder to go faster.' I think 'performance' is a great word for it, though, because there's so much energy coming out of the crowd. Sometimes when it worked it really felt like the bike was pedalling itself.

Those words, like York's, suggest that some kind of transcendence was taking place.

This ability to relax is crucial in these high-intensity situations agrees Dan Martin.

Obviously, there's a lot of times you're suffering and thinking how much it's hurting. It's just a natural reaction to being on the limit. But on occasions you do say to yourself, 'Wait, why am I grimacing like this?' If you actually step back out of that moment and just breathe deep and really relax, you don't need to breathe hard, to suffer or to pull faces. Generally, when you're racing up a mountain, you're actually not breathing really hard, because you're at threshold, which means you're not at maximum oxygen capacity. You're coping with the physical stress.

Like Woods, Martin underlines that moments like these are what he relished when racing and were actually what kept prompting him to push himself to his competitive limits, no matter what physical or psychological pressure he felt. 'I think there's a strange enjoyment in it,' he explains.

> Obviously, when you come to the bottom of a climb where the race is going to be decided, you can lose the gains that have been built with three weeks' work in one bad moment, with one mistake, so there can be nervousness or anxiety as far as your form is concerned. I wouldn't describe it as stress, though, because that's what we live for. I'd always much prefer to be racing on a climb than coming into a bunch sprint at 70kph – that's when you're stressed. There's a lot more within your control when you're climbing. You're not relying on the guy in front staying upright, for example.

To highlight his feelings and thought process at critical moments on climbs, the Irishman draws on the experience he had in winning his first and his last Grand Tour stage. The former came in the 2011 Vuelta that saw one of the first iterations of the Sky train, Martin being the quickest to the ski station of La Covatilla from a group that contained Bradley Wiggins and eventual race winner Chris Froome, as well as Dutchman Bauke Mollema and defending champion Vincenzo Nibali. He explains:

> My thinking was always that when I was on the limit, then everybody else was on the limit as well, so that was the time to attack. I remember attacking that day and thinking, 'What the hell are you doing?' But one of the things that often got me through was that my finish line was always at one kilometre to go. Once we got to 1k to go, if I was still in the group, I was always quite confident of winning the sprint.

So it was always kind of a case of I'd suffer and suffer until it was 1k to go, and then a different process would take over, almost like a sprinter's mentality. I remember fighting so many times and suffering so much and then as soon as I'd pass that one-kilometre-to-go mark everything kind of became easy.

Another aspect of having that thought process, he adds, is that with age and experience he learned to create and recreate that thinking for every kilometre of a climb, focusing on each kilometre as it came. 'People can get carried away with thinking, say, that the Tourmalet is seventeen kilometres long and seeing the climb as a whole rather than breaking it into pieces,' he says.

His final Grand Tour, on the 2021 Giro d'Italia stage to Sega di Ala, the same day of Dani Martínez's frenzied urging of teammate Egan Bernal, required a different kind of focus as he broke away close to the foot of the steepling final ascent, ten kilometres from the line. 'That was very controlled, a forty-five-minute effort. You're teetering on the edge of the limit. It was more about breathing deeper and staying focused on the effort, keeping concentrated,' he says.

It's different if you're on your own as well, because in that situation I was very much in control of the effort and not having to follow the wheel, which is when you get sucked into the cycle of suffering because you're fighting to stay there. That's also probably why when you are alone and in control, you tend to go quicker. You're completely focused on what you're doing. You're the hammer. That's what you race a bike for.

Chapter 17

The new golden age

When, in 2020, the Tour de France raced towards Orcières-Merlette five decades on from one of the most celebrated climbing exploits in racing history, the finale to the stage could hardly have been any more different to Luis Ocaña's solo success there in 1971 that put the Spaniard in the yellow jersey having ridden away from the apparently unsinkable Eddy Merckx as well as the rest of the peloton. Forty-nine years on, as Primož Roglič engaged his turbo over the final few hundred metres into the resort, there were almost twenty riders on the Slovenian's tail. What's more, his Jumbo-Visma team had just served up the best lead-out the race would see, not at the approach to a sprint finish but heading into and up the first-category final climb, Tony Martin, Robert Gesink, Wout van Aert and, ultimately, Sepp Kuss setting a blistering tempo into the Champsaur valley resort.

In its analysis of that stage and Jumbo-Visma's rise that had led to its anointment as the strongest team in the sport, *Cyclingnews* stated that, 'team director Richard Plugge must be delighted at how his project for a Dutch powerhouse in cycling has already come to fruition. Plugge must be thinking about Ineos Grenadiers' principal Dave Brailsford in the same way David Cameron spoke of Tony Blair: you were the future once.' That assessment looked justified as the Dutch team continued to dominate in the mountains, first helping Roglič into the yellow jersey and then to push his lead out to a minute by the La Planche des Belles Filles time trial on the penultimate day, enough of a buffer to secure the title it seemed. Yet, right at the death, Tadej Pogačar turned Jumbo's future past historic.

The young Slovenian's almost wholly unexpected success demonstrated that innate talent and instinctive brilliance can triumph over pacing and power meters. To an extent, his was a repeat of Julian Alaphilippe's performance the previous year. However, rather than leading a merry dance at the front end of the race and then trying to hang on as the Frenchman had done, Pogačar worked his way forwards from back in the pack, his form and momentum building through mountain stage victories at Laruns and on the Grand Colombier and into his final coup in the Vosges. In retaining the title in 2021, he showed the same élan, success in the opening time trial being followed up with a series of flamboyant performances in the mountains, culminating in back-to-back victories in the Pyrenees.

Were these performances outliers, a show of superiority from a rider who looks destined to amass major titles for seasons to come? Or were they a sign of a fundamental change in the approach to strategy within the sport, one that will see a shift away from climbing based on calculation (watts per kilo divided by distance and multiplied by the number of riders) and towards a purer style of racing, pitting rider against rider? There's a head and a heart answer to these questions.

In the first instance, it should be stressed that cycling's application of a science-led approach to racing and, above all, to training, has changed the complexion of the sport for the better. In combination with more and better controls as well as the Athlete Biological Passport, doping appears to have been reduced, and substantially according to most experts, although it is evident that the boundary between legitimacy and prohibition is still being tested. At the same time, though, performance has gradually become so data-led that spontaneity, racing on 'feel', appears to have lost its place. Soon after Pogačar won his second Tour title, one professional told me of a race where a rival had clearly been stronger than everyone else but had failed to deliver the attack that would almost certainly have demonstrated that fact because he'd ridden up each climb looking at the numbers on his power meter, clearly holding to the figure that he'd been told to. In the end, riding to that number rather than going beyond it meant that he finished on the lowest step of the podium rather than the highest.

Talking to Andy Hampsten about how racing changed over his career, he pointed out that this tendency to see science as always having the correct answer and, as a consequence, riding to your numbers first became apparent when heart-rate monitors were popularized in the early 1990s, when he was with Motorola. 'Both Doctor Max Testa and Eddy Merckx, who was working with us, said to throw them away, that they provided negative biofeedback,' says Hampsten.

> Testa felt that we should just be trying to go faster and that the key marker for that was your speedometer, and that you should just try to go quicker by being more efficient, by relaxing something or changing gear, instead of looking at your heart rate and thinking, 'This is great, I've got my number down.' I'm sure back in the team feed where you download your data, you'd think, 'I'm in good shape, I was at my anaerobic threshold, I was in zone whatever. No one can blame me. That is my best.' But Eddy Merckx's point was, 'No, you've got to go beyond that.'

Although the sometimes blind adherence to numbers hasn't been all-encompassing, thanks to both the amount and the quality of the data that they deliver on training and racing performance power meters have subsequently become the omnipresent technological tool that's depicted as putting a brake on flair, with Team Sky portrayed as the principal thrill-killers. There have been calls from a few riders, but more especially from lots of ex-pros and event organizers, for power meters to be banned from racing, but racers are now so well acquainted with their numbers from training that this move would probably make little difference. It should also be borne in mind that Sky's mountain 'train' was no more than an inevitable refinement of tactics employed by so many predecessors, from Fausto Coppi's Bianchi team through to Lance Armstrong's US Postal, the British team gaining an edge by employing hugely talented and very well-paid riders like former world champion Michał Kwiatkowski to train for a very specific role on the climbs, riding for substantial stretches of time at a high pace until their true climbing specialists came to the front, the strategy defensive but aggressive, boring but impressive.

The quest to escape from the perceived tyranny of numbers has led race organizers to seek out a variety of solutions – short stages, cobbles, gravel, finishes on viciously steep climbs long and short . . . Sometimes these novelties work and produce something spectacular – the 2021 Giro stage that featured the 'white roads' of Tuscany is a good example of this – but spicing routes up in this fashion can result in them becoming predictable in a different way because they often tend to favour a certain kind of racer, *puncheurs* in the Julian Alaphilippe and Mathieu van der Poel mould who can rip a peloton apart on a climb.

Watching these attempts to encourage chaos instead of control, I think back to a conversation I had with then rider and now directeur sportif Tejay van Garderen in 2018 when he voiced the concern that 'organisers are trying to manipulate the *parcours* because they only want to see climbing, only explosions, they want something unforeseen to happen every day . . . They're trying to make every race exactly the same with exactly the same guys winning, with lots of attacking.' The likes of Alaphilippe and van der Poel are undoubtedly good box office, but stage races, and especially the three-week soap operas that are the Grand Tours, need their sub-plots, those days when other kinds of riders, breakaway specialists and sprinters for instance, are the focus.

What's more, my heartfelt sense is that riders don't need to be impelled towards 'explosions' because they're already moving away from risk aversion and embracing a more aggressive style of racing, and that this has been particularly apparent in the mountains, where the train is no longer the predominant force at all times and long-range attacks are back in vogue.

Several factors have played a part in this. Dan Martin says the primary one is the Pogačar effect, the emergence of a dominant Grand Tour rider who sees racing as a game that should be played rather than a discipline where order needs to be imposed. Says the Irishman of his former teammate:

> Tadej's brought a different style of racing in and teams are trying to figure out how to beat him. The only way they can is to be aggressive and try to isolate him, although he still seems to be winning. His style of racing is definitely changing things around and forcing teams to rethink stuff.

The thrills served up by the peloton's star *puncheurs* Julian Alaphilippe, Mathieu van der Poel and Wout van Aert have contributed to this captivating mix, with the result, says Martin, being 'Some of the most entertaining races of the last decade have been in the recent seasons because of the individuals involved.' Add in the uncertainty created by Covid restrictions that led to more uncompromising racing when events did go ahead, as well as a growing inclination among teams to entertain, to look for the instant hit that a stage victory brings rather than devoting all their resources to a push for a high overall finish that might not capture any headlines at all, and cycling's future looks enthralling.

Sky's successors Ineos have been part of this trend. The lavishly backed British team has cast off *catenaccio* for a strategy that's more free-form, the transformation prompted by Tao Geoghegan Hart's thrilling victory against all expectations at the 2020 Giro. 'We've done the train, we've done the defensive style of riding and won a lot doing that, but it's not as much fun, really, compared to this, is it?' Brailsford said in Milan after the young Briton had ridden away with the *maglia rosa* in the mountains during the final week. 'At the end of the day, the sport is about racing, it's about emotion and the exhilarating moments of racing, and that's what we want to be.'

Cynics point to the fact that Ineos's ranks no longer feature the peloton's outstanding Grand Tour racer and that they've been forced into ditching their winning formula by the advent of Pogačar, and this has undoubtedly played a part in this radical switch of philosophy. Yet the team's performances in the wake of Geoghegan Hart's victory suggest that their riders have been unshackled, exemplified in 2021 by Egan Bernal's Giro victory and Richie Porte's success at the Critérium du Dauphiné. It's embodied, above all, by the verve and cunning of Richard Carapaz, who has said of himself that, 'The warrior in me comes out when I'm on the bike.'

If anything, the Ecuadorean is too eager to attack, but a Giro title, podium finishes at the Tour and Vuelta, and victory in the Tokyo Olympics road race in 2021 are testament to the effectiveness of his ballsy attitude. During that year's Tour, when he finished third overall after persistent harrying of Pogačar in the mountains, his teammate Kwiatkowski opined, 'I think he has been attacking too much, to be honest,' the Pole then adding, 'I guess he just believes he can win the Tour de France and if you sit on the wheels you're never going to win. That's just Richard. The belief is there and he will keep on trying. Sometimes it's difficult to make a difference, but it's in his nature, his style.'

Another equally significant reason for optimism is the increasing investment in women's racing that's concurrent with its rapidly growing profile. Whether you regard 2022's first edition of the Tour de France Femmes as a completely new race, which organizers ASO were keen to brand it, or as an overdue relaunch of previous iterations of an event that was launched in 1984 as the Tour de France Féminin, the eight-day event should provide a vital narrative in the mountains that's often been missing from women's stage races due to the paucity of press and, above all, TV coverage. Although there was criticism of a route that didn't feature any of the Tour's legendary high places, the two concluding stages into the Vosges have been well chosen from a competitive and historic perspective. I'm convinced that fans and the media will respond enthusiastically to this race and that it will become a pivotal event on the calendar, revealing the new lineage of the queens of the mountains, who will finally be feted in the same way as the kings long have been.

Writing this in my home in the Pyrenees on an icy December morning with cloud, rain and occasional flurries of snow cloaking the hairpins zigzagging up the far side of the Barguillère valley towards the 2019 Tour de France summit finish of Prat d'Albis, I can feel a warming rush of adrenaline as I think ahead to the season to come. Three decades on from my first experience of these mountains and of the Tour de France, at the start of a period when the sport became mired in deception and controversy, my sense is that not only is the sport in a much better place but it has entered a golden age of racing that will perhaps stand comparison with similar periods in the past, the post-war Coppi–Bartali–Bobet–Anquetil years, for instance, and the 1970s and 80s when Merckx, Hinault, Fignon and LeMond were in their pomp. While familiar problems remain, the perennial issue of finding and retaining sponsors most obviously, questions relating to the safety and health of riders, and, inevitably, doping – this is cycling, after all – I've never felt as much anticipation for racing, to see what exploit the likes of Alaphilippe, Vos, van Aert, Vollering and van der Poel will serve up next.

This more dynamic spirit is most evident in the hills and mountains, where the racing spectacle is once again matching the setting for drama. I got a glimpse into this standing at the roadside just below the little ski station at Luz Ardiden that hosted the final summit finish of the 2021 Tour de France, just 50 kilometres or so from the Col de Marie-Blanque where I first encountered the race. I'd ridden up there from Luz-Saint-Sauveur on a chilly, but perfectly clear October morning the previous autumn, the only cyclist on the climb that culminates with a wiggle of tightly packed hairpins to reach the one weary-looking building that is the resort. I stood at the top, the sun warming me, looking back down the road as it snaked down the mountainside for four or five kilometres, reflecting on what a remarkable arena it is.

Nine months on, I drove back up the climb to watch the finish of the 2021 Tour's final mountain stage from a point very close to where I'd so recently stood, the snaking road now lined with tens of thousands of fans, that impression was fully confirmed as I was reminded once again that it's on the climbs that cycling's magic happens. The racing was exceptional, not a train in sight as Richard Carapaz, Jonas Vingegaard, Enric Mas and Tadej Pogačar sparred with each other coming up through those bends, the latter defending his yellow jersey with a string of attacks, the final one decisive. I watched every rider pass, the first of them on their limit as they fought to defend their overall position, but many that followed cruising and smiling now that the mountains were almost over and the finish in Paris was almost in sight. At the back were a handful of Deceuninck riders, the blue jerseys of Michael Mørkøv, Tim Declercq, Dries Devenyns and Davide Ballerini in a wind-deflecting wedge formation around the green jersey of points leader Mark Cavendish, his physiological torture almost over. It was an experience to be treasured. A time not to wonder why they do it, but to delight in the fact that they do.

Epilogue

We're late arriving at the checkpoint at the foot of the climb to Hautacam. The car's headlights light up a temporary sign that informs: 'No vehicles will be allowed to pass after 22h00'. There's a slow-moving line of cars into the roundabout where the climb begins, the driver in each one pausing when they reach the front to plead with the gendarmes blocking the route upwards. Inevitably, given that it's now well past eleven, their entreaties are in vain and they're soon circling away to the left and back into the darkness on the main road as instructed.

After a couple of minutes, it's our turn. I point to the top of the windscreen, bringing the young gendarme's attention to the press accreditation sticker. It's the golden ticket to Hautacam, and she waves us through.

According to the *Tour de France Road Book*, the race bible, we're 13.6 kilometres from the top, although I know from a previous visit a couple of years before that the road continues on above the tiny ski station – passing the giant mechanical toboggan that my kids had to be dragged away from after two hours of ups and downs – to reach the Col de Tramassel, a start point for numerous walking, cross-country skiing and snowshoeing trails, and which also boasts one of the most spectacular views I've seen anywhere in the Pyrenees.

But that's for tomorrow. All we can see for now is the back-end of a white van, which creeps through every bend and switchback, partly hindered by its length and low wheelbase, but also by people in the road. Some have pots of paint and rollers, and step back from their mid-road daubings to let us pass, carrying off some of the emulsion used to identify favourites on our tyres. Most, though, are in party mode, waving and cheering at every vehicle, sound systems blaring techno and French pop, the smell of barbecues ever present. In the back seat, my teenage kids and the dog – yes, I am the kind of idiot who takes a dog to a bike race – are at full volume too. The cacophony of shouting, cheering, barking and Bigflo et Oli would be bedlam in almost any other situation, but at this moment it's impossible to avoid being swept up in the delirium, which I add to by hooting the horn as we inch by each gaggle of partygoers.

As we clamber higher and higher, my spirits start to become tempered by a nagging concern. I've been looking for places where we might pull over and set up camp, but every nook is filled. The 2022 Tour has been one of the most thrilling of recent years, possibly of all time, and Hautacam has been invaded by hordes of cycling fans, all set on witnessing the final mountain duel between two-time defending champion Tadej Pogačar and his Danish rival Jonas Vingegaard, who holds the yellow jersey thanks to a remarkable show of tactics and collaboration by his Jumbo-Visma team a few days earlier at the lofty and remote Col du Granon in the Alps.

We keep climbing, all the way into the car park at the ski station, where there is space. I gesture to the windscreen again, but this time the stewards and gendarmes are unrelenting. This is where President Emmanuel Macron's security detail will be located tomorrow, one of them tells me. We're told to look elsewhere.

We continue upwards to the car park on the Col de Tramassel, but it's filled with TV trucks, circled in a protective corral to prevent incursion by hostiles. The meadows just beyond are empty, but barricaded, set aside for the arrival of the Tour's publicity caravan the following afternoon.

We retrace a couple of hundred metres to a rough track lined with camper vans. The gradient increases, becoming too steep for these behemoths and there, finally, is a gap, albeit one at a 30-degree angle. We pull out our three small tents and pitch them in a line on the edge of the ballast-covered track, overlooking the toboggan run and ski station. It's now well past midnight, too late to be cooking dinner, and we're hurried under cover by gathering mist, clinging and damp.

While the kids and the dog sleep soundly, my wife and I are defeated by the gradient. She wakes up halfway through the night to find she's slid off her pillow and out of her sleeping bag to the bottom of the tent, while I can't get comfortable with all of the lumps and potholes. Eventually, I get up and take the dog for a walk up the track. As we climb, the sky starts to lighten a touch, and I can see that the mist has dropped into the Lavedan valley way below. The beauty of this inversion grows with the glow of dawn, reddening the top of the cloud, illuminating the bustle already taking place around the finish line, the road towards it gradually emerging from the dissipating gloom as the heat begins to build.

After breakfast, we tramp down the track, across the meadows and down past the finish line to find a place on the barriers. After years of doing this, we're professionals now. We've got folding chairs, a shelter for the dog and enough supplies to keep us going all day. We set up camp for the day and settle down to watch people riding past, waiting for indications that the publicity caravan is approaching.

In the early afternoon, the first motorbikes fly into view around the hairpin below us, heralding the publicity caravan's arrival, and my daughter outlines the tactics for this part of the day. We're each assigned positions a few dozen metres apart in order to optimize our collection of publicity-caravan goodies/tat. Among the former is the gingham bucket hat promoting Cochonou sausage products – like the polka-dot jersey, this is an emblem of the Tour – and the green Škoda T-shirts that the kids use as nightwear. Our harvest is decent, although we'll have to stick to existing pyjamas for another season.

Once the caravan has passed, weaving upwards into that cordoned-off meadow somewhere above us, there's a two-hour wait for the race to arrive. A quickening flow of Garde Républicaine motorbikes is the first signal that it's closing. Then comes the distant sound of helicopters, their clatter increasing as they track the lead riders, who are ascending Hautacam's lower ramps. The mountain's mobile transponder is so overloaded with users that we've got no idea what's going on, so I walk around the bend above us and within sight of the big screen at the finish line and watch Vingegaard's Jumbo-Visma teammates tear the yellow jersey group apart.

Tiesj Benoot begins the evisceration of the Dane's rivals. When the solid and round-shouldered Belgian pulls aside with 11 kilometres remaining to Hautacam's summit, Sepp Kuss, slight even by cycling's slimmed-down standards, takes over, the American dancing on the pedals with the typically staccato bob of a pure climber, pushes the pace a notch higher. The speed's not quite fierce enough to prevent Thibaut Pinot sashaying away on a solo sortie in that same dartingly insistent style, but there will be no race-redefining win for the *chouchou* of the French fans. Kuss gradually brings their favourite to heel.

Just before the five-kilometres-to-go banner, Kuss runs out of bounce and swings aside, bringing the latest incarnation of 'The Human Locomotive' to the front of the Jumbo train. The nickname was coined for Learco Guerra, a much-decorated Italian powerhouse of the 1930s, and fits Wout van Aert perfectly. The Belgian has the brooding good looks of a matinée-idol of that era. This has been van Aert's Tour as much as Vingegaard's. Resplendent in the green jersey of the points competition leader, he's won two stages, will win a third two days hence and held the yellow jersey for four days. He's left his imprint on every kind of terrain and he quickly does so again.

As on the Granon, Pogačar loses contact with a touch more than four kilometres remaining. Van Aert hurtles on with Vingegaard hitched to his wheel for another half kilometre or so before running out of steam, leaving the Dane to finish off the textbook display of teamwork by Jumbo. Passing us, on the very final bend where the car of race director Christian Prudhomme with President Macron alongside him is the only entity tracking him, he knows that the Tour is won, assuming he can pick his way through the minor obstacles of the last three days. Although there's a time trial still to come, there's no possibility of Pogačar upstaging Jumbo's leader as he managed to do two years previously at La Planche des Belles Filles, when his Slovenian compatriot Primož Roglič thought he had the yellow jersey won. Finally, the Dutch team has claimed what had been an elusive prize.

Seen in isolation, this final mountain stage of the 2022 Tour suggested that Vingegaard's success was redolent of the same tactical approach employed by Team Sky in their pomp, a train of powerhouse performers leading into the final climb, each completing a pre-decided stint of pace-making, then easing aside to allow another, usually smaller and more nimble, teammate to set the tempo. Yet, the foundation for the Dane's victory had been laid eight days earlier on the stage to the Col de Granon, where Jumbo adopted a very different strategy, a tag-team approach whereby its riders took turns roughing up Pogačar and UAE Team Emirates.

To understand how this tactic came about, let's first rewind to the 2020 Tour, in which Roglič and Jumbo were denied at the very last by race debutant Pogačar. The Dutch team made no secret of the fact they'd studied Sky's strategy and in that 2020 race they fielded what became apparent was a train every bit as formidable as any fielded by the British squad. They put on a demonstration of power riding on the first summit finish at Orcières-Merlette, laying down a blistering rhythm, with Tony Martin, Tom Dumoulin, Sepp Kuss, Wout van Aert, Robert Gesink and George Bennett all playing a prominent part before Roglič scooted away in the final few hundred metres to grab the stage win, just ahead of Pogačar.

And on they ploughed, always impressive, but never delivering a killer blow to Roglič's young compatriot. Indeed, by the time the race reached the penultimate stage, the mountain time trial to La Planche des Belles Filles, 41 of the 57 seconds that comprised Roglič's lead had been gained on the wind-hit stage into Lavaur at the end of the first week, when the UAE leader was caught behind a split in the peloton and ended up in the second group. For the most part, Pogačar, lacking the team support and the experience to take the initiative, had sat comfortably on Jumbo's coat-tails, effectively substituting the Dutch team for his own.

The sole occasion when Roglič gained time on his countryman in the mountains was on the Col de la Loze, where his 15-second gain was widely seen as an indication that the youngster was running out of juice. La Planche des Belles Filles proved, of course, that that assumption was abjectly wrong. Described by former time trial world champion Tom Dumoulin as 'the miner from Slovenia' due to his lack of finesse on a TT bike, Pogačar, who had beaten Roglič to the Slovenian time trial title three months previously, had enough left in his tank to turn his 57-second deficit into a 59-second advantage.

'We thought we had a good tactics and we thought we had a good lead on Pogačar before the last TT and it didn't happen. In hindsight, there were a few things that we would have done differently knowing the outcome, but in the race, we thought we were actually playing it pretty well,' Jumbo sporting director Grischa Niermann admits to me during the 2023 edition of Paris–Nice when reflecting on that race and its highly dramatic endgame.

The following year, Jumbo backed Roglič again, only for him to suffer a crash on the third day that ultimately forced him to abandon before the Tour reached the high mountains. It was here, though, that race debutant Vingegaard emerged as a Grand Tour racer of immense potential. Allowed a freer role following his leader's abandon from the race, the Dane dropped Pogačar on Mont Ventoux and then went head-to-head with the Slovenian on consecutive Pyrenean summit finishes on the Col de Portet and Luz Ardiden. Second to the defending champion and race leader on both of those latter occasions and, ultimately, second in Paris, Vingegaard gave Jumbo another card to play.

'We knew Jonas was really good,' Niermann explains, 'but he

surprised us in the Tour, especially in the second half, on Mont Ventoux and in the Pyrenees with how strong and good he is racing uphill. And so in 2022, we clearly went into the Tour with two leaders with Jonas and Primož because we knew that Tadej Pogačar is so strong. He's almost unbeatable one-on-one, and we thought we'd found a way to dismantle that, to drop him on the two most decisive stages of the Tour.'

Niermann stresses how pivotal that stage over the Ventoux was. 'It wasn't only significant for us guys, but I think for everybody in the whole peloton. It was the first moment in maybe almost a year and a half that Pogačar had shown a sign of weakness, or at least that he couldn't follow for the first time. It gave us hope that we could manage it again. I think it also gave a lot of other teams hope. They also saw that Pogačar is only a human being, although a very special one,' says the German team director. Vingegaard confirms how critical it was, telling me, 'I think that's the day that changed my mindset, from not thinking I could drop him to actually thinking, "OK, I actually have a chance of riding away from him and dropping him on a long climb." That really changed a lot for me.'

In the wake of the 2021 Tour, Merijn Zeeman, another of Jumbo's sporting directors who focuses on the technical aspects of racing, looked for different approaches to sporting success, fired by the adage, 'If you do what you did, you get what you got.' Just as Dave Brailsford had done when Sky were in their pomp, he looked outside the sport for inspiration, turning most notably to Manchester United manager Erik ten Hag. 'I wanted to understand from him: how do you arrive at tactics? What for you is the essence of your sport? Before you make a game plan, what's behind it? I had the opportunity to talk to him about that several times,' Zeeman told Dutch national broadcaster NOS.

He also set up a working group comprising members of Jumbo's backroom staff, including its most experienced sports directors, Niermann and Frans Maassen. Zeeman explained:

> We also asked guys who collect the data in the background to get thinking. With central questions like: what can we do better, what are we not doing well, what are our competitors doing? We held a lot of sessions. All through the winter. With great talents like Wout van Aert, Primož Roglič, Jonas Vingegaard and Steven Kruijswijk in your team, you can come up with different tactics. Just as good football coaches have good football players at their disposal with which to win matches, you can also plan when you've got good riders at your disposal.

Niermann, as he does every year, took on the task of looking over the Tour route in forensic detail, driving thousands of kilometres across France in between his management commitments at races. Underpinning of all this was one question: where are Pogačar's weaknesses? 'We kept on looking for those. What are his pitfalls, where is his weakness, what kind of team does he have, where can we hit them? And how do you translate that to our qualities on the course?' Zeeman underlined.

Pogačar's racing data and past performances were analysed, as were those of his key teammates. Among the other avenues Jumbo's researchers went down was picking over the two-time Tour champion's comments in the media, including an appearance in November 2021 on Geraint Thomas's podcast, *The Geraint Thomas*

Cycling Club. In the midst of a light-hearted and very laidback discussion of many things racing with the 2018 Tour winner, Pogačar offered an illuminating insight into his weaknesses on the bike. He said of his rivals:

> They shouldn't be scared of me because I can crack really fast. I put out good power on not so long climbs, but sometimes the longer climbs are worse for me, and as for high altitude . . . I think they've already figured that out. If it happens that my team isn't so strong, long-range attacks can make it more difficult for us. For sure, trying to racing aggressively from a long way out with multiple riders – Ineos, for instance have a lot of leaders, so they can try a lot of things a different way. There can be a lot of things that crack me and anybody else. It's not that complicated.

As if to prove Pogačar right in that final assessment, Jumbo-Visma set about planning a mountain coup on the hitherto impregnable Tour champion. Knowing that he tends to be the strongest on short, steep ascents, Jumbo's working group decided that the key to it was trying to ensure that the Slovenian was forced to expend a significant part of his physical resources before a long, hard climb, preferably one well above the 2,000-metre mark, which is regarded as the symbolic barrier to high altitude. Their focus quickly settled on stages 11 and 12 of the 2022 Tour, which concluded with summit finishes on the Col de Granon and Alpe d'Huez, respectively.

These stages deliberately harked back to the 1986 Tour, won by American Greg LeMond after a race-long duel with his own La Vie Claire teammate and five-time Tour winner Bernard Hinault, making the final appearance of his career. The Frenchman had committed to assisting LeMond's quest for a first yellow jersey victory having leaned heavily on the American in winning the title the year before. Whether he lived up to that promise still remains the subject of debate, but what can be said for certain is that the 1986 Tour hinged on those two stages. On the first, to the 2,413-metre Granon, Hinault was dropped and lost the yellow jersey to his teammate. On the second, the pair finished hand-in-hand at Alpe d'Huez, their only rival, Urs Zimmermann, minutes in arrears.

Jumbo's harrying of Pogačar began early in the first week, but didn't appear to unsettle the defending champion, who took the yellow jersey on the short, uphill finish at Longwy on stage six, before outlasting Vingegaard the very next day on the much tougher finale at La Super Planche des Belles Filles, located at the top of a kilometre-long gravel road above the traditional finish. In the immediate aftermath of that stage, UAE climber George Bennett, who had joined Pogačar's team that winter after seven seasons in the Jumbo set-up, told me: 'There'll be one day where it just goes apeshit, a day when Roglič goes in the break, when Sepp [Kuss] drops everybody. We never get complacent and we expect more every day. Maybe it'll be a sprint stage and they'll put the big guys on the front in the crosswind.'

Bennett pitched this battle as being between 'the best rider I've ever seen in my life' and teams with strength in depth. 'Jumbo have an advantage of having two guys that are dangerous, they can set up a lot of situations. So we're gonna have a really, really big battle.' Then he added, with a broad smile, 'And, as a fan of cycling, I'm looking forward to it.'

Unfortunately for the Kiwi and for Pogačar, Bennett was forced out of the race the day before the Granon stage, the second UAE rider to succumb to a positive test for Covid. Jumbo, meanwhile, still had a full complement of riders, although Roglič was hampered by the injuries he'd sustained when he hit a hay bale that had ended up in the road during the earlier stage across Roubaix's cobbles into Arenberg. Although he'd popped a dislocated shoulder back in himself, he was unable to stand on the pedals and produce the rapid-fire accelerations that are his trademark as a consistent winner of major titles.

The Granon stage began with Pogačar in yellow, his lead 11 seconds on second-placed Lennard Kämna and 39 seconds on Vingegaard, with Geraint Thomas in fourth at 1'17" and the ailing Roglič thirteenth, almost three minutes back. Jumbo's pre-Tour plan had been to get two riders into the early breakaway, with the aim that they would provide Vingegaard with support later in the stage from the foot of the Galibier. Benoot and van Aert had been assigned these roles, with a view to their being able to set a fast tempo on the front of the yellow jersey group in the valley between the Télégraphe and Galibier, the two climbs that preceded the Granon. Once they were on the early slopes of the 2,642-metre Galibier, Roglič would attack.

However, Jumbo tweaked their strategy during the Tour's first rest day at Châtel, as head of performance Mathieu Heijboer later explained to NOS. 'We decided that we would attack earlier than planned. We decided that doing so on the Galibier would be leaving it too late. We wanted to create a surprise. We decided that Primož would try on the Télégraphe.'

The plan didn't go exactly as it had been laid out, although the difference was only one of personnel. Rather than Benoot, it was Christophe Laporte who ended up in the breakaway group with van Aert. Benoot, though, still played a significant role, leading out Roglič's attack towards the top of the Télégraphe, a steady climb from the vast Maurienne valley, a busy communications route from France's second city, Lyon, through the mountains into northern Italy. Set up by Benoot, Roglič accelerated, his move provoking a flurry of counterattacks, including by race leader Pogačar, who looked to reassert his authority. Soon after, Laporte was swept up, enabling Jumbo to enact the next part of their strategy, with the Frenchman keeping up the pressure on Pogačar, who kept looking back to see if his teammates were getting back up to this yellow jersey group.

The next key point was Plan Lachat, where, having travelled almost due south from the Maurienne, over the Télégraphe and through the ski station of Valloire, the road switches sharply back on itself across a stone bridge and begins to gain altitude much more quickly as it clambers towards the oxygen-thin Galibier. Here, Roglič attacked once again. Isolated from his teammates, Pogačar had to respond himself, as he had done lower down the pass. Soon, he and Vingegaard were clear on their own and engaged in a head-to-head battle to the summit of the Galibier, the pair of them still perfectly matched.

On the long descent from Galibier to the foot of the Granon, they caught and soon dropped van Aert, and it appeared Jumbo's plan was unravelling. However, the Belgian wasn't yet finished. Approaching the foot of the Granon, he led a group containing Roglič, Kuss and Steven Kruijswijk up to the yellow jersey group. Pogačar, who looked extremely relaxed and confident as he laughed and joked with the motorbike TV cameras, gained an ally too in Polish climber Rafał Majka. It was five against two as they raced onto the Granon, 11.4 kilometres long, its average gradient a fearsome 9.1 per cent.

Jumbo's tactic was more straightforward now. First van Aert set the pace, then fell back, this time for good. Then Roglič took it on, his pace proving too strong for Kuss. When Roglič yielded, Majka took over and for a few minutes UAE appeared to have restored order. Kruijswijk lost ground, leaving Vingegaard on his own with Pogačar and a key teammate. 'For ten minutes or so, when first Sepp and then Steven were dropped halfway up the Granon, we were afraid,' Heijboer later confessed. 'All of a sudden, the balance had tipped and after outnumbering them earlier [five against two], there was only Jonas left while Pogačar still had Majka. We thought that it wasn't going to work, that we'd done all that work for nothing and that the only chance we had left was Jonas's legs.'

What did the Dane have left? The answer to that came when Vingegaard made his first acceleration with 4.5 kilometres remaining on the Granon. He'd sensed that Pogačar was straining to stay on Majka's wheel and swept by the UAE pair. The Pole tried to respond to the Jumbo rider, but in doing so dropped his leader. Majka eased off to pace the yellow jersey, who had cracked badly. As Vingegaard flew on up the formidable pass, passing first Romain Bardet, then Nairo Quintana and finally Warren Barguil as he rode away for the stage win, the ashen-faced Pogačar barely turned his head as Geraint Thomas, David Gaudu and Adam Yates edged past him. After Majka finally wilted, the yellow jersey reeled on alone, eventually finishing almost three minutes down on new race leader Vingegaard, whose advantage on the Slovenian was 2'22".

'I was a bit surprised that the gap was so big,' Heijboer said. 'But from early on the Télégraphe we'd ridden full gas, attacked all the way to the top of the Galibier. We'd planned to make the race very hot because the more difficult it was the more convinced we were that we could open a gap.' Jumbo-Visma's social media accounts were more succinct: 'We love it when a plan comes together.'

The Dutch team's strategy could now turn to defence, Vingegaard parrying attacks by Pogačar in the final kilometres at Alpe d'Huez the next day, on the short and steep ascent up to the aerodrome at Mende two days later, at Foix three days on from that, and once again 24 hours later on the savage incline of the altiport runway at the Pyrenean resort of Peyragudes. Then came Jumbo's blitz of Pogačar's defences at Hautacam, which all but clinched the overall title for them.

'When you're in the mix you're probably a little biased about how good the race has been, but it was a great fight, a great show, and I think it was very good for the sport,' Grischa Niermann tells me. 'You also saw that Pogačar never gives up and always keeps trying, while we on the other hand had the right riders and the right tactics to cope with that and to turn it around and to put the pressure on him. I think that this was a really nice and very entertaining Tour de France.'

UAE team director Andrej Hauptman, who has been advising and working with Pogačar since he was in his mid-teens, agrees that the spectacle was impressive and confesses that this made up for the defeat to a degree. 'We're all human, everyone. There's no supermen here,' he tells me during the 2023 Paris–Nice. 'There are a lot of other great champions who are really good competitors at Tour de France, and if Tadej was as great as some claim he would win every race. In the end, though, even though we lost the 2022 Tour, we still had a great Tour and we will try to do [the] same or better this year.'

There was a hint of how UAE may try to achieve that during the 2023 edition of Paris–Nice, the first stage-race clash between Pogačar and Vingegaard since the previous summer's Tour. With two of the team's new recruits, Tim Wellens and Felix Großschartner, particularly prominent, UAE routed their rivals on the mid-length passes where their leader is always at his best, and Pogačar romped to victory in Nice, bagging three stage wins while reasserting his authority over Vingegaard. Both riders, though, were quick to underline that what happens at 'the Race to the Sun' in March will have very little bearing on events at the Tour four months later.

When being probed a little deeper into their motivation as racers, neither Pogačar nor Vingegaard admits to a particular pull towards the mountains, the reverence and love for highland terrain that the likes of Pierre Rolland, Dan Martin and Mike Woods acknowledge so effusively. Asking Vingegaard what emotions he feels when racing and training on big climbs, he responds quite practically, saying: 'I think the high mountains is where I'm the best, that's really where my strength is. So, for sure, that's also where I feel the most at home.' But he looks nonplussed.

It could be down to the fact that he's talking in his second language, or that, at 26, he's still relatively young for a racer. But there's also a sense that climbing is, for him, just one part of the competitive process that has to be prepared for and strategized. The sport has become so professionalized that the romance that's always been associated with the mountains has been stripped away by the extreme physical and psychological demands of every aspect of racing.

Dan Martin offered a sense of this when he retired from racing at the end of 2021, writing in his autobiography, *Chased by Pandas*, about how the drive for 'marginal gains' had led to riders handing over responsibility for themselves to sports scientists and other performance gurus in order to do things perfectly. 'The fear of fun had been passed down since time immemorial in this sport, but it was accelerating before my eyes,' says the Irishman. 'Time had to be spent in a sealed bubble, either racing or training. The rider didn't just give his body to his team, he entrusted his whole life to them. Some riders were afraid of pleasure. I was afraid of becoming a robot.'

When I press Vingegaard on his feelings when he won on the Granon and Hautacam, he looks bewildered momentarily, almost as if he's not considered these extraordinary moments in great depth, that he essentially considers these victories as the successful implementation of a plan that was long and detailed in its conception. 'When I think back, they were probably the two best performances that I've ever done, and I think I can be really happy and proud of how I raced those days and how high my level was,' he replies. He's a little more effusive when talking about the importance of his team on the Granon stage, explaining: 'You can never do anything without your team, and especially on a day like that. We made a big plan before the day and we succeeded in pulling it off, and it's even nicer when you can do this.'

Speaking to colleagues in the Danish media, I discover they're getting little more from Vingegaard. He's described as 'a nice guy', 'quiet', 'a little introverted'. When trying to add a little colour to his story, another colleague contacted the manager of the fish-packing factory in Denmark where Vingegaard worked part-time during his early pro years, only to be told that there wasn't much to say.

He is, it seems, the archetype of the racer who lets the bike do his talking for him, and he's shown himself to be marvellously eloquent in this. Yet, while there's flair, there's far less of the panache that you'd associate with most of the sport's pure climbers. The margins are so fine now that there's little scope left for riders that fall into this category, who will make up for their deficit on the flat, in crosswinds, in time trials, and on short, steep, punchy ascents by skipping flamboyantly away from the pack in the mountains. Every aspect of racing is worked on, every angle analysed and covered. Brilliance in the mountains is still critical to success and does, as the 2022 Tour emphasized, still make for an absolutely compelling spectacle, but it is dependent on hitting the right numbers as much as natural talent, on following plans pieced together by a working group.

Pogačar is a different beast, more engaging and easy to warm to, but fired by a desire for victory that hasn't been seen in the men's sport since Eddy Merckx, who acknowledges that the Slovenian has gone closer han anyone else to meriting the tag 'The New Cannibal'. He seems less focused on the process than Vingegaard, more instinctive and totally sure of his ability, to the extent that this impulsiveness worked against him on the Granon stage, where he opted to respond to Jumbo's attacks by trying to ride them off his wheel.

Like Vingegaard, though, he's just as baffled when asked if he feels particularly at home in the mountains and for the sensations they evoke in him. 'I don't know. Maybe . . . yeah. I've never thought about it,' he confesses. Then he adds: 'A climb is a climb. You need to push with power whether you know the climb or if you don't, it's more or less the same.' But a window opens into what really fires him when I ask about Jumbo's strategy on the Granon. Had they found a weakness in his armour?

There's a flash of anger in his eyes. Although he controls it quickly, his reaction hints at the extraordinary level of competitiveness that drives him on, offering a brief illustration of how he's likely to respond when attacked by his rivals. 'I don't know whether they found the weakness in my armour, because I just wear a jersey,' he says, laughing off the suggestion that he might have an inherent flaw that can be exploited again. 'They played it really, really well last year in the Tour and I had a bad day. I was perhaps going through the wall with my head some days but that's just normal in racing. This year we go again.'

That moment of irritation suggests he's been piqued by losing to Vingegaard, which his storming ride at Paris–Nice underlined. He was determined to show that both he and his team were on point. While insisting that his approach to racing won't change, he admits that Jumbo's tactical focus has led to him and UAE's management analysing how they might strike back in future. 'We've spent a lot of time within the team studying their way of doing things,' he says. 'I've also tried to get to know more about them individually. I'm convinced that tactical responses can be found to prevent them being so dominant and from harrying me in the way they did last year on the Tour. But in the end, what really counts is having the legs to respond to them. And I hope to have them.'

Pogačar is absolutely right in his final comment. No matter what the era, bike racing does ultimately come down to the legs, to the fact that 'a climb is a climb' and that you need to push with power whether you know it or not. There is no romance when you're riding flat out up a climb. The intense burning pain is all-pervading, the only balm to it the thought that your rivals might be feeling worse. All that matters is enduring it and, if that can be managed, reaching the top first.

Bibliography

Bacon, Ellis and Birnie, Lionel, *The Cycling Anthology*, London: Yellow Jersey, 2014.

Béoutis, Didier, *Julio Jiménez, L'horloger d'Ávila*, Paris: Éditions de la Société littéraire du Maine, 2017.

Best, Isabel, *Queens of Pain*, London: Rapha, 2018.

Bourgier, Jean-Paul, *Benoît Faure, Roi de la Montagne*, Toulouse: Le Pas d'Oiseau, 2019.

Chany, Pierre, *La Fabuleuse Histoire du Cyclisme*, Paris: Éditions ODIL, 1975.

Chany, Pierre, *La Fabuleuse Histoire du Tour de France*, Paris: Éditions de la Martinière, 1995.

Cudeiro, Cudeiro, Oscar, *El Tarangu*, Meres-Siero, self-published: 2016.

Diamant-Berger, Marcel, *Histoire du Tour de France*, Paris: Librairie Gedalge, 1959.

Foot, John, *Pedalare! Pedalare! A History of Italian Cycling*, London: Bloomsbury, 2011.

Fotheringham, Alasdair, *The Eagle of Toledo: The Life and Times of Federico Bahamontes*, London: Aurum Press, 2012.

Fotheringham, William, *Fallen Angel*, London: Yellow Jersey, 2010.

Fotheringham, William, *Merckx: Half Man, Half Bike*, London: Yellow Jersey, 2012.

Fotheringham, William, *The Badger*, London: Yellow Jersey, 2015.

Fournel, Paul, *Anquetil, Alone*, London: Pursuit, 2017.

Friebe, Daniel, *Eddy Merckx: The Cannibal*, London: Ebury Press, 2012.

Guimard, Cyrille, *Dans Les Secrets du Tour de France*, Paris: Éditions J'ai Lu, 2012.

Hutchinson, Alex, *Endure*, New York: William Morrow, 2018.

Laget, Françoise and Serge, *Jours de Fête*, Paris: Éditions Chronique, 2012.

Leonard, Max, *Higher Calling: Road Cycling's Obsession with the Mountains*, London: Yellow Jersey, 2017.

Mondenard, Jean-Pierre de, *Les Grandes Premières du Tour de France*, Paris: Hugo Sport, 2013.

Neila Majada, Ángel, *Vicente Trueba Pérez: La Pulga de Torrelavega*, Santander: Ediciones Tantin, 2005.

Pickering, Edward, *The Yellow Jersey Club*, London: Bantam Press, 2015.

Rendell, Matt, *Kings of the Mountains*, London: Aurum Press, 2002.

René Pottier, Cycliste Moretain (1879–1907), Le Mée-sur-Seine: Lys Éditions Amatteis, 2006.

I also drew heavily on back issues of *L'Auto*, *L'Echo des Sports*, *Le Miroir des Sports*, *La Vie au Grand Air*, at the Bibliothèque Nationale de France in Paris, and of *L'Équipe*.

Index

Picture Credits

First section: page 1 above, DeAgostini/Getty Images; 1 below, AFP/ Getty Images; 2 above Branger/Roger Viollet via Getty Images; 2 below Bob Thomas/Popperfoto via Getty Images; 3 above Olycom SpA/Shutterstock; 3 below L'Equipe/Offside; 4 above AFP via Getty Images; 4 below Roger Viollet via Getty Images; 5 above Olycom SpA/ Shutterstock; 5 below AP/Shutterstock; 6 above & below L'Equipe/ Offside; 7 above Gamma-Keystone via Getty Images; 7 below Gamma-Rapho via Getty Images; 8 above Gilbert Iundt/Jean-Yves Ruszniewski/TempSport/Corbis/VCG via Getty Images; 8 below, ullstein bild/Getty Images.

Second section: page 1 above L'Equipe/Offside; 1 below & 2 above, AFP via Getty Images; 2 below Photosport/Shutterstock; 3 above & below Cor Vos/Fotopersburo Cor Vos -Video ENG; 4 above L'Equipe/ Offside; 4 below John Pierce/Photosport/Shutterstock; 5 above Homer Sykes/Alamy Stock Photo; 5 below Lionel Bonaventure/AFP via Getty Images; 6 above & below Tim de Waele via Getty; 7 above Luc Claessen/Getty Images; 7 below Artur Widak/NurPhoto via Getty Images; 8 above Luca Bettini/AFP via Getty Images, 8 below Pete Goding/Belga Mag/AFP via Getty Images.

Acknowledgements

I would first like to express my gratitude to the current and former riders who gave me so much time and offered such detail and insight into climbing: Kenny Elissonde, Andy Hampsten, Liam Holohan, Dan Martin, Ashleigh Moolman Pasio, Quentin Pacher, Nicolas Roche, Pierre Rolland, Michael Storer, Inga Thompson, Lucien Van Impe, Michael Woods and Philippa York.

I would also like to thank all those who provided insight into specific issues relating to climbing: my journalist colleagues Klaus Bellon, Daniel Benson, William Fotheringham, Daniel Friebe, Chris Marshall-Bell, Owen Rogers, Sophie Smith, Gibus de Soultrait, Jeremy Whittle, as well as Tour de France director Christian Prudhomme.

The editorial team at Octopus have been hugely supportive of this book from the very start. My thanks go to editor-in-chief Trevor Davies and this book's editor Sarah Kyle, as well as Matthew Grindon, Karen Baker, Jaz Bahra, Nick Fawcett, Anna Doble, Clare Hubbard, Giulia Hetherington and Peter Hunt.

Once again, I've been able to count on the Elland Road-like support of my literary agent David Luxton, and Rebecca Winfield and Nick Walters at David Luxton Associates.

My thanks also to my friends Jim Hodgkins, Neville McKay and Matt Taylor for offering much-appreciated input.

My love and gratitude goes to my wife, Elaine, and my children, Lewis and Eleanor, for their support, feedback and patience during the whole production process.

Finally, I would like to thank all those riders who I've watched race up a mountain. As a sporting test and spectacle, nothing compares to it. *Chapeau* to all of you!